Praise for *When Britain Burned the White House*

"A stirring tale." —Max Hastings

"Peter Snow's account of this extraordinary event in British-American relations reads like a military thriller, each chapter raising the tension with a mass of detail and a kaleidoscope of characters who transform this book from what could have been a dry, chronological account into a riveting romp. . . . Snow adds an extra ingredient—a boyish enthusiasm for his subject. . . . A meticulous and fascinating account."
—*The Times* (UK)

"Superb. *When Britain Burned the White House* is an exemplary work of history—lucid, witty, and humane, with terrific pace and so evenhanded that it will surely be received as well in America as here."
—*The Spectator* (UK)

"Snow builds his account on the voices of those who fought and witnessed the campaign, from nervous U.S. militiamen to Ross, Cockburn, and Dolley Madison, the president's resourceful wife. Written with verve and insight, this is a fitting reminder of a remarkable interlude in a war that deserves to be better known."
—*BBC History Magazine*

Also by Peter Snow

Leila's Hijack War
Hussein: A Biography
Battlefield Britain (with Dan Snow)
Twentieth Century Battlefields (with Dan Snow)
To War with Wellington

When Britain Burned the White House

The 1814 Invasion of Washington

PETER SNOW

THOMAS DUNNE BOOKS
ST. MARTIN'S PRESS
NEW YORK

THOMAS DUNNE BOOKS.
An imprint of St. Martin's Press.

WHEN BRITAIN BURNED THE WHITE HOUSE. Copyright © 2013 by Peter Snow.
All rights reserved. Printed in the United States of America. For information,
address St. Martin's Press, 175 Fifth Avenue, New York, N.Y. 10010.

Maps drawn by Rodney Paull

www.thomasdunnebooks.com
www.stmartins.com

Library of Congress Cataloging-in-Publication Data

Snow, Peter, 1938–
    When Britain burned the White House : the 1814 invasion of Washington /
Peter Snow. — First U.S. edition.
        p. cm.
    Includes bibliographical references and index.
    ISBN 978-1-250-04828-8 (hardcover)
    ISBN 978-1-4668-4894-8 (e-book)
    1. Washington (D.C.)—History—Capture by the British, 1814. 2. United
States—History—War of 1812—Campaigns. 3. Maryland—History—War of
1812—Campaigns. I. Title.
    E356.W3S66 2014
    975.3'02—dc23

                                                                        2014010743

St. Martin's Press books may be purchased for educational, business, or promotional
use. For information on bulk purchases, please contact Macmillan Corporate and
Premium Sales Department at 1-800-221-7945, extension 5442, or write
specialmarkets@macmillan.com.

First published in Great Britain by John Murray (Publishers),
an Hachette UK Company

First U.S. Edition: August 2014

10 9 8 7 6 5 4 3 2 1

To all my grandchildren

Contents

List of Maps   ix

Introduction   1

1. Eager souls panting for fame   5
   17 August

2. The great little Madison   17
   17 August

3. Into the Patuxent   29
   18–19 August

4. A black floating mass of smoke   42
   20–22 August

5. Not till I see Mr Madison safe   55
   23 August

6. Be it so, we will proceed   67
   24 August, morning

7. Bladensburg: a fine scamper   82
   24 August, afternoon

8. Barney's last stand   94
   24 August, afternoon

9. Save that painting!   104
   24 August, evening

10. The barbarous purpose   114
    24 August, evening

11. The dreadful majesty of the flames   125
    24 August, night

12. Damn you! You shan't stay in my house   135
    25 August

13. Into the Potomac   148
    26–27 August

14. A tempest of dissatisfaction   156
    28–29 August

15. Do not attack Baltimore!   165
    End of August

16. Is my wife alive and well?   175
    End of August

17. The star-shaped fort and its banner   182
    1–11 September

18. Many heads will be broken tonight   193
    12 September

19. The Battle of North Point   203
    12 September

20. The rockets' red glare   211
    13 September

21. You go on at your peril   220
    13 September

22. Unparalleled in history   231
    Aftermath

Author's Note   241
Notes and References   247
Bibliography   277
Illustration Credits   289
Index   291

Maps

1. USA, 1814   x
2. Chesapeake Bay area   6
3. The advance to Washington, 20–24 August 1814   34
4. Battle of Bladensburg (1), 24 August 1814   78
5. Battle of Bladensburg (2), 24 August 1814   95
6. 24–25 August 1814   105
7. 12 September 1814   186
8. Battle of North Point, 12 September 1814   204
9. 13–14 September 1814   212

USA, 1814

CANADA

UPPER CANADA

York

Plattsburgh

VERMONT

NEW HAMPSHIRE

MASSACHUSETTS (MAINE)

NEW YORK

MASSACHUSETTS

CONN.

RHODE ISLAND

PENNSYLVANIA

Philadelphia

New York

NEW JERSEY

Baltimore

Washington

DELAWARE

MARYLAND

OHIO

VIRGINIA

KENTUCKY

NORTH CAROLINA

TENNESSEE

SOUTH CAROLINA

GEORGIA

LOUISIANA

New Orleans

ATLANTIC OCEAN

GULF OF MEXICO

0   250 miles

0   350 kms

Introduction

O N A S W E L T E R I N G August evening, a group of British soldiers and sailors sat down to a meal in the State Dining Room of America's White House. They hadn't been invited. They had invaded the capital of the United States, had seized the President's house and were now helping themselves to the meal that he and his first lady had prepared for their guests. To the British officers and men who'd been marching for days the food and drink were like a gift from the gods. Royal Navy Lieutenant James Scott wrote in his diary that the President's Madeira wine tasted like 'nectar'. It was 24 August 1814. Thirty years after the United States had won its independence, the British were back.

The extraordinary story of how these intruders, at the head of a British force of 4,500 men, came to occupy and then burn the city of Washington has become the stuff of legend. President Obama greeted Britain's Prime Minister, David Cameron, at the White House in March 2012 by reminding him that two centuries earlier his countrymen had 'really lit the place up'. Cameron replied that he was a 'little embarrassed' by what his ancestors had got up to. Tony Blair, an earlier Prime Minister, was typically a bit more flip: 'I know this is kind of late – but sorry!' Even Bob Dylan wrote a special couplet referring to Britain's burning of the White House for his song 'Narrow Way'.

The British invasion of Washington is not an episode in their history that Americans recall with much relish – any more than the French do the Battle of Waterloo. In Britain, very few people know it happened or even that there was a so-called War of 1812. It was actually one of the defining moments in the history of both countries. For America it was the only other time – before the terrorist attack of 11 September 2001 – that outsiders succeeded in striking at the core of American state power. But within three weeks the young republic was to transform utter humiliation into triumph. And Britain was to see one of the most daring and successful military enterprises in its history bring it face to face with the limits of its imperial power. These three weeks provide a revealing commentary on the personalities of the two nations, now inseparable friends, then bitter enemies. The story is greatly enriched by first-hand accounts from characters in all walks of life on both sides of the conflict. They are as compelling a group of eyewitnesses as any you'll find in history. All – even the military – speak with a disarming immediacy and candour about the bloodshed and destruction and the strengths and weaknesses of those in command.

Most of the British men who tell us how they came to be in the White House that night had fought their way through western Europe defeating the armies of the French Emperor Napoleon. Harry Smith, an ambitious young officer in the Rifles, had recently seen burning and destruction in plenty as he campaigned through Spain and southern France with the Duke of Wellington. His only regret in being posted to America was that he had to leave behind his devoted Spanish wife, who had accompanied him throughout the Peninsular campaign. He was now a senior aide to the army commander, Major General Robert Ross, another uninvited guest at the White House table. Ross wore on his neck the vicious and still unhealed scar of a wound he had suffered in a battle with Napoleon's men in southern France. He too had had to leave a much loved wife behind. Months earlier she had crossed the Pyrenees to treat his wound. She was now languishing at their home in Northern Ireland, deeply unhappy without him. His letters to her reveal a kindly and deeply sensitive man, tormented by news of her loneliness and depression. He had been beset too by doubts about his campaign: he would not have led his men into Washington but for the persistent needling of another man eating the President's dinner that night– the fiery Rear

Admiral George Cockburn. Cockburn's own words and the accounts of those who knew him testify to his sharp tongue and fearsome reputation. To the Americans he was a 'brutal monster' for the raids he had made on their coastal towns over the previous year. Cockburn had relished the hard-bitten life of a sailor from the moment he served as a frigate captain's servant at the age of ten. His chief aide was now James Scott, a dashing young sailor with an unashamed weakness for flirting with ladies no matter what language they spoke. He writes with delightful indiscretion about the debates within the British high command which he often attended. All of these men dined at the President's table that night and then set the White House on fire: it still bears the burn marks to this day. One prolific diarist who wasn't actually at the meal but who describes the scenes there and throughout those dramatic weeks in more detail than anyone else was George Gleig, whose adventures read like those of Bernard Cornwell's Richard Sharpe.

The principal American characters and the stories they tell are no less compelling. James and Dolley Madison presented America with a striking partnership between a cerebral and often withdrawn President and his warm-hearted, gregarious and very practical wife. He won undying fame as the key draughtsman of the American republic's constitution, but was a near disastrous failure as its commander in chief when the War of 1812 reached this dramatic climax. Dolley was widely acclaimed for her plucky conduct during those August days in 1814. The letters of James and Dolley Madison and their friends Margaret Bayard Smith and Anna Maria Thornton provide a candid picture of the President's attempt to manage a desperate situation, and the crushing humiliation of having to abandon his own home. Madison was let down by the conduct of two seriously flawed characters: John Armstrong, the Secretary of War, and his military commander William Winder. Both may have had their merits but they both failed each other and their country. The cast of American players in the drama has its winners as well as its losers: the energetic Secretary of State, James Monroe, and Sam Smith, the resolute American commander at Baltimore, both helped Madison restore

America's faith in itself. There are a number of soldiers too like John Pendleton Kennedy who give us a taste of how ordinary Americans weathered the storm. Kennedy dashed so quickly into action that he found himself wearing his dancing pumps on the battlefield. And if there was one clear American hero, it was Joshua Barney, the mastermind behind the team of flotillamen who caused the British much mischief. He had been a swashbuckling privateer in the American and French navies and claimed he had once kissed Marie Antoinette. Barney was eventually to die of the wound he received fighting the British.

The accounts of these central characters on either side are at the heart of what is the most striking episode in an otherwise almost forgotten war. It began in 1812 and ended in 1815 with no material gains for either Britain or America. In just one month in the summer of 1814 the fortunes of both sides rise and fall with spectacular impact. The sack of Washington is only an early highlight in a story that reaches its height at Baltimore three weeks later. What happened there did much to soothe America's sense of national humiliation at the burning of Washington.

The fierce struggle of August and September 1814 was one of the last bouts of fighting between two nations that later became the closest of allies. It defines the strengths and weaknesses of each: the British empire – overstretched and arrogant, but fielding a navy and army of experienced veterans who could sweep all before them; the young American republic, struggling with internal divisions but infused with a freshness of spirit and patriotic fervour. And underlying this often bloody conflict is the grudging respect that often marked dealings between the two sides. This was after all a battle between two supposedly civilised nations who spoke the same language, shared family ties and were neither of them bent on the other's outright ruin. It is notable how, just occasionally, the essential humanity of the two countries took some of the edge off the death and destruction.

I

Eager souls panting for fame

17 August

THE AMERICAN WATCHMAN on the aptly named Point Lookout awoke to an astonishing sight. Thomas Swann stood gazing at up to fifty warships flying the British flag anchored in the wide expanse of water at the entrance to the Potomac River in Chesapeake Bay. He'd never seen anything like it: mighty warships like the eighty-gun *Tonnant*, captured from the French at the Battle of the Nile and one of the champions of the British fleet at Trafalgar in 1805, along with several other seventy-four-gun ships of the line, as well as some smaller, faster frigates and, scattered among them, clusters of schooners and sloops of war. There were troop transports, which Swann reckoned must be carrying thousands of fighting men, and bomb ships which could cause devastation ashore with their long-range mortars. He was looking at the largest British force to hit the Chesapeake since Britain had tried and failed to crush the American revolution thirty years earlier. The bay was of great strategic importance: it commanded the approaches to the cities of Washington, Annapolis and Baltimore. Of the three, Baltimore was the largest and most prosperous with a well-protected harbour. But Washington had the prestige of being the home of Congress and the President.

It was dawn on 17 August 1814. Within hours the news would be in Washington some eighty miles away. War was about to come to the very heart of the United States. Swann, a lawyer and volunteer observer, sent an express letter to the War Secretary John Armstrong detailing the fifty-one ships he counted in the bay. One terrified American eyewitness in the coastal town of York wrote to his local newspaper that the appearance of this 'formidable' enemy fleet could

only mean 'our property destroyed, our dwellings in ashes, our wives and children homeless and defenceless'.

The previous evening the bay had echoed to the thunder of British cannon. It was a salute to the final squadron to arrive, carrying 2,800 troops from southern France. Robert Barrett, a midshipman on the frigate *Hebrus*, had all the enthusiasm of a young lad of fifteen just embarked on a life of adventure. 'It was a glorious and imposing spectacle to behold these noble ships standing up the vast bay . . . manned too with eager souls, panting for fame and opportunity to sustain the laurels they had gained in many a bloody field of Spain and Portugal.'

6

Another inspired by the 'glorious' sight 'of an English fleet standing up an enemy's bay with all sails set' was George Gleig. He was an eighteen-year-old subaltern with an amiable round face and curly hair, already a prolific and meticulous diarist. Until that spring he had been chronicling his adventures with the Duke of Wellington's army in the Peninsular War against the French. But that war was over. France's Emperor Napoleon had abdicated. And Gleig and his comrades had expected to go home. But pretty soon the rumour went around that the British veterans who'd fought their way through the Iberian Peninsula into southern France and others from the war in the Mediterranean would be off to America. With France defeated, now was the time to get the upper hand in another war that had become a futile drain on British resources – the conflict with the newly independent United States. The Americans were fighting the Royal Navy at sea and trying to seize parts of British Canada. Britain responded in the summer of 1814 with an enterprise designed to give the Americans what Britain's Military Secretary, Colonel Torrens called a 'good drubbing'. There was no plan to reimpose British rule.

The American war was a tiresome sideshow for the British. They had been fighting a war of survival against Napoleon, whose domination of the European continent they saw as the paramount strategic threat. And so when America's President James Madison declared war on Britain in June 1812, it seemed like a stab in the back. Madison was exasperated by what he saw as the intolerable excesses of the British empire. In applying a stranglehold on France, Britain had massively interfered with American ships trading with Europe. The Royal Navy also imperiously made a habit of impressing Americans into working on its warships – even if the men could demonstrate that they were American citizens. What was more, Americans driving west to settle in Ohio and beyond felt threatened by Britain's support for the indigenous Indian tribes who stood in their way. And so, even though the United States had won its independence from Britain a generation earlier, it felt forced to declare war against the old mother country again.

The war hadn't gone well for either side. The Americans tried and failed to seize slices of Canada. Former President Thomas Jefferson (before he was succeeded in the White House by James Madison in 1809) had boasted that conquering Canada would be a 'mere matter of marching'. The odds appeared to be massively in America's favour. Upper Canada's tiny population of less than 100,000 faced an American population of more than seven million. But it proved impossible for the American army to establish a permanent foothold across the frontier. And the British, although they possessed the most powerful navy in the world, suffered as much punishment as they inflicted in several naval encounters, and even had their Upper Canadian capital York (the modern Toronto) burned by an American marauding force in the spring of 1813. The parliament buildings there were reduced to ashes by soldiers who, the Americans claimed later, had run amok.

This debilitating war remained inconclusive. Lord Liverpool's Tory government in London was severely short of money after two decades of fighting the French. So he leapt at the opportunity of peace in Europe – with Napoleon's exile to Elba in the spring of 1814 – to deal a decisive blow against America. 'Now that the tyrant Buonaparte has been consigned to infamy,' thundered the London *Times*, 'there is no public feeling in this country stronger than that of indignation against the Americans . . .' Parliament, press and government switched the nation's attention from Europe to America in language that knew no bounds. The Americans were called 'loathsome' and 'hateful' for having turned on Britain when it was fighting a war with the French. America's President Madison was a 'serpent'. Resentment still burned strong in Britain at the humiliating defeat it had suffered in the American War of Independence. Now it was free to turn up the heat on its former American colonies. And the fleet that appeared in the Chesapeake in August 1814 was there to do just that.

George Gleig was happy not to go straight home after Napoleon's defeat. He was as keen as anyone, he wrote, 'to gather a few more laurels even in America'. But over on the flagship, the *Tonnant*, Harry

Smith, who'd seen rather more action than Gleig in the Peninsula, was much less happy. Two years earlier he'd rescued a beautiful Spanish girl of fourteen from British troops who'd gone berserk after their successful storming of the fortress town of Badajoz. Within minutes Smith proposed to her, and they married in the presence of Wellington, the Commander in Chief. Juana, Harry's new wife, had followed him through many a scrape in the years of fighting that ensued. And he now found it 'an awful trial' to part with her. 'I knew I must leave behind my young, fond and devoted wife, my heart was ready to burst.' They spent their last few days together in a little skiff floating down the river from Bordeaux enjoying the 'beauties of the scenery', and he finally left her 'insensible and in a faint'. Now Smith, who'd made his name as an energetic and forthright captain on Wellington's staff, was attached to a new army commander, Major General Robert Ross. The Duke of Wellington himself showed no enthusiasm for the war in America. He had always believed that wars should have clearly defined and achievable goals: the American war had neither. But he admired Ross, who'd been one of his senior commanders in Spain and southern France, and the Duke was glad to see him presented with such a promising command.

Ross was a Northern Irishman from Rostrevor in County Down, and he had done Wellington proud in the Peninsula. He had been awarded a medal for his leadership at the Battle of Vitoria the previous summer. He was notably courageous in battle, occasionally reckless: he had a habit of leading from the front and lost a number of horses killed under him. His men were devoted to him: he would occasionally entertain them by playing his violin. An American prisoner who was to meet him later said of Ross that 'he was the perfect model of the Irish gentleman of easy and beautiful manners, humane and brave . . . and his prisoners had no reason to regret falling into his hands'.

It was at the Battle of Orthez in February 1814 that Ross received the near fatal neck wound that brought his wife, Elizabeth – he called her 'Ly' – riding on horseback through the snow to look after him. In a letter to her brother, Ned, he made light of his wound: 'You will be happy to hear that the hit I got in the chops is likely to prove of mere temporary inconvenience.' But Ross was now worried about the deep depression that had seized Elizabeth when he broke the news that far from coming home he was off to another war in America. 'The prospect of your unhappiness', he wrote to his wife in mid-July, 'dismays me considerably. The care which our young ones require ought to make you consider the care of yourself of the most infinite consequence. Do, my Ly, somehow dispel all those gloomy ideas . . .' Concern for Elizabeth was to hang like a dark shadow over Ross throughout the next gruelling weeks. He wrote to reassure her that he believed the contest with America would be over by the end of the year 'so as to restore my Ly to me. What a joyful meeting after the most melancholy separation we have ever had.' His letter went on to give a hint that he hoped he would come back with a generous share of any prize money. As the army commander in the operation, he told Elizabeth, 'any advantage to be derived from it will I trust fall to my lot'. Like his naval colleagues Ross expected the campaign to add handsomely to his earnings.

Ross was fortunate in two key aides, both still showing the scars of their own wounds in the Peninsula: Harry Smith was one, George de Lacy Evans the other, a lieutenant, one rank junior to Smith. Both of them were burning with ambition and enthusiasm for the mission. Evans was a tearaway young cavalry officer who was given a medal for leading his dragoons in repeated charges at the Battle of Vitoria in 1813. Ross wrote to his wife that he was 'much pleased' with his staff officers. 'In addition to Smith, the Brigade Major, who improves much upon acquaintance, I have a Mr Evans of the Quarter Master General's department who is an extremely intelligent active fellow and' [as if that wasn't commendation enough] 'an Irishman.' Both competed energetically to influence Ross, though Smith was less impressed with his chief than was Evans, and Ross may have detected this. Certainly the general went out of his way as the campaign progressed to try to promote George Evans to the same level as Harry Smith. It was enough to inject a touch of jealousy into Smith's spirit of comradely rivalry with Evans.

Within minutes of arriving in Chesapeake Bay Ross met the admiral who was to be the driving force of the British blitzkrieg of the next few weeks, Rear Admiral George Cockburn. Cockburn had impressed Nelson with his fierce self-confidence and courage at the Battle of Cape St Vincent off Portugal in 1797 and at several engagements in the Mediterranean. Here in America he had been causing terror and destruction in the Chesapeake for the last eighteen months. People in coastal towns lived in fear of their homes being burned and their tobacco crop and other valuables being seized and sold for profit by Cockburn's marauding troops. He was often seen accompanying his men ashore – he relished being involved in the action – in his admiral's two-cornered hat and familiar jet-black uniform jacket with gold epaulettes. By the end of 1813, he was being attacked in the American press for behaviour it described as 'brutal' and 'savage'. The *Boston Gazette* called him 'the notorious barbarian Admiral Cockburn . . . there breathes not in any quarter of the globe a more savage monster than this same British admiral. He is a disgrace to England and to human nature.' Another newspaper reported the offer of 'a reward of one thousand dollars for the head of the notorious incendiary and infamous scoundrel, and violator of all laws, the British Admiral Cockburn, or five hundred dollars for each of his ears on delivery'. Cockburn's aide-de-camp, James Scott, who witnessed much of the fighting, welcomed the raging reaction of the American press. 'It exposed their weakness in the eyes of the world,' he wrote in his diary. 'The abuse and vituperation . . . out Heroded Herod; there was no crime no outrage however flagitious that was not placed to his account.' Scott reports that the admiral's raids did indeed spread fire and destruction and earned piles of prize money, and that Cockburn often put himself in danger by plunging into the middle of the action. To Scott the admiral had always been a hero – from the moment he joined Cockburn's frigate HMS *Phaeton* way back in his early teens. And he also claims that Cockburn was renowned for his gentlemanly gallantry. When on one raid his men burst in upon a party of young women and sent them scuttling in panic into a corner of the room, Cockburn arrived and assured them they would come to no harm. 'The courtly demeanour of the Admiral and promises of protection restored the roses to their smiling countenances and they learned that the enemy and the gentleman may be combined without disparagement to either.'

Cockburn was not in fact as unscrupulous as he liked his enemy to believe. He applied strict rules of engagement. Towns that surrendered to his raids he would spare; towns that resisted he would burn. Livestock and other food, he insisted, should be paid for, never looted, again always providing there was no opposition. As even one early twentieth-century American historian observed: 'The harassing of the shores, however, was carried out in a mild and gentlemanly fashion – private property being respected, or if it were levied upon, payment was made unless the owners offered resistance.' In practice the presence of American militia in many towns made a clash inevitable. And once battle was joined Cockburn abandoned restraint: burning, plunder, confiscation, all were fair game. And the outcome was often so savage that one British officer, Colonel Charles Napier, who served with Cockburn, complained: 'Strong is my dislike to what is perhaps a necessary part of our job, viz, plundering and ruining the peasantry . . . it is hateful to see the poor yankees robbed and to be the robber.' Napier made no secret of his contempt for what he saw as Cockburn's 'impetuous' way of conducting raids. Napier was one of Wellington's grizzled Peninsular veterans who'd delighted in killing Frenchmen at Bussaco and Badajoz, but he had his doubts about fighting fellow Anglo-Saxons: 'It is quite shocking to have men who speak our own language brought in wounded; one feels as if they were English peasants and that we are killing our own people.' To one British seaman, Frederick Chamier, the type of warfare in which he was engaged with George Cockburn was 'a blot on our escutcheons . . . We most valiantly set fire to unprotected property and notwithstanding the imploring looks of the old women, we, like a parcel of savages, danced round the wreck.'

But to most of his men Admiral George Cockburn was a hero. A young British midshipman watched Cockburn's men rampaging through one town on the Virginia shore, capturing a pile of tobacco and several American schooners. 'It's almost impossible to depict my boyish feelings and transport when at the close of this spirit-stirring affair I gazed for the first time in my life on the features of that undaunted seaman, Rear Admiral George Cockburn, with his sunburnt visage and his rusty gold laced hat – an officer who . . . on every occasion shared the same toil, danger and privation of the foremost man under his command.' James Scott, Cockburn's ADC, recalls one day when the temperature reached 90 degrees, and some of Cockburn's men threw themselves on the ground saying they couldn't move a step further. Cockburn jumped off his horse and 'addressing the brave fellows who lay stretched on the ground in an encouraging tone, he said, "What! Englishmen tired with the morning's walk like this; here, give me your musket; here, yours my man; your Admiral will carry them for you."' Scott, already scarcely able to stand in the heat, found himself carrying two of the men's muskets. 'But it had the desired effect of rousing the men afresh, and, headed by their chief, we reached the boats without one man missing.'

Ross and Cockburn were under command of a vice admiral who was one rank senior to each of them. He was Sir Alexander Cochrane, whose flag flew on HMS *Tonnant*, which had retained her French name since she had been seized by the British at the Battle of the Nile. Cochrane had begun this enterprise no less aggressively than the plain-spoken George Cockburn. He had a long-term grudge against the USA. His brother had been killed at Yorktown, the last major battle in the War of Independence with America thirty-three years earlier. Cochrane was somewhat of an expert in the field of amphibious warfare: he had landed an army in Egypt in 1801, and supervised an assault on the island of Martinique in 1809.

Cochrane had received a letter from Britain's commander in Canada, General George Prevost, telling him of the 'outrages' the Americans were committing in their raids on Canada, and Cochrane promptly responded by ordering his subordinates such as Cockburn to carry 'retributory justice into the country of our enemy . . . to destroy and lay waste such towns and districts upon the coast as you may find assailable'. Cockburn of course had been doing that ruthlessly to towns that picked a fight with him for the past year and a half, and was delighted to receive a letter in July asking for his advice about a plan of action for the new task force. Cochrane's central strategic objective was to cause the Americans so much punishment on the east coast that they would be forced to reduce their pressure on Canada. He had been deliberating for some time about where to attack once Ross's army arrived from Europe. Annapolis, Baltimore and Washington were all possible targets, perhaps Philadelphia up the Delaware River. 'I will thank you for your opinion,' Cochrane wrote to Cockburn. He didn't have to wait long for his answer. Cockburn made it clear that he had no doubt what the approaching task force should do. It should strike where it would do most damage to the upstart republic's pride and prestige. The target should be the city that was now the capital of the United States – Washington.

He had already confidently reported that he had found America to be 'in general in a horrible state . . . it only requires a little firm and steady conduct to have it completely at our mercy'. And then in mid-July he despatched a fast schooner with a letter he marked 'secret' to Cochrane, who was still building up his force in Bermuda. Cockburn said he now believed it was the perfect opportunity for a thrust at the very heart of the enemy's power – their seat of government in Washington. And he added: 'I feel no hesitation in stating to you that I consider the town of Benedict in the Patuxent, to offer advantages for this purpose beyond any other spot within the United States . . .' The town, he said was forty-four or forty-five miles from Washington by a good road. And, he went on, within forty-eight hours of landing the troops, 'the City of Washington might be possessed without difficulty or opposition of any kind'. Cockburn added that Benedict offered a sheltered spot on the Patuxent River at which to unload the troops. In the rich country around it they would find plenty of supplies for the army and horses to drag their heavy guns. What was more, added Cockburn, once the Americans had suffered the blow of losing their capital, the other cities like Annapolis and Baltimore would soon fall as well.

Cochrane and Ross were not so sure. Nor was another admiral, who joined them from Britain, Edward Codrington. 'We are now on our way to the Chesapeake,' Codrington wrote to his wife. '(Mind you don't tell the Yankees!)' He was the only one of the admirals in America who had fought at Trafalgar nine years earlier. As captain of the *Orion*, Codrington had received the surrender of the French *Intrépide* at the cost of only one of his own men against 200 French dead. He was now to command the fleet under Cochrane. The Admiralty had intended to give Cochrane a force of 20,000 men. It had now been reduced to just 4,500. This must have been a shock to the Commander in Chief, who from now on allowed an element of caution to dilute his passionate loathing of the Americans. And in this he found an ally in Codrington. Before he arrived in the Chesapeake Codrington had expressed caution about going all out for a major target like Washington: 'I feel extremely anxious that we should succeed in the first attack we make; and I should prefer even a minor object with something like certainty, to a point of more consequence which might be doubtful.' Both men knew that if the Americans could get their act together they would outnumber the British several times over. But Ross's men were battle-scarred veterans who had thrown the French out of Spain, and they would face untried and poorly trained American militia. Cochrane was inclined at least to give Cockburn's plan a chance.

There were actually four British admirals on the fleet assembled in the Chesapeake on 17 August. They included Rear Admiral Pulteney Malcolm, who had led the convoy that brought Ross's troops across from France. Three of the admirals, confusingly, had names that start with a C. Alexander Cochrane, the vice admiral and Commander in Chief, was to supervise the campaign aboard his flagship, the *Tonnant*; Edward Codrington, a rank below him, was to be the day-to-day manager of the fleet, often exerting a restraining influence on his chief; the third was the pugnacious George Cockburn, who now relished the prospect of accompanying General Ross on his land operations.

By the time the American government in Washington *did* know that the British had arrived in force, Cockburn, in two days of meetings on the *Tonnant*, swept away any doubts that remained in the minds of Ross and Cochrane. Washington it would be. They would sail as far as they could up the Patuxent River on Thursday 18 August, land the army at Benedict and march on the American capital. Two other diversionary moves would be made. One force would sail up the Potomac, another into the northern reaches of Chesapeake Bay. Anything to confuse the enemy, divide their forces and keep them guessing about the real target. Would the British attack the city of Baltimore, Annapolis – or Washington?

2

The great little Madison

17 August

AMERICA'S CAPITAL WAS still little more than an oversized village with only 8,000 inhabitants. 'To a Bostonian, or a Philadelphian,' wrote one of Madison's cabinet ministers, 'Washington appears like what it really is, a meagre village; a place with a few bad houses and extensive swamps, hanging upon the skirts . . . of a thinly-peopled, weak and barren country.'

But it was a village with monumental pretensions. It had been chosen by America's first President, George Washington, to be the capital of the new nation. The broad avenues and imposing buildings of state were already partly in place. The two wings of the great stone Capitol – the Senate on the north side and the House of Representatives on the south side – were complete, lavishly adorned with vaults and columns in the classical style and topped with domes. Next to them stood the Library of Congress with more than 3,000 leather-bound volumes in a chamber eighty feet long. Way off to the west along the still largely bare but broad Pennsylvania Avenue stood another group of palatial buildings: the executive offices, the Treasury Building and, in the centre, in solitary grandeur with a generous space around it, the White House, usually referred to at that time as the President's House.* An ornate whitewashed Georgian mansion, it looked very much as it does today – but without the north and south porticos. It is a striking fact that what is arguably the world's most iconic

---

* The brilliant whitewash that has given the building its name was first applied as early as 1798, two years before it was occupied by a President, in order to seal the porous Aquia Creek sandstone of which it is constructed.

17

building, the seat of today's most powerful leader, has changed little in size and shape from the time it was built.

America's second President, John Adams, moved into the mansion briefly on its completion in 1800, and was succeeded by Thomas Jefferson in 1801. Jefferson was one of America's most esteemed Presidents but he was unmarried and had no taste for grand social occasions. It was his successor, his close friend and Secretary of State James Madison, and his wife Dolley, who brought the place alive. It was a curious paradox because Madison was anything but a flamboyant personality. He had a slight, almost shrivelled frame no more than five foot four inches tall. He dressed usually in black, looked rather severe and had a thin and rather diffident voice. 'As to Jemmy Madison,' wrote the waggish American author Washington Irving, 'ah poor Jemmy! He is but a withered little apple-john.' Another said he was like 'a schoolmaster dressed up for a funeral'. Madison was a studious man. He was unostentatious and unassuming when in company. But he had a charming smile, and eyes that were penetrating and expressive. His conversation sparkled with wit and anecdote and he had a fluent command of language, which had people listening to him in fascination. He was recognised as the intellectual force behind the US constitution: he had played a central role in designing the new republic.

His wife Dolley could hardly have been more different. She was a buxom, warm-hearted woman with twinkling eyes – eyes that one observer said 'wrought havoc with the hearts of the Quaker lads'. She was a natural hostess. She radiated an open bonhomie and disarming friendliness that made her White House the centre of Washington society from the moment James Madison became President in 1809. Dolley was born a Quaker, but by her mid-twenties she had left her modest upbringing behind her and was a vivacious and highly eligible widow in Philadelphia. Her first husband had died of yellow fever when she was twenty-five, leaving her with a small son, John Payne Todd. Young men would stop in the street to admire the 'Widow Todd'. 'Really, Dolley,' said her friend Elizabeth Collins, 'thou must hide thy face, there are so many staring at thee.' Only a few months after her first husband had died, Dolley wrote excitedly to another friend that she was about to be introduced to 'the great little Madison'. She wore a mulberry-coloured dress for the occasion with an 'an exquisitely dainty little cap from which an occasional uncropped curl would escape'. James Madison, the intense, unmagnetic but already celebrated political genius, was immediately captivated. He fell for her – passionately. He told Dolley's cousin Catherine Coles that he thought so much of Dolley in the daytime that he 'lost his tongue', and 'at night he dreams of you'.

They were married in September 1794, and so began one of the most unlikely but successful Presidential partnerships in American history – the thoughtful, preoccupied husband and the outgoing, vivacious wife. 'Her smile, her conversation, and her manners are so engaging', remarked one congressman, 'that it is no wonder that such a young widow with her fine blue eyes . . . should indeed be a queen of hearts.' George Washington met her at a Washington party in 1795 and remarked afterwards, 'Mrs Madison was the sprightliest partner I've ever had.' 'She was humble-minded, tolerant and sincere,' wrote her grand-niece Lucy Cutts, 'but with a desire to please and willingness to be pleased which made her popular, and always a great friend and support to her husband.' She called him her 'darling little husband'; she combed his hair and wrote letters to him when he was ill. After James had won the Presidential election in 1808, his defeated opponent, Charles Pinkney, remarked, 'I was beaten by Mr and Mrs Madison . . . I might have had a better chance had I faced Mr Madison alone.'

When James became President in 1809, Dolley redecorated Jefferson's dowdy White House with sumptuous furnishings: Jefferson's study was reborn as the State Dining Room with a large portrait of George Washington by Gilbert Stuart as its centrepiece. Dolley Madison's drawing room adjoined the State Dining Room: it was elegantly furnished with pieces rather more delicate than the giant sideboard next door. The main, much larger drawing room stood in the centre of the south front with a door opening on to the terrace. Dolley embellished it with elegant mahogany furniture and rich red velvet curtains, which cost her a crippling $4 a yard. They were matched by red velvet cushions on the newly designed Grecian-style chairs; each chair bore a gilded and varnished US coat of arms.

Each Wednesday the Madisons held an open house which became famous for its informality and the easy way in which Dolley drew together people of all political persuasions. While the President would retire to a corner to talk politics, his wife would be chatting to everyone, an unmistakable focus of fun and fashion. She was blessed with a rich memory. One guest observed that she always found time to speak to everyone and never forgot a name. At one drawing-room party she wore a pale buff-coloured velvet dress with a very long train, a Parisian turban of the same buff-coloured velvet and white satin, with two Bird of Paradise plumes, and a pearl necklace, earrings and bracelets. Her friend Margaret Bayard Smith wrote that 'she looked like a queen'. Washington Irving described her as a 'fine, portly, buxom dame, who has a smile and pleasant word for every-body'. Dolley had a passion for ice cream, which was generously served at her parties, and she was often seen to take a pinch of snuff from a little silver box she carried around. One of her guests observed that she was 'not in the least a prude, as she once told an old bachelor and held up her mouth for him to kiss'. By 1814 Dolley Madison's 'drawing rooms' had become an established part of fashionable life in Washington.

One of the ironies of the time was that the White House was largely staffed by slaves. Even the country estate owned by one of the prime architects of America's liberal constitution, the comfortable Madison family mansion at Montpelier in Virginia, housed 120 slaves. Like two other early Presidents with tobacco plantations in Virginia, Washington and Jefferson, Madison depended on slave labour. However uneasy the deeply principled James Madison might have been about slavery, he felt he had no choice. He and his wife treated their slaves with obvious humanity, but they never freed them. Madison's own personal servant, Paul Jennings, was devoted to his master. He later wrote that he never saw Madison lose his temper and 'never knew him to strike a slave; neither would he allow an overseer to do it'. If a slave was reported as stealing, rather than punish the man Madison would have a private talk with him.

Each year as the busy Washington social season drew to a close in the summer, the Madisons would spend some time at their country house Montpelier 100 miles to the south-west. Their elegant Georgian mansion, which still commands a tranquil view of the Blue Ridge Mountains, offered a welcome retreat from the heat and bustle of Washington – particularly in wartime. But in 1814, after a break there in May, they spent the summer in the White House. Too many alarm bells were ringing in the capital.

Well before the British fleet arrived in the Chesapeake, warning of London's newly aggressive attitude had reached Washington. A senior American envoy exploring peace prospects in London wrote to a colleague in Washington that the end of the war in Europe and the defeat of Napoleon had transformed the situation. 'A well-organized and large army is at once liberated from any European employment, and ready, together with a superabundant naval force, to act immediately against us. How ill prepared we are to meet it in a proper manner no one knows better than yourself.' We hear that there are voices in Britain which 'revel in the idea of burning the cities and towns, the mills and manufactories of that country [the United States]; at the very least, they talk of forcing Mr Madison from his seat and new modeling the government'.

James Madison knew very well how ill prepared America was for a determined attack from Britain. In the first two years of the war his forces had at least managed to hold their own against the might of the British empire. Fighting on land had been indecisive, and at sea in a number of encounters American warships had done notably well. But things were already changing. The British were reinforcing their army in Canada, and the havoc Cockburn's squadron was causing much nearer home was becoming intolerable. Many Washingtonians blithely dismissed the idea that the British would strike as far inland as the new capital. But the Madisons had watched Cockburn's raids with deepening anxiety. As early as the spring of 1813 Dolley wrote to her cousin about the 'fears and alarms that circulate around me'.

She said people were expressing 'reproach' that her husband's government was not doing enough to prepare. Quite the contrary, she said, 'considerable efforts' were being made for defence and she added that, although she was a Quaker, 'I have always been an advocate for fighting when assailed . . .' As for Cockburn, rumours were flying around that he was threatening to burn the White House over her head and carry her off to London to parade her in the streets. Dolley said she wasn't one to 'tremble' at any threat Cockburn might make. By the summer of 1814 she was more concerned about threats to her husband, the President, than to herself. 'I am not in the least alarmed at these things but entirely disgusted and determined to stay with him.'

James Madison's reaction to Cockburn's depredations was to seek the help of someone who was already an American naval hero, Joshua Barney. He would now play a spectacular role in the events of summer 1814. Born in a coastal village in Maryland in 1759, Barney angered his father by announcing at the age of ten that he'd had enough of school and wanted to go to sea. His father managed to resist for only two years, and at the age of twelve Barney was a sailor on his brother-in-law's brig. By the time he was fifteen he had established such a command over his fellow crewmen that he became captain when his brother-in-law died on the voyage. In the American War of Independence Barney led a daredevil life of adventure as an American privateer. He seized a number of British ships, and when captured himself and locked up in a British gaol in Plymouth he escaped dressed as a British officer. In 1782 he was sent to Paris to deliver papers to the US mission there. We are told by Barney's biographer, his daughter-in-law Mary, that Queen Marie Antoinette was so impressed by the young naval officer that instead of offering him her hand to kiss she offered her cheek. Once Britain and America were at peace Barney found himself in Napoleon's navy and still capturing British ships. But with the start of the War of 1812 he was back in America skippering a privateer schooner, the *Rossie*, which seized no fewer than eighteen British ships in four months. With a record like that it was hardly surprising that, when Barney suggested building a special flotilla of shallow-draught barges to fight Cockburn's marauding British fleet in Chesapeake Bay, President Madison agreed. His Naval Secretary, William Jones, wrote to Barney: 'Your force is our principal shield and all eyes will be upon you.' 'I am anxious to be at them,' Barney replied.

The idea was that Barney's barges, which were built over the winter of 1813–14, would be able to harass and perhaps disable Cockburn's warships in the shallow waters in and around Chesapeake Bay. Barney's and Cockburn's ships clashed twice in the River Patuxent on the west side of the bay in June 1814. The battles were a disappointment for both sides. Barney's men fought bravely but they managed to do little damage to the bigger British warships. And each time the British gave chase, Barney's flat-bottomed barges retreated into shallow water. By the end of June Barney's flotilla was tucked away so far up the river that the British were unable to get near it. It was secure enough but impotent. Madison had no effective floating naval force to counter the enemy armada that might sail into view any day.

As warnings of a substantially increased British threat reached him that summer, Madison's most important task was to make sure that the country's defences were in order and that the right people were in command. And this is where Madison got it spectacularly wrong. There were three key people in positions of power under the President. The most controversial of the three was the fifty-five-year-old John Armstrong, whom Madison had appointed Secretary of War eighteen months earlier. He was intellectually able but an arrogant man, who, as Tacitus famously said of the flawed Roman Emperor Galba, appeared to everyone to be capable of ruling until he tried it.* Both Jefferson and Madison gave Armstrong jobs that he notably failed in. His main weakness was his abrasive, intolerant and occasionally indolent personality. He began his life opposed to the old Jeffersonian Republican party. The principled view of Republicans like Jefferson and Madison was that a standing army

---

* 'Omnium consensu capax imperii, nisi imperasset' (*Histories*, Book 1, section 49).

could threaten the democratic will of the people. They were determined to resist pressures for the powerful central government which their Federalist opponents demanded. The Republican party was strong in the centre and south of the country, the Federalists in the north-east. Armstrong started as a Federalist from Pennsylvania and believed in a strong central state with a regular army. His views changed over the years and by the time he was forty he described himself as a Democratic Republican. Jefferson appointed him Minister to France in 1804 but his high-handedness soured relations between the two countries. Things got so bad that Napoleon complained that the American government was 'not represented here; that its minister does not know French; is a morose man with whom one cannot treat'.

When war broke out with Britain, Armstrong became a brigadier general and, because Madison wanted support from the northern states, he appointed him Secretary of War in 1813. Armstrong won approval for speeding up the promotion of some promising young officers, but soon lost it again when he massively overstepped his powers by taking command of the army fighting British Canada on the Great Lakes. It didn't help: the campaign was a failure. In 1814 he again interfered in the northern campaign which was as inconclusive as it had been the year before. Madison had every reason to dismiss Armstrong, but he didn't. He did however issue an order on 13 August 1814 reducing Armstrong's powers in a number of areas, which only served further to worsen the fragile relationship between the President and his War Secretary.

All this led to increasing tension between Madison and the second key figure in his administration – James Monroe, his Secretary of State. Monroe, a highly ambitious and very competent man, had long loathed Armstrong. Monroe was another Virginian, like Madison and Jefferson. Unlike Madison he had distinguished himself as a soldier in the Revolutionary War. He had made his mark too as a diplomat: he had been America's Minister in London and Paris. Aged fifty-six in 1814, he was tall, with a healthy physique and broad shoulders. He tied his hair at the back with a black ribbon. His gaze was strikingly clear and direct. Jefferson thought him so honest that 'if you turned his soul inside out there would not be a spot on it'. Whether Monroe was jealous of Armstrong or just downright disapproved of him, he did everything in his power to persuade Madison to dismiss him. When Armstrong took over command in the north, Monroe wrote to the President arguing that it was dangerous for a government minister to perform the duties of a lieutenant general. The constitution, he pointed out, demanded a separation of powers. By December 1813 Monroe was going even further – telling Madison that Armstrong was corrupt, promising officers promotion in order to win their support. 'It is painful for me to make this communication to you nor should I do it if I did not most conscientiously believe that this man if continued in office will ruin not you and the administration only but the whole republican party and cause.' If this dysfunctional relationship between two key members of his cabinet was not bad enough, Madison made one further disastrous mistake. In the belief that the American capital was at risk from any British attack on the mainland, he appointed Brigadier General William Winder the commander of a new military district which comprised the two vital cities of Washington and Baltimore. Winder was the nephew of Levin Winder, the Federalist Governor of Maryland, the state that surrounded Washington DC. Madison no doubt believed that Maryland's support would be critical if Washington were threatened by a British invasion and so he may have believed that the elevation of the Governor's nephew might help secure the capital. William Winder, a somewhat insecure thirty-nine-year-old, had only limited military experience. But the omens were hardly promising. He had succeeded in getting himself captured in a clash with the British a year earlier. Madison was promoting an undistinguished soldier to buy a political favour.

The President appointed Winder without consulting his Secretary of War, John Armstrong. He was already beginning to doubt Armstrong's competence for the job, although he still stopped short of taking Monroe's advice and dismissing him. Armstrong was naturally upset. He also believed, rightly, that Winder was completely unsuitable for the job. He resented the fact that Madison had ignored the candidate he'd suggested. The scene was set for an administrative catastrophe. The Secretary of State and Secretary of War despised each other, and both of them believed they had more military competence than the man their President had appointed Commander in Chief.

It was against this unpromising background that James Madison called a meeting of his top advisers at the White House on 1 July. The curious paradox was that of the four men with responsibility for the defence of the capital it was the man with the least military experience, Madison himself, who was the most concerned. He had told a colleague in June that what might prompt the British to make Washington a target was its weakness and the 'éclat that would attend a successful inroad upon the capital, beyond the intrinsic magnitude of the achievement'. The President had written to Armstrong as early as 20 May 1814 that of all the places likely to be targets for British attack 'the seat of government cannot fail to be a favourite one'. Armstrong didn't believe Washington was in any danger. He had done little or nothing as Secretary of War to provide for coastal defences or any plan to obstruct an enemy advance on the capital. Monroe didn't yet seem too worried. As for William Winder, it was only after he got his feet under his desk that he suddenly woke up to the enormity of the task before him if an enemy were to advance on the capital.

The problem was that the United States had no ready force to confront such an emergency. The regular army – in line with the governing Republican party's long-held suspicion of a standing army – was small and mainly occupied in the north on the Canadian border. There were in theory over 90,000 men in the country's militia who could be summoned. They were drafted able-bodied men, who mustered for training only once or twice a year. There were volunteer companies as well – young lads eager for action, dressed in a wide variety of exotic uniforms, as rich in enthusiasm as they were poor in professional military skills. But they were not easily assembled, particularly if the call was from a different state. Winder's problem was that the militia were the property of the states, not of the central federal government. The most available of the militia, Maryland's, up to 6,000 strong, was already being deployed in defence of Maryland's main city Baltimore by Governor Winder. He understood his nephew's predicament, but the state of Maryland was his main concern. The unfortunate William Winder had even less success with Pennsylvania, whose 5,000 militiamen turned out to be unavailable because the state's militia law had expired. An assistant to Pennsylvania's Governor wrote apologetically to Winder that the 'deranged state of our militia system prevented a more prompt compliance'. Winder spent the next few weeks desperately working on Virginia's Governor for a contribution of 2,000 men and continuing to press Maryland's. Armstrong suspected that the Virginians were more concerned to guard against possible slave risings on their plantations than against any attack on the nation's cities.

But it was worse than that. When Winder looked to Armstrong, his political boss, for help, he got none. On 9 July he wrote a plaintive letter to Armstrong saying that as things were going he was being promised only a very small force to defend his territory if the British appeared. 'Should Washington, Baltimore or Annapolis be their object, what possible chance will there be of collecting a force, after the arrival of the enemy, to interpose between them and either of these places?' And he went on: 'If the enemy's force should be strong, which, if it come, it will be, sufficient numbers of militia could not be warned and run together even as a disorderly crowd, without arms, ammunition, or organization, before the enemy would already have given his blow.' Winder then went on to appeal to Armstrong to call out 4,000 militia without delay. He got no immediate reply. And throughout the next six weeks, his appeals to Armstrong fell on deaf ears. Since the Secretary of War did not believe there was a threat to Washington, he was going to do as little as he could to provide men or equipment to Winder, whom he anyway resented and despised. Armstrong said he believed the best way to instill fighting spirit in the militia was to field them only when the enemy actually appeared in view. Winder complained that the Secretary of War was for using the militia only 'on the spur of the moment'.

It wasn't just Winder who was pressing Armstrong. The commander of Washington DC's militia was Major General John Van Ness, a hard-headed realist and an influential Washington banker. He pressed Armstrong repeatedly to do something about the defences of Washington. Each time, Van Ness recalled, he was brushed off – 'the Secretary generally treating with indifference, at least, if not with levity, the idea of an attack by the enemy'. Van Ness communicated his alarm to Monroe without effect, and even to President Madison, who referred him back to Armstrong. Virtually nothing was done. Van Ness wasn't alone. Other senior officers were bewildered by the inaction too. One irate colonel wrote to a military colleague that he would be only too ready, if it were his job, to provide the forces to defend the city. There were plenty of ways in which 'impediments could be thrown in the way of the enemy', he said. 'How long are we to be the laughing stock of the world? . . . The enemy can with a small force destroy Washington in its present situation . . . Surely it might and ought to be protected . . . ?'

Throughout July and for the first two weeks of August the unfortunate Winder rode frantically around the countryside and in and out of the cities of Washington and Baltimore which were only thirty miles apart. He was desperate to do what he could to resist the British invasion that reports from Europe were warning of. He spent every hour of every day trying to secure himself an army and asking himself what he would do with it once he had it under his command. And then on 17 August his worst fears were realised. He was given the news from Point Lookout that the British fleet had arrived. But where would it land its troops and what would be their target?

3

Into the Patuxent

18–19 August

WASHINGTON AND THE Chesapeake are notorious for the fierce heat of August and the sudden storms that disturb the normal sultry calm. It was not the month to be in the US capital. The rivers that snaked towards Washington from Chesapeake Bay, the Potomac and the Patuxent, were reputed to be so dank and feverish that you risked your health venturing anywhere near them. When the *Tonnant* first anchored in the bay, Admiral Edward Codrington noted that the temperature on deck was 133 degrees Fahrenheit, though in his cabin he found it a bearable 83. On the morning of 17 August, as the ships prepared to move off from their assembly point at the mouth of the Potomac, George Gleig watched the sky, which had started 'calm and serene', suddenly cloud over and the water 'began to rise in black waves tipped with foam'. The crews began to fear that a hurricane was about to arrive, but the scare quickly vanished, and the invasion fleet was soon under way.

In faltering winds Cochrane and Cockburn led the main force out of the Potomac into the bay and then north to the mouth of the Patuxent. All the time flag signals flew back and forth preparing the men for the landing. They were told to take three days' worth of rations as well as their blankets, weapons and ammunition. The plan was to beach the troops halfway up the river at Benedict – some fifty miles from Washington – at dawn the following morning. But by evening they had only just reached the mouth of the Patuxent. The river was narrow in places and the depths uncertain. It would be foolish to tackle the Patuxent at night. Cochrane decided to anchor just outside the river until the first light of dawn.

The next morning the wind was hardly more helpful. But there was just enough for the ships to make it up the first few miles of the Patuxent. 'The wind was light and contrary,' wrote one artilleryman, 'and the ships were compelled to beat up equally against the breeze and tide. They were consequently curiously intermingled and passing each other upon opposite tacks.' It must have been an extraordinary sight. Harry Smith found himself looking back at the ships struggling up the river behind him and thinking it looked like 'a large fleet stalking through a wood'.

Dozens of vessels of all sizes inched their way upstream. Huge queues of warships heaved themselves round from one windward beat to the other. For the frigates, sloops, brigs and schooners it was a swifter and easier passage; for the troop transports it was a tortoise-like crawl. And all the time the monotonous cries of the men on the lead lines warned of the quickly changing depths and bosuns shouted at the sailors to haul in or ease the braces and the sheets. Cochrane, determined to follow his landing force as far as he could up the river, left the *Tonnant* at anchor and shifted his flag to the frigate *Iphigenia*.

Those who had time amid all this activity to glance ashore were immediately struck by the beauty of the country on either side. Gleig thought it compared pretty favourably with home. 'The sail up sur-passes even that up the Thames, the woods are so fine, the cottages so beautiful and the cultivation so rich.' He saw fields of Indian corn and 'meadows of the most luxuriant pasture . . . whilst the neat wooden houses of the settlers, all of them painted white and sur-rounded with orchards and gardens, presented a striking contrast to the boundless forests which formed a background . . .'. A young midshipman called the river 'lovely and romantic . . . how bountiful nature has been in her gifts to this favoured country'. It was indeed fertile land. This was Maryland, rich in pasture for cattle, rich too in corn and tobacco. Cockburn's raids had stripped much of it in the past few months. But to the troops who'd been cooped up afloat on the Atlantic for ten weeks, Maryland looked like paradise. It would be solid ground beneath their feet, and it was teeming with fresh fruit and livestock. In places the banks were bustling with people too:

'astonished slaves rested from their work in the fields contiguous; and the awe-struck peasants and yeomen of this portion of America beheld with perturbation, the tremendous preparations to devastate their blooming country'.

Ross organised his men into three brigades of between 1,100 and 1,500 men each. He had four regiments to call on. All had a distinguished record in the war with Napoleonic France. There was the 85th Light Infantry, the Buckinghamshire Volunteers. Wellington had been generous in his praise of their stand at Fuentes d'Oñoro three years earlier where they lost fifty-three men. From then on they had shared in every savage battle he'd fought. George Gleig had joined them as a young subaltern at the bloody siege of San Sebastián in 1813. Now the 85th formed the core of Ross's 1st Brigade under Colonel William Thornton, who had led them through all their fiercest encounters in the Peninsula. Thornton's outstanding courage, bordering on recklessness, would be one of the highlights of this campaign.

The 2nd Brigade was formed of men from the 4th and 44th Regiments. The 4th King's Own was one of the oldest regiments in the army: it had fought for William III at the Battle of the Boyne in 1690, and it had fought with Wellington throughout the Peninsular War from 1808 to 1814. The 44th had spent the last few years fighting the French in the Mediterranean under Colonel Arthur Brooke. Another Northern Irishman, without Ross's flair but with much of his experience, Brooke had signed up with the 44th East Essex Regiment back in 1793 and fought with them against the French in Egypt. He would now command the second of Ross's brigades and his beloved 44th was part of it.* He records in his diary how disappointed his men had been when they were told they were not going home but to America. 'All this', he wrote, 'could not be very agreeable from the general to the drum boy.'

---

* There were two battalions of the 44th: Brooke's was the 1st Battalion; the 2nd fought with Wellington through the Peninsula but did not travel on to America. I have for simplicity referred to Brooke's 1st/44th as the 44th.

Finally the 21st North British (later Scots) Fusiliers would form the bulk of Ross's 3rd Brigade. They fought for the King against both Jacobite rebellions, of 1715 and 1745, and were in the front line against Bonnie Prince Charlie at Culloden, where the second of those uprisings was conclusively defeated. Their commanding officer and now brigade commander was Lieutenant Colonel William Paterson. He was out to avenge the humiliation the 21st had suffered when it was part of the surrender at Saratoga in the American War of Independence. A further 1,000 marines and some 700 sailors brought the total number to around 4,500.

By the evening of Thursday 18 August the ships had managed to penetrate several miles up the Patuxent. There had – to their astonishment – been no sign of any attempt by the Americans to interrupt their progress. A couple of guns on an elevated section of the river bank could have caused havoc. But there was not even a rifle shot. As they anchored for the night the brigade commanders issued their detailed orders for the landing which would begin at first light.

At five the following morning, Friday 19 August, a gunboat was anchored off Benedict in case the Americans offered any resistance to the landing. Eight miles downstream a gunshot gave the signal for the troops to clamber over the sides of the ships and into a fleet of smaller boats which would ferry them up to Benedict. Each man was heavily loaded with weapons, clothing and rations: the soldiers carried muskets, powder and at least sixty balls; the officers – like Gleig – pistols and sabres. As well as his weapons and food, Gleig brought a telescope and a cloak to sleep in. Slung over his left shoulder was a haversack containing, among other things, a spare shirt, a pair of stockings, a foraging cap and three pounds of salt pork and two and a half pounds of biscuit. Gleig knew the march ahead would be a lot tougher than in the Peninsula. There were no tents for shelter, no horses to ride, no mules to carry their kit, and the heat was as intense as anything they'd experienced in Spain.

The armada of small boats had to row eight miles against the stream to Benedict: a daunting challenge. For Gleig it was a nightmare. 'How it came about, I know not, but in my eagerness to reach *terra firma*, I sprang with five dozen men and one brother officer, into a broad-bowed punt which, being supplied with no more than a couple of oars, moved against the stream at a rate of half a mile per hour.' Gleig faced the prospect of a sixteen-hour voyage 'under a broiling sun'. 'Boat after boat, and barge after barge passed us by, without bestowing upon us any other notice than a volley of jokes, or repeated peals of laughter; till at length a worthy midshipman took pity on us and threw us a line.' This lucky break saw Gleig ashore at Benedict by noon. More than 4,000 fully equipped men were successfully disembarked. Only three artillery pieces were landed, one 6-pounder and two 3-pounders. Because Ross could not be sure he would find horses to drag the guns and their store wagons, he would have to rely on a squad of a hundred sailors to do it.

Benedict today remains the 'small straggling place' Gleig described in 1814: a few houses scattered on a low-lying river bank where the river narrows and shoals. When the British troops landed they found it deserted. The news from Point Lookout had sent people scuttling for safety. Again, there was no sign of American opposition. The men made the most of what for many was their first chance to luxuriate on dry land for weeks. Some stretched their limbs. Others just basked at full length on the grass. Fires were soon blazing and camp kettles boiling. The more adventurous, like Gleig, went off to see what they could find. They all knew Cockburn's orders that there should be no plundering of local property unless resistance was offered. Perhaps to reinforce this, a warning had been circulated that the Americans might well have poisoned any food or drink that they left behind. This didn't stop Gleig and a few soldiers, who found a dairy farm near by, from devouring a pot 'of delicious cream, which occupied one of the shelves'. George Chesterton, a twenty-year-old artilleryman scarcely out of school in England – his uncle was a French general – had been inspired to join up by stories of derring-do in the war against Napoleon. He was quick to seize the chance to go on land. He and an adventurous friend rowed ashore and 'signalised our first landing in America by the timely capture of some sheep'.

Later in the day Ross moved his men up to high ground behind

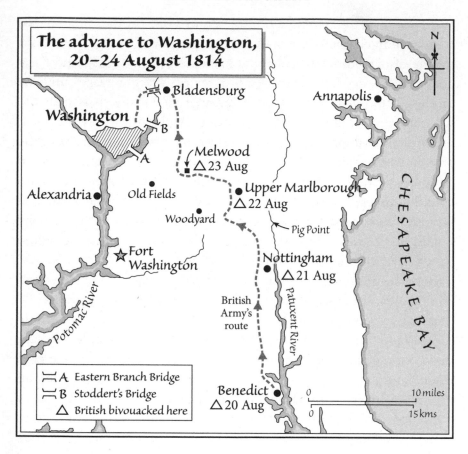

The advance to Washington, 20–24 August 1814

Bladensburg
Annapolis
Washington
B
Melwood
△23 Aug
Upper Marlborough
△22 Aug
Alexandria
Old Fields
Woodyard
Pig Point
Fort Washington
Nottingham
△21 Aug
British Army's route
Patuxent River
Potomac River
Benedict
△20 Aug

⊢∃A Eastern Branch Bridge
⊢∃B Stoddert's Bridge
△   British bivouacked here

0   10 miles
0   15 kms

Benedict. The troops prepared to bivouac for the night and, in case the Americans staged a surprise attack, pickets were posted in a wide circle and the three guns placed with lighted slow matches beside them. But 'Jonathan', the British soldiers' nickname for their enemy, was nowhere to be seen. (In colonial New England Jonathan was such a common name around Boston in 1776 that the British had called all American revolutionary soldiers 'Jonathan'.)

Ross could now make his plans for the next few days in the light of the orders he'd received from London. The army commander was a cautious strategist. He had to match the ambitious objective that Cockburn had persuaded him and Cochrane to accept with the guidance he had received earlier from Lord Bathurst, the Secretary for

War. Ross had been told Cochrane was in overall command, but he, Ross, was in charge of any troops on shore. Bathurst had made clear that it was for Ross to explain to Cochrane the pros and cons of any course of action, but 'you will consider yourself authorized to decline engaging in any operation which you have reason to apprehend' would lead to failure or undue losses. And Bathurst imposed an important strategic limitation on Ross's freedom of action. The British government was not after all out to reconquer the United States but, in the jargon, to 'give them a good drubbing' in order to secure acceptable peace terms. The force Bathurst had despatched with Ross was not strong enough to do more than hit and run. It was not an army of occupation. So Bathurst's orders went on: 'You are not to engage in any extended operations at a distance from the coast.' This rather vague but clearly important stipulation was to haunt Ross and Cochrane for the next few weeks. How far was 'at a distance'?

Another problem for Ross – and for Cochrane – was that these orders made no allowance for the third figure who was sure to insist on a key role in any military adventure on shore – George Cockburn. Cockburn had one clear and immediate responsibility. He would lead a cluster of small boats to attack and destroy Joshua Barney's American flotilla bottled up in the upper reaches of the river. Ross would march his army along the bank in parallel, so that each could come to the other's aid if they ran into opposition. Once that had been achieved, Cockburn would have little formal authority apart from command of a few hundred sailors in his force. But Ross knew that the man who had urged him and Cochrane, the Commander in Chief, to go for Washington was unlikely to allow himself to be left out of the action. Cockburn, for his part, may have feared that either Ross or Cochrane, or both, would have second thoughts about allowing the army to push on to Washington once the first objective had been achieved. He was determined not to allow them to flinch. He also managed to get a defiant message through to the American President. In conversation with John Skinner, a go-between who dealt with prisoners on both sides, Cockburn remarked: 'I believe, Mr Skinner, that Mr Madison will have to put on his armour and fight it out. I see nothing else left.' Skinner lost no time in reporting this to Madison himself.

Bathurst's orders had also touched on another highly sensitive issue – what to do about American slaves who wanted to desert and might even be ready to rise against their white masters. America was racked by deep unease and even dissension about slavery. It was part of everyday life on the tobacco plantations of Virginia – like those of the late George Washington, Jefferson and Madison, and on the cotton farms in the deep south. But in the northern states slavery was either disapproved of or illegal. But everywhere there was widespread fear of a slave revolt. Margaret Bayard Smith, a luminary of fashionable Washington who became a close friend of Dolley Madison, described the country's slaves as 'our enemy at home'. She wrote in her diary back in 1813, 'I have no doubt that they will if possible join the British.' The son of Madison's Vice President, Elbridge Gerry Junior, wrote in his diary: 'Should we be attacked, there will be great danger of the blacks rising, and to prevent this, patrols are very necessary, to keep them in awe.' Tempting as it might be for British commanders to provoke a black rebellion, Lord Bathurst was adamantly against – on moral grounds. 'You will not encourage any disposition which may be manifested by the negroes to rise upon their masters.' Humanity, he said, forbade any idea of prompting warfare that 'must be attended by atrocities'. If individual slaves wanted to desert or join the British 'Black Corps' of negroes – that was permissible, but the slaves should immediately be freed.

The irrepressible George Cockburn, in his eighteen-month Chesapeake campaign, had already recruited blacks. He was for stretching Bathurst's rule as far he could, short of openly promoting a slave rebellion. He told his Commander in Chief, Cochrane, that the blacks who'd managed to desert to the British side were 'getting on astonishingly and are really very fine fellows . . . they have induced me to alter the bad opinion I had of the whole of their race'. Cockburn's ADC, James Scott, writes of the 'runaway negroes, who flocked over to us in such numbers that every transport which brought us provisions and naval supplies generally returned with a live cargo of blackies, their wives and children'. Cochrane himself believed that with the blacks properly armed and backed by a large British force, 'Mr Madison will be hurled from his throne'. One of Cockburn's naval officers recalled: 'A great many black slaves, with their families, used to take advantage of our visits to come away with us. Some of their first exclamations were, "Me free man; me go cut massa's throat; give me musket," which many of them did not know how to use when they had it.'

Not all slaves were attracted by British offers of freedom. One who preferred to chance his luck on the American side was Charles Ball, who spent his life escaping from slave masters and somehow managed to make a living claiming that he was free. In August 1814 he had been hired as one of Joshua Barney's crewmen. He was employed as a part-time seaman, part-time cook in one of the barges in Barney's flotilla.

Barney was one of the first to flash the news to Washington that the British had landed. At nine o'clock that Friday morning he sent off an urgent letter to Madison's Secretary of the Navy, William Jones. Barney wrote, 'Sir, One of my officers has this moment arrived from the mouth of the Patuxent, and brings the enclosed account.' He detailed a full list of the ships that had anchored and went on: 'A large number of small boats are now under way standing up the Patuxent, with a number of men, with a determination to go to the city of Washington as they said yesterday. They have taken all the horses in this part of the world . . .' Barney's letter went on to say that people had heard Cockburn boasting he would dine in Washington on Sunday after destroying Barney's flotilla.

If earlier reports had caused alarm in Washington, Barney's provoked panic. Everything that weekend was terror and confusion. There was now no doubt that a British army was on American soil and as little as two days' march away, bent on the destruction of at least one major US city. But which one? The Potomac River led only to Washington; the Patuxent offered an approach to Annapolis and Baltimore as well. The fact that there were now three possible targets heightened the confusion. Jones's reply to Barney, written at lunchtime that same day, Friday 19 August, said: 'Appearances indicate a design on this place, but it may be a feint, to mask a real design on Baltimore.' As for Barney's flotilla, Jones was emphatic that it should not be allowed to fall into British hands. 'You will run no hazard of capture . . . should he advance upon you with an overwhelming force, you will effectually destroy the flotilla by fire, and with your small arms, retire as he advances, towards this place, opposing by all means in your power, his progress . . .'

William Winder was frantic. 'The innumerably multiple orders, letters, consultations and demands . . . can be more easily conceived than described,' he said, 'and occupied me nearly day and night . . . and had nearly broken down myself and assistants . . .' The beleaguered Commander in Chief had to admit that, of the 15,000 troops that were supposed to be available from the four neighbouring states, only a few hundred were in the field to confront the conquerors of Napoleon. Winder wrote another desperate letter to the Secretary of War John Armstrong. 'Would it not be advisable', he asked, 'to make an appeal to the patriotism of the country, at the present moment, for volunteers, without regard to their legal obligations as militia men?' Anything to get a force in the field. Forget the red tape.

Winder reckoned Annapolis, Maryland's capital thirty miles east of Washington, was the British target. The only senior cabinet minister, apart from Madison himself, who now believed that British sights were set on Washington was James Monroe, the Secretary of State. When the news came in from Point Lookout, the morning before, Monroe went to see the President. 'I remarked that this city was their object,' Monroe reported later. 'He concurred in the opinion.' Monroe also wrote to Armstrong: 'The movement of the enemy menaces this place among others . . . in a more imminent degree than any other.' But then, demonstrating his contempt for Madison's military chiefs, Monroe offered to go to Benedict himself and report back what the enemy was up to. Madison agreed, and at lunchtime on the Saturday Monroe, whose job was supposed to be foreign affairs, rode off, like a glorified intelligence officer, to scout the front line with an escort of dragoons.

No doubt Monroe relished the risk he was taking. He was something of a Revolutionary War hero: he had been injured at the Battle of Trenton in 1776, and he'd become a colonel before the end of the war, in his early twenties. By Sunday morning, even though he'd left his telescope behind, he was able to make out the forest of British masts at Benedict and send a written report back to the President. The British were still disembarking, but he couldn't make an estimate of their numbers. He said he wasn't sure they were headed for Washington, but 'the best security against this attempt is an adequate preparation to repel it'.

The commander of Washington's own District of Columbia militia, Major General John Van Ness, had long been vainly pressing Armstrong to build proper defences. When he heard that the British had entered the Patuxent, he again urged Armstrong to take immediate steps to defend the city. But the Secretary of War replied: 'Oh yes! by God, they would not come with such a fleet without meaning to strike somewhere, but they certainly will not come here: what the devil would they do here?' Van Ness disagreed. The British, he said, were out to capture or destroy America's seat of government. 'No, No!' retorted Armstrong. 'Baltimore is the place, sir; that is of so much more consequence.' Armstrong also did his best to belittle Van Ness. In a letter to a friend he said Van Ness was 'a fellow who has not military knowledge enough to command a Corporal's Guard'.

Van Ness, in despair at Armstrong, then called on Winder and found him 'hesitating and undecided' about what sort of force he needed from the District of Columbia. To which the exasperated general replied that Winder should order out every militiaman he could. Winder agreed to make another effort. But who should command them? As they were talking, Van Ness began to suspect that there might be a conflict between him and Winder about which of them would be in charge. He, Van Ness, after all was a major general, Winder only a brigadier general. At a later meeting he tackled Winder, who prevaricated. Van Ness then called on Armstrong, who said he'd ask the President to decide. The President left it to

Armstrong, and Armstrong effectively ruled in Winder's favour. Van Ness promptly resigned. It was managerial chaos.

While most people now began feverishly discussing what to do and where to go to escape the expected British onslaught, there were a few young lads whose hearts were stirred at the prospect of fighting to save their homes. One such was John Pendleton Kennedy. He was an eighteen-year-old law student in Baltimore with a strong romantic streak. He'd long found his law studies 'inscrutable, dreary mystification' and he leapt at the chance of being a soldier, a calling he described as 'all sunlight and captivating glitter'. Kennedy joined the 5th Regiment of the Maryland militia. 'Here I was,' he wrote, 'just out of college, in a very dashy uniform of blue and red with a jacket and leather helmet, crested with a huge black feather . . . with my white crossbelts, pure as pipe-clay could make them, my cartridge box and bayonet and a Harper's Ferry musket of fourteen pounds . . .'

Kennedy spent most of his time at Fort McHenry, Baltimore's great defensive bastion at the entrance to the inner harbour. He hugely enjoyed his bouts of military training there. He loved the eating and drinking, the storytelling and the joking. 'Nothing', he wrote, 'is more natural than this association of youth, military ardour and susceptibility to the charms of female society . . . I visited a great deal among the young belles of the city and rather piqued myself upon the importance of belonging to the army.'

So, when the news broke that the British army had landed, Kennedy was delighted to get the order to march that Sunday morning. 'It was a day of glorious anticipation', he wrote, 'with all the glitter of a dress parade . . .' As they marched through the streets the pavements were crowded with admiring but anxious spectators, and the windows were filled with women: 'friends were rushing to the ranks to bid us goodbye – many exhorting us to be of good cheer and do our duty; handkerchiefs were waving from the fair hands at the windows – some few of the softer sex weeping as they waved adieux to husbands and brothers.' At every corner Kennedy found himself being cheered as he and his comrades moved briskly along to familiar music: banners fluttered in the wind and bayonets flashed in the sun. 'What a scene it was, and what a proud actor I was in it! I was in the ecstasy of a vision of glory, stuffed with any quantity of romance.' Kennedy knew he was marching to a real war: the enemy had landed and he was sure to meet them on a field of battle in a few days. Along with the marching soldiers went a wagon train carrying all the stores needed for the campaign – cartridge boxes, spare ammunition and powder. Officers rode swaggeringly up and down on horseback 'with a peculiar air of urgent business'. Kennedy's account of the march that followed, as the day became hotter, provided a vivid illustration of the ordeal that soldiers on both sides had to endure at the height of a Maryland summer. 'We could not have been tramping over those sandy roads, under the broiling sun of August, with less than thirty pounds of weight upon us.' His pack weighed ten pounds, his musket fourteen. He carried three or four score of musket balls. 'But we bore it splendidly, toiling and sweating in a dense cloud of dust, drinking the muddy water of the little brooks . . . taking all the discomforts with a cheerful heart and a steady resolve.'

Kennedy recalled that on the first night of the march he and his comrades, who'd been used to a comfortable life, believed 'the idea of a supper of fat pork and hard biscuit was a pleasant absurdity which we treated as a matter of laughter'. They massively overcooked the pork and ended up with 'a black mess which seemed to be reduced to a stratum of something resembling a compound of black soap in a semi liquid state . . .'

Kennedy's regiment was part of a force of some 1,500 militiamen under General Tobias Stansbury from Baltimore, which finally responded to Winder's call. At last some Americans were beginning to wake up to the need to assemble a force to stop the British.

4

A black floating mass of smoke

20–22 August

JOSHUA BARNEY, THE commodore of the American flotilla of barges, had been in many scrapes before. He'd fought for his life in desperate naval battles with spars, sails and rigging crashing on the deck all round him. He had harried Cockburn's powerful fleet with his shallow-draught gunboats with negligible loss of life. But now he and his flotilla were trapped in the upper reaches of the Patuxent. Like James Monroe, Barney's scouts had seen the scale of the British landing force. Barney knew it would be suicide to lead his gunboats downstream to Benedict and make an assault on the much larger British ships.

At seven on the morning of Saturday 20 August Barney sent a message to the Navy Secretary in Washington. What was he to do about the British threat to his little fleet and to the American capital? 'No doubt,' he wrote, 'their object is Washington, and perhaps the flotilla.' There had been talk of dragging the flotilla's barges across land from the Patuxent to the South River a few miles north-east, but Barney had scotched that. Spies and other disaffected local people, angry at Madison's failure to protect them from the British, would be quick to tell the enemy where the flotilla was. If it managed to escape to another river, the British would soon have it bottled up again. The Navy Secretary's reply was blunt and to the point: destroy the flotilla rather than let the British seize it. Barney should then lead the flotillamen back to help defend Washington. 'Your force on this occasion is of immense importance and is relied upon with the utmost confidence.' Barney's dream of foiling the Royal Navy on the water was to end in heartbreak, but he and his men would soon play a vital role in the fight for the capital.

William Winder, America's commander in the field, after his near breakdown a day earlier managed to pull himself together sufficiently to send off some cavalry to tackle the British. He told them 'to fall down upon the enemy, to annoy, harass and impede their march by every possible means, to remove or destroy forage and provision . . . and gain intelligence'. And the next day, Sunday the 21st, Winder rode to the Woodyard, a convenient assembly point about halfway between Washington and the Patuxent River, to meet what troops he could muster in a further effort to disrupt any British advance.

General Ross was in no hurry to move forward. His men were still disembarking from the ships on the Saturday morning, and George Gleig and Lieutenant Williams, another young officer in the 85th, reckoned they had time to go off and do some private foraging. Others had been on the rampage before them, and they found little left in the way of livestock and vegetables. They finally came to a cottage whose garden, pigsty and poultry pen had been thoroughly ransacked. 'There was a wretched old woman here,' reported Gleig, 'who began to weep bitterly as soon as she beheld us.' They assured her they meant no harm, and then applying the rules of conduct that others had clearly ignored, they astonished her by paying 'a quarter dollar piece' for her last fowl. But no sooner had they sat down to tuck into their lunch than the bugles sounded. They stuffed what they could of the meal into their haversacks, buckled on their gear and hurried off. Gleig and his men were light infantrymen. They found themselves in the leading brigade – led by Colonel Thornton – of about 1,200 men including 'a hundred armed negroes'. As they stood, lined up and ready to march, Robert Ross and his staff rode up to shouts of applause. 'The General pulled off his hat, smiled and bowed to his soldiers.' On his order to march off there was 'another hearty cheer'.

The high spirits didn't last for long. It was the time of day when the heat of the sun was at its fiercest. There wasn't a cloud in the sky and the air was still. The notorious humidity of this part of America's eastern seaboard soon had the men sweating into their clammy woollen uniforms. Three months at sea had made them utterly unfit for a long march. They were weighed down by their muskets and ball ammunition, by the spare clothes and three days' rations they were carrying in their packs. Gleig saw more men fall behind from fatigue that day than on any march in the Peninsula. 'Never, perhaps, did an army exhibit such symptoms of deficiency, not in courage but in bodily strength, as we all exhibited this day.' Ross kept them struggling on for only four and a half miles before he called a halt. Gleig and his men were put on picket duty at a nearby farm, and were immediately confronted by a bad-tempered, weather-beaten old farmer. 'He was a keen democrat, a thorough Yankee and abhorred the English with all his heart ... he spoke much of the iniquity of the invasion but comforted himself by anticipating the utter destruction of those engaged in it.' But he was hospitable enough to produce some peach whisky which went down well with his uninvited British guests. After the oppressive heat of the day the British, sleeping in the open, had to endure a night of thunder, lightning and drenching rain.

In spite of Winder's dispositions, the British saw no sign of any enemy horsemen. Vulnerable though the large British force was without its own cavalry, it was left undisturbed. Ross had the men up again two hours before dawn, and his newly invigorated army marched all the way to the small town of Nottingham sixteen miles to the north. It was, as the nineteenth-century American historian Henry Adams described it, a 'midsummer picnic ... through a thickly wooded region where a hundred militiamen with axes and spades could have delayed their progress for days, the British army moved in a solitude apparently untenanted by human beings till they reached Nottingham ...'.

All the way there they were accompanied in the river to their right by Admiral Cockburn and a fleet of up to forty British shallow-draught boats and tenders on the lookout for Joshua Barney's flotilla. At around midday when both Ross and Cockburn were passing Lower Marlborough, the two men met on the river bank for a talk.

Cockburn was anxious to keep up the momentum of the British advance on the two agreed objectives – the destruction of the flotilla, and the attack on Washington. Ross was committed to the first but nervous about the second. Washington was still some forty miles off – inland. He was haunted by Bathurst's instruction that he should never stray too far from the coast and he was aware that it was he, not Cockburn, who would bear the responsibility if anything went wrong with what would be a highly ambitious undertaking. His two aides, Harry Smith and George de Lacy Evans, were enthusiastic advocates of the plan to target Washington, and saw it as their job to help the general wrestle with his doubts and keep him on mission. Smith thought Evans a fellow as 'goodhearted . . . as ever wore a sword'. He admired Ross too, and wrote of him as a 'dear friend', but he observed that the general was 'very cautious in responsibility – awfully so, and lacked that dashing enterprise so essential to carry a place by a *coup de main*'. It was clear to Cockburn and to the two aides that Ross had not yet fully steeled himself for the job. But the immediate task was to eliminate Barney's flotilla, and on that the two men were agreed. The next day Cockburn would push on up the river and hunt down the flotilla.

The army stopped for the night of Sunday 21 August at Nottingham. It had spent most of the day in woodland, and for the first time there was a skirmish with the Americans. A corporal standing beside Gleig said, 'What is that? Do you see something, sir, moving through those bushes on the right?' Gleig looked where the man pointed and saw the glint of what appeared to be a weapon. He had the bugle sounded and his men raced forward and the Americans soon made off leaving one dead. It was, said Gleig, a 'trifling affair' but it put the British on the alert. They were now in tobacco country and Gleig and his mates prepared themselves a bed of tobacco leaves in the shelter of a barn. 'With a fire blazing before us and the remains of our supper taken away, we reclined pipe in hand, and drinking cup hard by, within the porch of the hospitable barn chatting . . .'

★

45

The American who was closest to all this action was still James Monroe, the Secretary of State, who was eagerly reliving his life as a Revolutionary War veteran, keeping as close an eye as he could on the British movements. He was lucky to avoid capture as he circled around Benedict and then rode up the road towards Nottingham. Indeed one report claimed he was just leaving Nottingham when the British entered it. He wrote to President Madison that the British were pushing up the Patuxent heading for Barney's flotilla 'or taking that in their way, and aiming at the city . . .'. Madison wrote to Monroe that they should be ready for the British to 'risk everything . . . If the force of the enemy be not greater than yet appears and he is without cavalry, it seems extraordinary that he should venture on an enterprise to this distance from his shipping. He may however count on the effect of boldness and celerity on his side, and the want of precautions on ours.' On Sunday evening Monroe turned up at the Woodyard and met William Winder who – to his delight – addressed him as 'Colonel Monroe'. They talked briefly and then Monroe, utterly exhausted, retired to bed, leaving Winder to spend the night, as he himself described it, 'writing letters and orders to various officers and persons'. Finally at dawn on Monday 22 August the American commander, who cannot have had much sleep, ordered off the first substantial detachment of around a thousand troops to confront the British at Nottingham. It was the first serious attempt to oppose them three full days after they had landed.

That same morning in the upper reaches of the Patuxent a small detachment of Joshua Barney's flotillamen under Lieutenant Solomon Frazier meticulously laid powder trails to the magazines on each of the seventeen gunboats in the flotilla. It was anchored as far up the river as Barney's men had been able to penetrate. Barney himself and the rest of his force – dragging with them five large guns (two that could fire 18-pounder shot and three 12-pounders) – had abandoned the flotilla the night before and made for the Woodyard to reinforce Winder.

It was eleven o'clock before Cockburn's fleet of small ships rounded a bend above Pig Point and spotted Barney's pennant on the sloop *Scorpion* anchored at the head of the long line of his flotilla barges. 'Here, then,' recalled James Scott, Cockburn's aide-de-camp, 'was the boasted flotilla. We had brought them to bay, and in a few minutes we should see what they were made of. The Admiral, dashing on in his gig, led the attack.' But seconds later they saw smoke issuing from the sloop. The order was given to lie on their oars and 'the Scorpion, like the venomous insect she was named after . . . turned the sting of death upon herself, and exploding, blew stars, stripes, broad pendant and herself into a thousand atoms'. Each of the boats behind, save one, then blew up as well. 'It was a grand sight; one vast column of flame appeared to ascend and lose itself in the clouds; from the summit of the evanescent flash issued a black floating mass of smoke, which, quickly unfolding itself in curling wreaths, gradually but quickly obscured the heavens from our view.' Only one vessel escaped and was captured. The British sailors looked on in 'blank dismay . . . and all was disappointment and despair . . . [Barney] had the reputation of being a brave old seaman, but it was the general opinion throughout our fleet that on the appearance of the British flotilla he should have struck one blow for the honour of his flag . . .'

Scott was sent off in Cockburn's gig to reconnoitre the shore. He was passing some bushes when suddenly a shot whizzed past his ear. Scott couldn't see anybody, but Cockburn called across the water to him, 'He is below you, Scott, he is below you.' 'I jumped down,' wrote Scott, 'and found myself within arm's length of an American seaman.' Scott leapt on him and secured his sword arm. Cockburn shouted at him not to kill his opponent. So the American narrowly escaped 'acquaintance with an excellent piece of cold steel'. Midshipman Samuel Davies recalled that two of Barney's 'damn rascals' were 'very near shooting the Admiral'. They were captured, he added, and turned out to have been ex-British sailors who'd deserted a Royal Navy warship and who would be hanged when the expedition was over.

The self-destruction of Barney's flotilla removed a force that has been extolled particularly by American commentators for its pluck and effectiveness in confronting the most powerful navy in the world at the time. In truth it was little more than a tiresome irritant to the Royal Navy, more renowned for what its flotillamen and their commander had achieved before and after the clashes in the Patuxent. Theodore Roosevelt, in his naval history, said, 'it is very certain that the gunboats accomplished little or nothing of importance'. Barney's barge force has been overrated, though the fighting skill and bravery of his flotillamen were second to none, as we shall see.

While Barney had been making his arrangements for the scuttling of his flotilla, William Winder set off from the Woodyard with the men he had managed to muster to do battle with Ross's main force. James Monroe went with him. 'I entertained a hope', Winder said later, 'to have given the enemy a serious check . . .' But he did nothing of the sort. First he learned that the cavalry he'd sent out to harass the British march the day before had retired without landing any effective blow. And when he did come within reach of the British, who'd started out from Nottingham at seven that same morning, he found they'd halted in a deliberate effort to confuse him. They'd stopped at a crossroads. Which way would Ross go? Would he lead his men straight on along the road that led to the Woodyard and Washington – the one Winder's men were on – or would he head north to Upper Marlborough, a small town twenty miles from Washington? If they'd taken the Woodyard road to Washington, Winder might have had no choice but to fight. As it was, the British took the right fork and headed for Upper Marlborough. Rather than provoke an all-out battle with the British as they marched off, Winder withdrew his men way back to a spot called Long Old Fields. He was probably wise. The British had a force far superior in numbers and experience to the relatively small detachment Winder had moved off that morning. But it had been a futile day's marching to and fro for the Americans, who'd been alerted as early as 2 a.m. Winder had lost a day, had exhausted and disheartened his men and had yielded valuable ground to the enemy. If he was to stop the British closing on the American capital his only chance now was to intercept them west of Upper Marlborough. That would have to wait until the next day.

To the relief of Ross and Cockburn and the astonishment of many Americans, Winder had done little or nothing to attack or obstruct the British advance. Charles Ball, an ex-slave fighting with Barney who'd helped scuttle the flotilla, reckoned US commanders should have taken action in the woods on the way from Benedict. 'One hundred Americans would have destroyed a thousand of the enemy by felling trees and attacking them in ambush.' Joshua Barney and his 400 flotillamen and guns reached the Woodyard around noon. Barney had had to endure the distant sound of his vessels exploding one by one, and was naturally eager to engage the enemy. But no sooner had he arrived than he was, we're told, 'astonished to perceive the whole army in motion of retreat'. He thought this was 'precipitate and injudicious'. Winder rode up and did his best to explain to Barney that when he had learned the British were on their way to Upper Marlborough, he felt he had to pull back in order to intercept any march on Washington. Barney concluded that Winder was a near-useless commander in chief. James Monroe watched Winder's fruitless marching and counter-marching with increasing anxiety. He sent a message to President Madison saying 'the enemy are in full march for Washington. Have the materials prepared to destroy the bridges . . .' He added an afterthought before he sent it: 'You had better remove the records.'

One man who took his cue from James Monroe was Stephen Pleasonton, a clerk in the State Department. He decided that the department's books and papers including some priceless documents drawn up in the first years of the American Revolution were too valuable to risk seizure by the enemy. He bought some coarse linen bags, crammed the documents and books into them and began to pile them on to carts to take them off to the other side of the Potomac. Just as he was lugging one load of papers down the passage that separated the State Department from the War Department, John Armstrong, the Secretary of War, appeared on his way to his room. He stopped a moment and Pleasonton later recalled him saying that 'we were under unnecessary alarm, as he didn't think the British were serious in their intentions of coming to Washington. I replied that we were under a different belief, and let their intentions be what they might, it was part of prudence to preserve the valuable papers of the revolutionary government, comprising the declaration of independence, the laws . . . the correspondence of General Washington . . .' and several other documents. The doughty Pleasonton first had the carts taken to a mill just above Georgetown. But, judging it unsafe to leave them there, he had other wagons take them thirty-five miles off to a farm in Virginia where they stayed safely locked up for weeks. There were conscientious clerks in the Capitol too. Two assistants found an ox cart to rescue precious papers from the House of Representatives; another wagon carrying papers from the Senate lost a wheel and later turned over. But all the documents were in the end safely stowed away.*

There were military stores to be moved too, great stacks of gunpowder kept in Washington's naval headquarters on the Potomac waterside. Its commandant, Commodore Thomas Tingey (pronounced Tinjy), was very proud of his Navy Yard and anxious to stop such lethal material falling into British hands. He instructed his trusty and resourceful orderly, Mordecai Booth, to move what powder he could out of the city to safety. Booth acted instantly, as if his life and career depended on the outcome of his mission, documenting his every action in a special report for his boss. He had a fretful day procuring wagons to transport the powder. In the general panic wagons were in huge demand. He had no way of securing them apart from declaring that he was confiscating them for Commodore Tingey. One after another people made their excuses. Few drivers were impressed by his efforts to commandeer their vehicles. He almost had a stand-up fight with a pair of men driving

---

* Stephen Pleasonton died in 1855 and was buried in the Congressional Cemetery in Washington. One hundred and fifty years later the damaged and barely readable gravestone of this modest hero of the Republic was restored thanks to the exertions of the writer Anthony Pitch, author of the book *The Burning of Washington*.

one wagon. 'They made use of such language as was degrading to gentlemen – I had no one to enforce the detention of the wagon and it was hurried off in opposition to my positive command to the contrary – and except I had used violence [I] could not have prevented it.' After exhaustive efforts Booth managed to secure four wagons, loaded them with 120 barrels and two casks of gunpowder and had them transported safely out of the city. Tingey rewarded his dedication by removing Booth's family to safety. 'Seeing my children out of the reach of a ferocious and vandal enemy was delight indeed . . .' Booth remarked.

British troops were now less than a day's march away. Within hours they could be in Washington. There were those who believed the British might be headed elsewhere, but to most people that looked a slim chance. What had seemed unthinkable only a few days earlier was now an imminent nightmare: the capital of the United States under enemy occupation. Evacuation was now everyone's imperative, belongings first. And, after that, the ultimate guarantee of personal safety was a horse ready saddled in the stable. The streets were quickly full of wagons piled with furniture and everything else in the house that could be moved. Of course no one doubted that the army would fight to defend the city, but it was a brave family that would await the outcome of the battle. In the White House the President and Dolley Madison watched the signs of panic everywhere around them as their fellow citizens voted with their feet.

James Madison felt he had to join his men in the field. He was no soldier, but in the only other war the United States had fought George Washington had always been at the head of his troops. Madison thought he had no choice: he had at least to show himself to the army and talk to his generals. But he feared for his wife's safety alone in the White House. Madison asked Dolley if she could manage on her own. 'He enquired anxiously whether I had [the] courage', she recalled later, 'or firmness to remain in the President's house until his return . . . and on my assurance that I had no fear but for him and the success of our army, he left me, beseeching me to take care of myself, and of the cabinet papers, public and private.' Madison set off accompanied by a small party of aides including his Attorney General Richard Rush and Navy Secretary William Jones. They reached a farm near Long Old Fields, where the main US force would spend that Monday night.

Winder and his troops arrived the same evening and settled down near by. They took up position only seven miles short of Washington. The pressure was mounting on America's beleaguered commander to make a stand. He was told that President Madison had arrived and that his party had been joined by the War Secretary John Armstrong. They would all meet with the President at six the following morning.

The American camp that night was halfway between the capital and the British at Upper Marlborough eight miles away. One contemporary military expert said that Winder was taking a risk camping there and exposing his 'disorganized' army to attack from General Ross's British veterans. One officer commented, 'I made up my mind that if Ross, whose camp I had reconnoitred in the evening, was a man of enterprise he would be upon us in the course of the night and being determined to die like a trooper's horse I slept with my shoes on.' It was a tense night. And the exhausted troops were further disturbed by a sentry's false alarm at 2 a.m. It was the second time they'd been roused and drummed into battle order in the small hours.

Ross and his army arrived in Upper Marlborough in the early afternoon of Monday 22 August after another hard day's marching. They were delighted by what they found there. George Gleig described the town as 'one of the most exquisite panoramas, on which it has been my fortune to gaze'. That didn't stop him going off and helping himself to 'five fowls . . . a loaf of bread, a sack of flour and a bottle of peach whisky'. The place was a patchwork of prosperous houses and rich meadows offering the army abundant supplies and its inhabitants, reported Ross's aide George de Lacy Evans, 'consist of a very respectable class, they have claimed protection on the promise of neutrality . . .'. Evans could not have been talking about most of the people of the town who had fled on the British approach, but one of the most 'respectable' who had stayed was Dr William Beanes, a well-to-do physician with a particularly elegant and spacious house. He immediately opened it to Ross, offering him food and lodging in the crusty accent of his Scottish ancestors although he had been born in America. 'He professed moreover', wrote Gleig, 'to retain the feelings as well as the language of his boyish days. He was . . . hostile to the war with England which he still persisted in regarding as his mother country.' The British officers were made very welcome and, when he supplied them with all the food they needed, he was paid for it in full. 'The wily emigrant was no loser by his civility,' remarked Gleig. Beanes wasn't the only local Marylander ready to do business with the British. Cockburn and Ross had had little trouble picking up spies – and not just among the black slave population – ready to guide them through the countryside. America was divided about the war. Many, particularly in mercantile New England, felt the dispute with Britain was a mistake and would be murderous for their maritime trade. And in the Chesapeake area disenchantment with Madison for failing to protect them from Cockburn's rampages had severely strained the patriotism of some.

That evening in Upper Marlborough Robert Ross had another attack of nerves. He was thirty miles from his ships. Barney's flotilla had now been successfully eliminated. He had given 'Jonathan' a severe fright. An advance on Washington – still fifteen miles away – was a daunting challenge for an army of little more than 4,000 men with no cavalry and only three small guns. Maybe he should proclaim 'Mission Accomplished' and return to Benedict. Ross recalled that Vice Admiral Cochrane, his Commander in Chief waiting with the ships, had had his doubts about Washington. Ross's staff sensed the general's renewed unease; he may even have talked openly about it to them. The ambitious George Evans hadn't fought gallantly in India, Persia and the Peninsula only to be cheated of the final act in Washington. Evans and the equally impatient Harry Smith saw their leader's commitment to what would be the crowning triumph of their mission ebbing away. They quietly agreed to send for George

Cockburn. As evening fell Evans leapt on his horse and galloped off to the upper reaches of the Patuxent to entreat Cockburn to ride back with him. Only the forthright admiral would be able to convince Robert Ross once and for all to lead his British army on to Washington.

5

Not till I see Mr Madison safe

23 August

GEORGE COCKBURN SPENT the evening of Monday 22 August
on the naval tender *Resolution* anchored in the upper Patuxent.
He had a lot to congratulate himself about. He had accomplished the
extinction of Joshua Barney's flotilla without the loss of a single man.
He had seized around ten merchant schooners, which had been protected by the flotilla, and loaded them with a vast haul of tobacco.
True, he hadn't led his men triumphantly into battle and grabbed the
flotilla before it could be blown up, nor had he killed or captured
more than a handful of the flotillamen. Four hundred had escaped.
They had distinguished themselves in fighting his navy ships earlier
that summer and would now be a valuable reinforcement for the
American ground troops in the defence of Washington. But Cockburn
was sure that Ross's British veterans would be more than a match for
any force that Madison and Winder could put into the field. And
Cockburn hoped that his meeting with Ross that morning had
removed any remaining doubts in the general's mind about the
wisdom of pressing on to the American capital. It was time to report
his success to his Commander in Chief, Alexander Cochrane, in his
flagship further down the river. Cockburn wrote that his vessels had
'advanced as rapidly as possible' towards Barney's barges, but the
British sailors 'saw clearly that they were all abandoned and on fire
with trains [of powder] to their magazines, and out of the seventeen
vessels which composed this formidable and much-vaunted flotilla,
sixteen were in quick succession blown to atoms and the seventeenth
(in which the fire had not taken) we captured'.

Before Cockburn had finished writing this letter, George de Lacy

Evans rode up with the bad news that Ross's doubts had returned yet again. He asked if the admiral would accompany him to Upper Marlborough in the morning to stiffen the general's resolve. He even brought a spare horse with him for Cockburn to ride. Evans writes that Cockburn promptly agreed to this 'with his characteristic zeal'. But the admiral made no reference to any of this in the letter he now completed and sent off to Cochrane, other than to end it with the words that Ross had 'been good enough to send his aide de camp [Evans] to inform me of his safe arrival with the army under his command at Upper Marlborough'. Cockburn was walking a tightrope. He knew that Cochrane had his doubts too about the Washington plan and that of the expedition's commanders he, Cockburn, was the only one consistently behind it. In fact Cochrane had that afternoon written a message to Cockburn implying that the operation should now be wound up. Writing at 5.30 p.m. Cochrane said: 'I congratulate you most cordially on the destruction of Barney's fleet and think as this matter is ended, the sooner the army get back the better . . .' This message may not have reached Cockburn some thirty miles up the river till after he'd set off to see Ross the following morning. Evans says Cockburn did not read it till 24 August. If it *did* reach him before that, he chose to ignore it.

Cockburn was up early on the 23rd and soon riding with Evans and his own aide-de-camp James Scott to see Robert Ross. They hadn't far to go. It was only five miles to Upper Marlborough and, once there, he soon persuaded Ross to banish his doubts to the back of his mind and order his men to be ready to march on towards Washington. According to Samuel Davies, a midshipman who was in close attendance on Cockburn, Ross began by saying that he – like Cochrane – believed it was impossible to take Washington with such a small army. Cockburn replied that nothing was impossible with the kind of soldiers he had led through France and Spain. When Cockburn went on to say that he himself would happily go to Washington and 'either conquer or die', reported Davies, 'we gave three cheers'. Once again Ross allowed himself to be persuaded. 'It is perfectly fair to conclude', Evans writes in his official memorandum with deliberate understatement, 'that the presence of the Rear-Admiral may not have been, as in fact it was not, without a favourable bias.' Cockburn himself wrote later that he went to 'confer with Major General Ross as to our further operations against the enemy, and we were not long in agreeing on the propriety of making an attempt on the city of Washington'. Ross also agreed – to Cockburn's delight – that the admiral would accompany the army to Washington together with a contingent of seamen and marines. Cockburn would now be at Ross's side to keep him on course if he looked like deviating again. Evans recorded: 'Admiral Cockburn yields unqualified assent to the propriety of the operation contemplated and volunteers his services with the marines and seamen.' James Scott was sent off to report to Alexander Cochrane: 'I was despatched to the Commander in Chief with the news of the flotilla's destruction and the intended descent upon the capital.'

George Evans expressed his satisfaction at the way things were going in his daily 'memorandum of operations'. The army was clearly getting into its stride after its enervating time at sea and was much more effective than when it had first disembarked. There were, he wrote, plenty of supplies of cattle and horses, which local people were ready to provide 'on receiving the established prices'. What was more the army was receiving intelligence from slaves who were 'zealous, intelligent and highly useful' and from 'some of the white inhabitants [who were] by no means incorruptible . . . in fact a sort of espionage exists on which there is already some reason to depend . . .'. He went on to remark that although the enemy had twice the numbers the British had and were 'accumulating', the Americans had 'leaders devoid of talent and experience', and 'the troops are without confidence and discipline . . .'.

Most of the British troops were too busy enjoying a restful morning in the relaxing surroundings of Upper Marlborough with its plentiful sources of food to care about their army commander's dithering earlier that morning. But junior officers like George Gleig could sense something was wrong. The day before at Nottingham he had noticed that 'there seemed, indeed, to be something like hesitation as to the course to be pursued – whether to follow the gunboats, or to return to the shipping . . .' 'We remained [at Upper Marlborough] not only during the night, but till past noon on the following day. The hesitation which had caused the loss of a few hours at Nottingham again interfered, and produced delay which might have been attended with serious consequences . . .' Towards noon Ross made his appearance after his meeting with Cockburn and the troops were ordered to prepare to move off after lunch. 'The scruples which had, for a time, affected him were now overcome, and a push, it was understood, was about to be made against the city of Washington.' Gleig reports that the buzz went around that the general and the admiral were determined on 'insulting' the American capital. The word was put about that this would be retaliation for excesses committed by the Americans in burning towns like Newark and York (the modern Toronto) in Upper Canada. The men weren't too concerned about the reasons for the action, Gleig writes: 'it was sufficient for us to know that an enterprise was before us . . . we cared not from what motive it sprung – our only thought was to effect it'. By 2 p.m. the British army was on the move towards Washington – fifteen miles away.

That day, Tuesday 23 August, was the day on which the chaos on the American side induced by the bewildered leadership of William Winder reached its climax. By the evening his flurry of contradictory orders had driven his subordinate commanders close to despair. His misery was compounded by the fact that throughout the day the British still managed to keep him guessing about where they were headed. The American troops in their camp at Long Old Fields had had a disturbed night with one false alarm at 2 a.m., and the day that now dawned promised to be as sultry and sweaty as any that August. Winder himself had only managed, as he put it, to 'snatch a moment of rest . . . having waded through infinite applications, consultations and calls . . .'. At 6 a.m. he ordered his bleary-eyed troops to make ready to move and rode over to the nearby farm where he briefed the President. He was able to tell Madison he now had around 6,000 troops immediately available – over 2,000 at Long Old Fields and another 4,000 assembling around the village of Bladensburg which commanded a river crossing north-east of Washington. His cavalry were keeping an eye on the British, who were in Upper Marlborough eight miles east of them. They showed no sign of moving from there and he was inclined to move forward to intercept them. He did not know what the British intended. They could be headed for Annapolis, which Winder thought the most likely, or by one of two roads to Washington. Armstrong, who up to that moment had discounted any British move on Washington, then intervened to say that if Ross did move on Washington 'it will necessarily be a mere Cossack Hurrah, a rapid march and hasty retreat'. The best plan of action, said Armstrong, was to retreat to the Capitol in Washington and defend it with 5,000 troops and a battery of guns. On the success of this plan, said the War Secretary, 'I would pledge my life and reputation.'

Far from taking the advice of a man whose judgement he had every reason to distrust, Winder did almost precisely the opposite. He decided – initially – on a forward strategy. He had already ordered the force (which now amounted to more than 2,000 men) under General Tobias Stansbury around Bladensburg to move forward towards Upper Marlborough. He now ordered his force at Long Old Fields including Joshua Barney's flotillamen to move an advance party forward towards Upper Marlborough and to prepare to inter-cept any British move towards Washington. The word went around the American units that at last they were going to have a go at the British invaders of their country. At 9 a.m. James Madison reviewed the troops at Long Old Fields and wrote an upbeat letter to his wife. He said the troops he'd been with that morning were 'in high spirits and make a good appearance'. The latest and probably truest infor-mation about the enemy, he wrote, 'is that they are not very strong, and are without cavalry or artillery; and of course that they are not in a condition to strike at Washington'. He said they didn't look like moving from Upper Marlborough 'unless it be from an apprehension of our gathering force, and on a return to their ships . . . it is possible however they may have a greater force or expect one, than has been represented or that their temerity may be greater than their strength'. Madison told Dolley he might have to return to the camp; 'otherwise I hope I shall be with you . . . though perhaps later in the evening. Your devoted husband M.'

For a brief hour or two the President and his field commander allowed themselves to hope that the worst might not happen and that their hopelessly inadequate preparations might not be tested. Moreover another 700 militiamen from Virginia were expected to arrive in Washington at any moment under Colonel George Minor. They should have nearly 7,000 men ready to fight by the morning of the 24th. Madison turned his horse back towards the city, and Winder went off to try and meet up with Stansbury. He and his Baltimore men should now be well on the road from Bladensburg to Upper Marlborough.

But they weren't. Winder could find no sign of Stansbury. He was nowhere to be seen on the road from Bladensburg to Upper Marlborough. Stansbury had been waiting for a force of 800 men including a rifle battalion under Major Pinkney to join him. Stansbury didn't hurry forward and it wasn't till late on the Tuesday evening that his whole force was together. He decided not to exhaust his men by marching through the night. He would wait till dawn. At around teatime Winder, who'd been riding about looking for Stansbury, was tracked down by a staff officer from the force left at Long Old Fields. The British had moved off early that afternoon from Upper Marlborough and had advanced to within three miles of Long Old Fields. The American advance guard had loosed off a few musket shots at the British without hitting anyone, and then retired. Joshua Barney's flotillamen and a brigade of District of Columbia militia commanded by General Walter Smith prepared to hold the line at Long Old Fields. Barney, for one, relished the prospect of avenging the destruction of his fleet. He'd met Madison earlier in the day and the President had 'exhorted the men to be firm and faithful in their duty'. Smith reported later that he had proposed to Barney 'making a stand in our then position, with which, with his characteristic gallantry, he promptly acquiesced'. Smith was confident that they could throw the British back. His artillery in which 'it was ascertained we were greatly their superior, and for which the ground was admirably adapted, [was] so posted as to have the best effect; indeed, so strong did we deem our position in front, that we were apprehensive that the enemy, upon viewing us, would forbear to assail us by daylight'.

Twenty-four hours earlier Winder might have applauded this. He had 'entertained the hope of giving the enemy a serious check'. But the news that the British were on the move set Winder's mind spinning. Now he reversed his strategy and decided to pull his men right back to Washington. Winder said he was afraid the enemy might try and stage a night attack on the camp and cause havoc among the inexperienced militia. Smith and Barney were told to withdraw across the half-mile-long road bridge spanning the Eastern Branch River (today called the Anacostia). The men were now utterly exhausted. Smith wrote that they'd been 'under arms without intermission . . . night and day . . . for four days . . . with only two rations . . . during their different marches in advance and retreat . . . exposed to the burning heat of a sultry sun by day and . . . the cold dews of the night, uncovered'. All this, said Smith, 'could not but be severely distressing to men, the greater part of whom possessed and enjoyed at home the means of comfortable living'. Few militiamen were gritty outdoorsmen used to the hardships of soldiers and nights bivouacking under the stars.

It was no less distressing for Stansbury's men. They'd made it to Bladensburg, but they were now to face a night of marching and counter-marching as their commanders openly questioned the orders they had received from General Winder. When Winder learned that the various units had arrived too late at Bladensburg to move forward towards Upper Marlborough as he had hoped, he sent orders to them to take up a strong defensive position at Bladensburg on the high ground in and around the village on the east bank of the river, and defend it as long as possible. His message arrived at two in the morning of the 24th. He told Stansbury that he had retreated with his whole force from Long Old Fields to the city of Washington. Stansbury immediately sent for his senior officers and wrote later that 'they were unanimous in their opinion that our situation on that hill [at Bladensburg] could not be defended with the force then under my command, worn down with hunger and fatigue as they were, and that it was indispensably necessary for the security of the army that we should immediately retire . . . and take a position on the road between Bladensburg and the city'. With his officers agreed that they should ignore Winder's orders, the order to march was given at 3.30 a.m. It was a notable piece of disobedience by one of Winder's key commanders and exposed the flaws of America's loose military system. It meant that Stansbury abandoned his strong position on the east bank of the river, which would have been a formidable obstacle to the British advance when it came.

John Pendleton Kennedy was one of the luckier of Stansbury's militiamen. He'd arrived at Bladensburg with an early contingent and had had time to enjoy a relaxed supper of some stolen chickens, ham and coffee. 'Finding ourselves with an extra supply of candles, we indulged the luxury of lighting some three or four, which, being fitted into the band of the bayonet with the point stuck in the ground, gave an unusual splendour to the interior of our tent.' At 1 a.m. there was a false alarm and they all frantically sought their belongings in the pitch dark. 'Some got the wrong boots, others a coat that didn't fit, some could not find their cross-belts. I luckily was all right except that I sallied out in my [dancing] pumps.' He'd brought the pumps along hoping to be invited to the ball the President would give at the White House 'after we'd beaten the British and saved Washington'. Later in the night Kennedy was woken again for the march back across the river and down towards Washington. He couldn't find his boots: they'd been thrown on to the regimental wagon. He was still in his dancing pumps.

The entire American army had now abandoned the east side of the river. The road to Washington was suddenly wide open to General Ross's invading forces. And Ross hadn't – yet – lost a single man in action.

James Madison, who had only a few hours earlier expressed such optimism to his wife, was now in no doubt that he faced a fight for his capital. He had stopped on the way home to write another quick pencilled note to Dolley telling her that she should make ready to leave the White House. The British, he wrote, seemed stronger than they had been before and were 'marching on the city, with intention to destroy it'. She should make her arrangements to pack what papers she could and escape in a carriage 'at a moment's warning'. Dolley wrote a hasty letter to her sister dated Tuesday 23 August: 'I am accordingly ready. I have pressed as many cabinet papers into trunks as to fill one carriage; our private property must be sacrificed.' It was, she said, impossible to procure wagons for its transportation. 'I am determined not to go myself until I see Mr Madison safe, and he can accompany me, as I hear of much hostility towards him . . . disaffection stalks around us.' Apart from those who had always opposed the war with Britain, there was now an increasing number of people who felt that Madison and his military commanders were mishandling the crisis, and that he was to blame for the imminent prospect of death and destruction in the streets of the American capital.

There was now a mood little short of pandemonium throughout Washington. Dolley Madison's close friend Margaret Bayard Smith wrote that very few women or children remained in the city on that Tuesday evening. Earlier in the day she had been cheered by accounts 'that the enemy were retreating'. American troops, she recalled, were – at that stage – displaying 'a cheerful alacrity', and among the citizens of Washington there was a 'universal confidence . . . few doubted our conquering'. Now all those hopes were dashed. She said that she and her family had intended to remain at home but:

> we were roused Tuesday night by a loud knocking. On the opening
> of the door Willie Bradley called to us 'The enemy are advancing, our
> own troops are giving way on all sides and are retreating to the city.
> Go, for God' s sake, Go.' He spoke in a voice of agony and then flew
> to his horse and was out of sight in a moment. We immediately rose,
> the carriage and horses were soon ready, we loaded a wagon with
> what goods remained and about 3 o'clock left our house with all our
> servants.

She still felt it unlikely that the British would win possession of the city: the army would defend it and it wouldn't be defeated. 'I felt no alarm or agitation, as I knew the danger was not near. I even felt no distress at the idea of forsaking our home.' They travelled very slowly as it was dark: Margaret Bayard-Smith herself had to walk part of the way. Her three daughters, aged three, ten and thirteen, were 'quite delighted with our flight, novelty has such charms at their age . . . Even for myself I felt animated, invigorated, willing to encounter any hardship.' The family finally reached the house of a friend in the country, Mrs Bently, where 'all seemed security and peace'.

The family of William Jones, the Navy Secretary, were planning to escape too. He and his wife had been invited to dine that evening with the Madisons at the White House. But in the afternoon Mrs Jones wrote to Dolley saying 'in the present state of alarm and bustle of preparation for the worst that may happen, I imagine it will be more convenient to dispense with your hospitality today . . .'. Her husband, wrote Mrs Jones, was 'deeply engaged in despatching the marines . . . Lucy and I are packing, with the possibility of having to leave.' She said they had no ideas where to go, or how to transport their belongings. 'Our carriage horse is sick, and our coachmen absent . . .'

Fortunately for those in Washington the British army didn't march much further that day. After the odd skirmish with the advance guard of General Smith's men from Long Old Fields, General Ross called a halt in the grounds of a large house at Melwood. Cockburn was with him; Washington was now only a short march away. They could either approach it by the Eastern Branch Bridge across the wide Eastern Branch of the Potomac, or they could bear north and cross the river, where it was much narrower, by the bridge at Bladensburg. There was a third, rickety wooden bridge, halfway between them, called Stoddert's Bridge, but it could be easily destroyed, so was an unlikely choice. George Gleig was posted with his men as a picket in an elegant house – Gleig called it a 'chateau' – some miles from the British camp. They were treated to a sumptuous supper by the owner, a 'gentleman of extensive fortune', who appeared very friendly. But Gleig was suspicious that their host might be about to spring a trap and there was indeed late that night what looked like an attempt to attack them. 'Our situation was most ticklish ... Burrell [on sentry watch] came and told us the enemy were surrounding us ... I commanded the men to fire. The enemy halted and then, without so much as returning our salute, melted away.'

Ross and Cockburn were awaiting the return of James Scott, who had set off down the river in Cockburn's gig earlier in the day to tell the British Commander in Chief of their determination to press on to Washington. Vice Admiral Sir Alexander Cochrane received Scott on the *Tonnant*, his flagship, near Benedict and a heated debate followed between the admirals about the wisest course to follow. There were three admirals present, Cochrane himself and two others who, like George Cockburn, were as rear admirals a rank below him – Edward Codrington and Poultney Malcolm. Malcolm, whose failing eyesight soon had him writing to his wife, Clementine, for new spectacles, was feeling rather spare. He had convoyed Ross's troops from France but was now feeling redundant and clearly jealous of George Cockburn. 'I hope Cockburn will go home,' he was shortly to write to his wife, 'only because he is my senior. He is a dashing fellow and I attribute our excursion to Washington to his sanguine advice.' The key mover in the debate on Cochrane's flagship was Codrington, the experienced Trafalgar veteran who now commanded Cochrane's fleet. Scott recalls him 'appearing to think the attempt [on Washington] was too rash'. Cochrane himself had always doubted the wisdom of marching on the American capital. Malcolm, perhaps partly out of envy of Cockburn, was inclined to be cautious too. Ross was forty miles from the ships with an army that was a fraction of the size of the force that the Americans should be able to put into the field and he had virtually no horses or guns. True, Barney's flotilla was eliminated, but Cochrane, conscious all the time of Whitehall's insistence that the army should never stray far from the ships, determined not to allow success to turn into tragedy. Scott was despatched with Cochrane's reply to Cockburn, and instructed to eat the letter he carried if there was a chance of him being made prisoner. He was told to read its contents before he left and commit them to memory. 'I carefully perused and reperused the dispatch,' and the orders 'were to the following effect: that under all circumstances the Rear Admiral [Cockburn] had already effected more than England could have expected with the small force under his orders; that he was on no account to proceed one mile further, but, upon receipt of that order, the army was immediately to return to Benedict to embark; that the ulterior and principal objects of the expedition would be risked by an attempt upon the capital with such inadequate means'. And Scott recalled that the despatch concluded with 'a reiteration of the orders to return immediately'.

The Commander in Chief had pulled the plug on the whole operation. The invasion of Washington was off.

6

Be it so, we will proceed

24 August, morning

JAMES SCOTT TUCKED away the admiral's message and made all speed back to Upper Marlborough and then rode on through the night. 'It was very dark and we had some difficulty finding our way . . . we fell in with some of the enemy's cavalry, who however galloped off without molesting us.' He was relieved at not being caught and having to swallow Cochrane's note. 'I was right glad when the bivouac fires of our friends appeared in sight,' runs his account. And he was shown to the shepherd's hut where Cockburn and Ross had bedded down for the night. It was 2 a.m. 'I found both of them stretched out on their cloaks, enjoying the rest which the severe fatigues of the preceding day must have rendered so grateful.'

Scott gave the Commander in Chief's letter to Cockburn. The admiral read it and then handed it to Ross. The general took one look at it and then remarked that there was now no alternative but to return. He had always had his doubts, now he had no choice. They had to abort the operation. 'No!' replied the admiral. 'We cannot do that; we are too advanced to think of a retreat; let us take a turn outside and talk the matter over.' Scott says he and the general's two staff officers, George Evans and Harry Smith, were:

> at a short distance and could not avoid hearing what passed as they walked to and fro in earnest conversation. 'If we proceed,' said our energetic commander [Cockburn], 'I'll pledge everything that is dear to me as an officer that we shall succeed. If we return without striking a blow, it will be worse than defeat – it will bring a stain upon our arms. I know their force – the militia, however great their numbers, will not – cannot stand against your disciplined troops. It is too late,'

continued the Admiral, 'we ought not to have advanced – there is now no choice left us. We must go on.'

He was determined to convince Ross that there was absolutely no alternative. Cockburn had to persuade Ross that even if they could have called off the enterprise earlier on, there could now be no turning back. He knew that the final call in this major strategic decision was not down to him but to the general. This was a land operation. The admiral was not in command. He led only a handful of sailors and marines. Ross led the army.* But Cockburn was taking as great a risk – perhaps more of one – than Ross: the admiral was flouting the orders of his direct naval superior; Ross enjoyed a certain autonomy as the commander of the land force. Scott says the discussion went on – with Evans also pressing Cockburn's case – till, suddenly, at daybreak Ross gave in. 'The General had been much excited, and at this moment, striking his hand against his forehead, he exclaimed, "Well. Be it so, we will proceed."'

Ross immediately passed on orders to his other commanders and the army was soon on the march. Evans wrote in his official memorandum that the Commander in Chief, Vice Admiral Cochrane, had sent a message recommending 'in strenuous terms' an immediate retreat, which 'the general . . . with the entire concurrence of the rear admiral did not hesitate to disregard'. Talk of a possible retreat had caused widespread disappointment among the men. Ross's caution was by now a byword throughout the ranks: it wasn't just Harry Smith, George Evans and Cockburn who thought the general too hesitant. But when they heard the advance on Washington was on again, 'a low murmuring burst of enthusiasm involuntarily escaped from the lips of the officers and men, sufficiently indicative of the spirit that animated the hearts of the gallant band'.

---

* It's an interesting twist that Ross's aide George de Lacy Evans, writing later on, claims that in a recent Cockburn biography the admiral's role has been greatly overplayed: he could not, as the biographer suggests, have 'determined to make an attack' on Washington: that was Ross's role. Cockburn had no more authority to order the army to advance than 'the youngest midshipman' (Evans, *Facts*, pp. 1–4).

Cockburn had persuaded Ross to take a huge gamble. If they failed, their careers would be at an end. In a letter to his wife a week later, Ross wrote: 'at the moment the attempt was made upon the city of Washington, I felt apprehension of the consequences of failure'. They would be disowned by Cochrane for disobeying orders. The British government, press and public would condemn them for recklessly transforming a moderate success into a fiasco. The odds against them were high: their army was dangerously far from its base with its rear quite unprotected; their 4,500 men faced a potential enemy twice or three times their number; British infantry alone would have to tackle American guns, cavalry and footsoldiers on ground of their choice; their enemies would be fighting for their capital, their homes and their families. But Cockburn – and Ross, whether he finally gave way to his own inner conviction or to Cockburn's impassioned persistence – could count on one proven asset that now had to be decisive: the quality of their soldiers. Ross would lead a force whose battle honours were the admiration of the world. In the last two and a half years they had crushed the armies of Napoleon in victory after victory in the field, from Salamanca to Toulouse, and they had blasted their way into strongholds like Ciudad Rodrigo and Badajoz that made Washington look defenceless. These gritty veterans of the war in Europe would confront an army of untried, poorly trained part-timers. And the experience of the last week was promising: any professional opponent would have used every opportunity to harass the invading army's flanks and rear and plant impediments in its way. The British had suffered only the most trivial pinpricks and there had been no attempt to use trees or other obstructions to block their route. The die was cast. For Cockburn, Ross and their army it was now either victory or disgrace – even death.

The last-minute hiccup in the British high command – and the brief chance of a reprieve for the city – was imperceptible to the frantic population of Washington. One eyewitness of the panic in the capital that night at 1 a.m. on 24 August said, 'I cannot find language to express the situation of the women and children, who are running the streets in a state bordering on distraction; their husbands, father and brothers all under arms, scarce a man to be seen in the city. Enemy reported to be 13,000 strong.' Each family had the agonising decision to make: should they leave their homes to the mercy of the British, if they were to enter the city, or should they stay and risk all? Very few decided to stay.

Winder still believed there was a chance the British would head for Annapolis. But if their target was Washington, which even he had now come to believe the most probable, there were two possible approaches. They could march west and cross the long Eastern Branch Bridge. Or they could thrust north-west to Bladensburg and cross the much shorter bridge there. Bladensburg had the obvious attraction to the British of being the lowest point where the river was fordable if the bridges were destroyed. But Winder still wasn't sure.

He decided his best option was to withdraw his army direct to the city itself. He had left the lower, longer bridge intact in order to allow his army to do that. And it was across it that he dragged the exhausted troops and heavy guns he had held at Long Old Fields throughout the day. Once they were across there was every reason to blow all the bridges up. He ordered the captain of the Washington artillery to supervise this operation, and eight barrels of powder were sent up from the Navy Yard in small boats to be ready to do just that. But somehow the bridge was never destroyed. According to George de Lacy Evans, Ross deliberately kept the Americans guessing by taking a road which initially led towards both bridges – the bridge across the Eastern Branch and the bridge at Bladensburg. The third, wooden Stoddert's Bridge was set alight and destroyed on Winder's orders in the early hours of the 24th. If Winder had expressly destroyed the long Eastern Branch Bridge once all his men were across and effectively ruled out that approach for the British, he could have concentrated his army at Bladensburg. But throughout the night and until ten o'clock the following morning he remained unsure which bridge the British would use, and those hours of uncertainty further strained the tolerance of a number of his commanders.

Through what must have been the longest night of his life, William Winder rode backwards and forwards from one unit to another desperately trying to reconcile the deployment of his forces with his uncertainty about the British objective. He called Benjamin Burch, Washington's artillery captain, out of his tent and asked him to carry out 'one of the last good acts which it might ever be in my power to do for my country that night' – to guard the Eastern Branch Bridge. Burch, who recalled that his men were 'so fatigued they could hardly stand by their guns', had to haul his artillery to the end of the bridge in the pitch dark and stay alert all night. Winder didn't relieve him and his men till ten o'clock the following morning. He called in Joshua Barney's flotillamen to replace Burch, so that Burch and his gunners could hurry to Bladensburg to stop the British there. Another late-night call Winder made was on Commodore Tingey, who was fast asleep in his house at the Navy Yard. Was there enough gunpowder on its way to blow up the bridge? he asked. Tingey said several casks were ready to move, but Winder told him to increase the quantity. He then went back to the bridge to make sure it was properly guarded, and finally back to his headquarters 'about three or four o'clock, much exhausted, and considerably hurt in the right arm and ankle from a severe fall which I had into a gully or ditch on my way to the Navy Yard'. In between all this shuttling to and fro Winder had been trying to communicate with the commanders of the two halves of his army, General Smith in Washington whom Winder couldn't track down in his camp, and General Stansbury who had taken matters into his own hands at Bladensburg. Winder was furious. 'I learned about this time, with considerable mortification, that General Stansbury, from misunderstanding or some other cause, instead of holding a position during the night, in advance of Bladensburg, had taken one about a mile in the rear . . . and was at this moment on his march into the city.'

Stansbury was now well on his way towards Washington with his brigade, having ignored Winder's earlier order to resist any British assault at Bladensburg. He now received another message from Winder repeating his insistence that he, Stansbury, should stay at

Bladensburg. It was daylight by now and Stansbury called another meeting of his top staff: 'I laid the letter [from Winder] before them.' One of his top commanders said the men were 'worn down and exhausted . . . and that he should consider it a sacrifice of both officers and men to seek the enemy at any considerable distance from General Winder's force . . .' Once again they all agreed to ignore Winder's orders and continue towards Washington. Stansbury and his commanders were convinced that they had a far better chance of thwarting any British assault in a favourable defensive position nearer Washington than eight miles away to the north-east at Bladensburg. It was a blatant challenge to Winder's authority.

It wasn't only Winder's subordinate commanders who were expressing unease and even contempt for their Commander in Chief. One of those who had dined with the President at the farm near Long Old Fields the previous night was a respected intellectual and pillar of Washington society, William Thornton. He was born in the British Virgin Islands and had trained in medicine at Edinburgh University before travelling to America. He was now a fifty-five-year-old doctor and architect, who had among other things designed the original US Capitol buildings for George Washington. The Thorntons were close to the Madisons but that didn't stop William's forthright wife Anna Maria – no doubt reflecting her husband's views – writing in her diary of the 'great error in [which] Winder and all engaged'. It was a mistake pulling the army back across the bridge into Washington, 'which gave the troops an opportunity of dispersing, particularly those who had families or homes in the city'. Winder, she said, should have destroyed the bridge and concentrated his whole army at Bladensburg. 'Instead of this the troops were marched off their legs.'

Winder's problem was not only his own bumbling: he was poorly served by his colleagues and subordinates. Stansbury had openly disobeyed him. Others failed to respond to his urgent calls for action. The Virginia militia, who'd arrived in the city on Tuesday the 23rd under Colonel George Minor, were eager to reinforce the army but were without weapons and ammunition. Anxious to lead his men to the front Minor reported his requirement to the President, who referred him to the War Secretary John Armstrong. Armstrong told him the arms could not be obtained that night and he should report to a Colonel Carbery in the morning. But on the Wednesday morning there was no sign of Colonel Carbery. After searching for him for hours Minor sought out Winder himself, who personally signed an order to the armourer to equip the men. 'On my arrival at the armoury, I found that department in the care of a very young man, who dealt out the stores cautiously, which went greatly to consume time.' For example, said Minor later, his own officers, keen to get the job done, counted out the flints their men needed, but 'the young man had to count them over again before they could be obtained . . .'. The result of all these delays was that Minor's men were not in time to reinforce Winder.

Even when Winder woke that morning after an hour or two's sleep he still couldn't be sure where the battle for Washington would be fought. At nine o'clock President Madison came to his headquarters. For an hour he discussed the crisis with Winder, James Monroe, the Secretary of State, now acting as an alternative battlefield commander, Richard Rush, the Attorney General, William Jones, Navy Secretary, Thomas Tingey, the Navy Yard commander, George Campbell, the Treasury Secretary, and – a late arrival – War Secretary John Armstrong. Madison recalled that he and his ministers grew increasingly impatient at Armstrong's absence and expressed surprise when he finally turned up. Campbell in particular was quick to criticise Armstrong. He'd met the War Secretary the night before and asked him in a forthright manner why the army had waited this long and retired this far before confronting the enemy or at least doing much more to harass their advance. Surely to make the fate of the city depend on a single battle, to be fought on their side by raw, inexperienced troops, was too much of a risk? Campbell was surprised to find that Armstrong appeared to agree with him, and so he pursued him further. Had Armstrong offered his advice, and was he ready to make suggestions to Winder about how best to proceed? Armstrong replied that he had left all that to Winder: to express his own opinion might be 'indelicate and perhaps improper unless he had the approbation of the Executive for so doing'. Campbell was astounded: 'surely feelings of delicacy . . . should not be allowed to come into collision with the public interest?' What on earth was the use of a war secretary if he wasn't ready to question and advise his commanders?

Campbell was so disturbed by this conversation that he raised it with the President at that morning's meeting. Campbell said he 'regretted the reserve apparently observed by the Secretary of War', to which Madison replied that he was sure Armstrong was able to volunteer his opinion and that Winder would listen to him. Not, it appears, without your say-so, replied Campbell. Madison agreed to talk to Armstrong. 'I could scarcely conceive that General Armstrong could have so misconstrued his functions and duty as Secretary of War; that he could not but know that any proper directions from him would receive any sanction that might be necessary from the Executive.'

Armstrong's extraordinary detachment had already prompted Madison to doubt his judgement. The morning meeting only strengthened the President's view that his War Secretary was living in a different world. Armstrong's determination not to be involved in matters that were clearly within his remit was thought particularly odd in view of the fact that he later admitted he'd just received a note from Winder 'asking counsel from me, or from the government'. Madison asked Armstrong point blank – close enough to the Attorney General Richard Rush for him to remember the words – whether he had any advice or plan to offer. 'He replied that he had not.' He then added his forecast of what would be likely to happen in any battle between America's army and the British. 'As it was to be between regulars and militia, the latter would be beaten.'

By this time – around ten o'clock – the first definitive message arrived relating to the whereabouts of the British. They were marching direct on Bladensburg. They would clearly attempt to cross the river at the bridge there and then descend on Washington. Winder, suddenly all action, ordered his whole army – including General

Smith's men in Washington – to put on all speed to Bladensburg and take up a defensive position there. Stansbury and his men were also ordered finally and emphatically to retrace their steps to Bladensburg. This time Stansbury promptly agreed. Winder departed, leaving Armstrong with Madison, who was clearly now deeply anxious about the likely outcome of a battle for Washington with his two top military men, Armstrong and Winder, so obviously at loggerheads. Madison later wrote that he turned to his War Secretary and 'expressed to him my concern and surprise at the reserve he showed at the present crisis, and at the scruples I understood he had at offering his advice or opinions . . .'. And Madison went further. He said he himself would go to the front line and be 'near at hand . . . to remove . . . any difficulty on the score of authority' between Armstrong and Winder. Madison, who had no military experience, was in such despair at the prospects for the battle for Washington that he felt he had to go to the battlefield and oversee it himself. Armstrong rode off, soon to be followed by Madison and Richard Rush. Rush was by far the most junior member of the cabinet, but he was close to Madison: the President trusted him and felt comfortable with him at his side. As the two men rode away, Campbell, the Treasury Secretary, fearful for the President's safety, handed Madison his brace of duelling pistols.

John Pendleton Kennedy, still in his dancing shoes, was one of Stansbury's men who had marched back and forth through the night. By morning he was ready to drop. 'I slept as I walked. At every halt of a moment whole platoons laid down in the dusty road and slept till the officers gave the word to move on. How very weary I felt.' At length they were allowed to lie in a field of stubble and grab some sleep. 'Mine was the sleep of Endymion. When I awoke I was lying on my back with the hot sun of a summer's morning beaming upon my face.' By 11 a.m. he and all the other troops under Stansbury's command were back at Bladensburg.

The only unit that was being left behind in the rush to Bladensburg was that of Joshua Barney still guarding the lower Eastern Branch Bridge, even though the enemy were now clearly headed elsewhere.

Winder had denied Barney's flotillamen a battle with the British the day before; now it looked like they'd miss the decisive battle for Washington. Barney had no time for Winder: his daughter and biographer Mary Barney calls Winder 'the commanding general, if indeed he could be properly so called'. He was now fuming about his pointless assignment on the bridge. Then suddenly the President rode past on his way to Bladensburg and greeted him. Barney immediately asked permission to abandon his position and move his men and guns to join the army at Bladensburg. He said it was absurd for his formidable force of flotillamen to be wasted where they were. 'A midshipman with half a dozen men' could stop the enemy crossing the bridge. John Armstrong quoted Barney saying the job could have been done by 'a corporal and six men'. Madison agreed. Barney and his men should move at once to Bladensburg. They would be a useful reinforcement. They were to prove more than useful: they would play a vital role in preserving the honour of the United States.

The British army had been on the road to Washington since 5 a.m. For a time Ross persisted in keeping the Americans guessing by sticking to a road that led to both the still-intact bridges. But by 9 a.m. he was clearly on the road to Bladensburg. It would have been more direct to approach the capital across the Eastern Branch Bridge, but Ross knew it would be a simple matter for the Americans to deny access by destroying a small section of it. The river was too wide to cross anywhere south of Bladensburg without a massive amphibious operation.

There was a nervous moment when some American sharpshooter took shots at Ross and Cockburn and their aides. 'Three or four of these gentlemen', James Scott recalled, 'were suddenly discovered above us on a high bank secured by a paling. The acting Quartermaster General [none other than the eager George de Lacy Evans] was the first to observe them, mounted the bank by the slope leading up to their hiding place, clapped his spurs into the flanks of his charger and gallantly taking the pales, leaped into the thick of them . . .

they instantly threw away their rifles and scampered into the brush-wood . . .'

For the first few hours of the day the British army had to make its way through difficult wooded country, but by 9 a.m. the country had opened out, the road had widened and the going had become easy. George Gleig saw increasing signs of life on both sides. The sight of villages, farms and rich meadows cheered up the troops – many of whom were beginning to flag. 'To add to the general spirit of exhil-aration, the bugles of the light corps sounded a lively march, and the troops moved, in spite of the heat and weakness, merrily, gaily and rapidly.' But the high spirits didn't last long. 'The sun beat upon us in full force; and the dust rising in thick masses from under our feet, without a breath of air to disperse it, flew directly into our faces . . . I do not recollect a period of my military life during which I suffered more severely from heat and fatigue . . . it is not surprising that before many hours had elapsed numbers of men began to fall behind from absolute inability to keep up.' At around ten o'clock Ross called a halt. 'We threw ourselves upon the grass and in five minutes the mass of the army was asleep. My eyes were closed before my head hit the ground . . .'

Ross gave his men an hour to rest, then, clearly energised by the prospect of a showdown with the Americans, he ordered his army on under an unyielding sun. It wasn't long before his troops were plainly wilting again, 'some of the finest and stoutest men in the army being literally unable to go on'. The British forces were hardly in a state to fight a battle, but by noon that is exactly what they realised they would have to do. They began to discern a great cloud of dust rising a mile or two to their left, and then 'on turning a sudden angle in the road . . . the British and American armies became visible to one another. The position occupied by the latter was one of great strength and commanding attitude.' But Gleig observed that as the Americans were composed chiefly of militia they 'exhibited to our eyes a very singular and very awkward appearance. Sufficiently armed, but wretchedly equipped, clothed part in black coats, others in blue, others in ordinary shooting-jackets, and some in round frocks . . .

The Battle of Bladensburg (1),
24 August 1814

Laval's cavalry

Sterett

to Georgetown

Baltimore guns

Bladensburg

Thornton

Schutz

Pinkney

STANSBURY

Ragan

ROSS

Scott

WINDER

Peter

Barney

Kramer

to Upper
Marlborough

SMITH
DC
militia

Miller

Beall

to Washington

0   ¼ mile

0   400 metres

they might have passed off very well for a crowd of spectators, come out to view the approach of the army which was to occupy Washington.' Some, dressed in blue jackets, looked to Gleig like regular troops, but the rest 'seemed country people, who would have been more appropriately employed in attending to their agricultural occupations'.

The British had reached the outskirts of the village of Bladensburg on the east bank of the river. It was the very village that General Tobias Stansbury and his large American force had occupied twelve hours earlier before Stansbury had decided to withdraw and head back towards Washington – against Winder's orders. As Ross looked down on Bladensburg from the high ground of Lowndes Hill, he saw the Americans fast taking position on the other bank of the river. Their number was clearly greater than his. The village on the east bank, beneath him, appeared unoccupied. His scouts reported that it was indeed empty, and he decided promptly to advance down the hill, through the village and across the narrow bridge that led straight into the heart of the American position. Robert Ross was now eager for battle, all his caution swept away. He was seized by the almost reckless enthusiasm that had prompted him to plunge into battle against the French at Vitoria and Orthez. Courage and forthright leadership had won him the devotion of his troops in the Peninsula and the admiration of the Iron Duke. Now he would display it again. With only a few minutes of briefing his various commanders, and without even waiting for the whole of his army to arrive, he ordered his men into the village and across the bridge. Ross was playing for the highest stakes. Defeat would mean an almost certain court martial.

By eleven o'clock that morning, Wednesday 24 August, the United States President and his Commander in Chief were on the field at Bladensburg. It was a short ride – six miles north-east of the capital. There they found Stansbury's and Smith's forces together with a number of other units rapidly taking positions on the west bank of the river. James Monroe, the Secretary of State, was there too, busily deploying the units where he thought fit. Madison had agreed to let him leave the earlier meeting in Washington and ride ahead of the others to see what he could do. Madison's first thought was to cross the bridge and see what was happening in the village on the other side. He was well on his way when William Simmons, an American scout who'd been keeping an eye on Ross's approaching army, rode up to him in great haste. 'Mr Madison, the enemy are now in Bladensburg.' 'The enemy in Bladensburg!' gasped Madison in surprise. Simmons then watched the President and his party all turn their horses and ride back at speed to the American lines. 'I called out aloud: "Mr Madison, if you will stop, I will show them to you;

they are now in sight.'" But they all rode off very fast except Richard Rush, the Attorney General, who told Simmons he doubted that there were British in Bladensburg. But the sight of a few British redcoats gathering in the village street was enough to send Rush galloping off to safety. His hat flew off and Simmons had to shout at him to come back for it.

With every sign that a battle was about to begin, Madison and Rush had time for a brief meeting with Monroe, Winder and Armstrong. One of Madison's reasons for coming to Bladensburg was to reassure Armstrong that he could readily offer advice to Winder about where to place his troops and how to fight the battle. Winder had said he wanted advice: Armstrong should feel free to offer it and he, the President, would be there to show that this was in order. Madison recorded every detail of what followed in his own personal memorandum of what happened that day: 'I asked [Armstrong] whether he had spoken with General Winder on the subject of his arrangement and views. He said he had not. I remarked that though there was so little time for it, it was possible he might offer some advice or suggestion that might not be too late to be turned to account.' Armstrong and Madison then rode up to Winder, but 'the unruliness of my horse prevented me from joining in the short conversation that took place. When it was over, I asked General Armstrong whether he had seen occasion to offer any improvement in any part of the arrangements. He said that he had not; that from his view of them they appeared to be as good as circumstances admitted.' Armstrong persisted in keeping himself at arm's length from any responsibility for the city's defence. Moments later the first shots rang out. Rush's memory of this many years later was of British rockets flying over their heads as they sat on their horses. Armstrong and Winder 'were in close view of the front line, as was the President, doing what they could do to encourage the resistance'. Madison now observed to his three cabinet ministers that it was time for them to withdraw and leave matters to the 'military functionaries'. Armstrong later remarked that after these words from the President: 'I now became, of course, a mere spectator of the combat.' He was no doubt relieved that Madison was apparently freeing him from any further involvement – but he may also have been smarting at his own failure to play a stronger hand.*

Madison and his ministers rapidly retired to the rear. Some, unkindly, said later that the President fled from the field. One typically hostile voice in the opposition newspaper *Federal Republican* accused the President of being 'the first to fly . . . and on his very countenance bore the marks of fear and trembling'. Other, less biased reports say Madison waited near the battlefield with Rush until they learned the outcome of the battle before returning to Washington. Back home Madison had left his wife to supervise the preparation of a meal for himself and his cabinet at the end of a hard day. 'Mrs Madison ordered dinner to be ready at 3 as usual,' recounted Paul Jennings, the White House servant. 'I set the table myself and brought up the ale, cider and wine and placed them in the coolers, as all the cabinet and several military gentlemen and strangers were expected.'

The President and his guests would never sit down to the dinner, and James and Dolley Madison would never spend another night at the White House.

---

* Madison was not the last President to be present on an active battlefield. President Lincoln actually came under fire twice at Fort Stevens in Maryland on 11 and 12 July 1864.

7

Bladensburg: a fine scamper

24 August, afternoon

I T WAS SOON after midday on Wednesday 24 August that the Battle
of Bladensburg began. The Americans had the advantage of numbers and location: there were around 6,000 of them in defensive
positions facing Ross's army of 4,500, which had to attack across a
river. On the American side veterans like James Monroe knew that
they were not facing the bungling British army they'd defeated in their
fight for independence thirty years earlier. But most American troops,
inexperienced though most of them were, were fired up with patriotic
enthusiasm. They were defending their young country against an
enemy who'd sailed from the other side of the ocean to ravage their
capital and burn their homes. 'As for me – not yet nineteen,' wrote
John Pendleton Kennedy, describing his march down from Baltimore,
'I was too full of the exaltation of the time to think of myself – all
my fervor was spent in the admiration of this glittering army.'

On the ground – as Gleig, Scott and Ross himself noted – the
Americans held a commanding position on the west bank of the river.
They occupied partly wooded ground that sloped down from a ridge
one and a half miles away. The stream in front of them was 50 yards
wide with only a narrow bridge offering the British a crossing point.
Stansbury had prudently ordered forty horsemen with axes to cut
away the bridge. But in the rush to take up their positions that morning someone had overlooked Stansbury's command to destroy it.
'Why this order was not executed, I never could learn.' The river
was fordable 100 yards further upstream, but if the bridge was there,
the British would use it.

This wasn't the only failure of foresight on the American side. The deployment of their forces was woefully maladroit. Their units were strung out in three lines so widely separated from front to rear that they could give little support to each other, and none of the lines was long enough to avoid being outflanked to left and right. The weakest of the three lines, the front line facing the river crossing, was the one that should have been the strongest. The place to stop the British was where they were most vulnerable – crossing the river. The only American firepower with the range to hit the bridge was a battery of six 6-pounder guns placed about 300 yards from the crossing. The gunners struggled – in the short time they had – to conceal their cannon behind embrasures which had been designed for much bigger guns. So they had little protection and they had only scant infantry support on either side of them.

Closest to the guns was Major William Pinkney with his two companies of riflemen. Pinkney was a distinguished lawyer and diplomat: he had been Minister to Britain and President Madison's Attorney General. He now suddenly found himself in the very front line of the battle for Washington. He commanded around 150 men from Baltimore armed with rifles, which were proving far more effective than the old musket. Both fired musket balls propelled from the barrel by the blast of a powder cartridge stuffed down it and ignited by the spark from a flint released by a trigger. But the musket's barrel was smooth. The ball that shot out of it quickly lost its range and accuracy: you were lucky to hit someone you were aiming at 100 yards away. The most effective range of the musket was under fifty yards. The groove of rifling spiralling its way up the inside of a rifle's barrel sent the ball spinning far more accurately over a longer distance. The rifle's effective range was between 200 and 300 yards. It was slower to load – the best soldiers could fire a shot from a rifle every thirty seconds compared to every twenty seconds from a musket. But when you could kill an enemy 300 yards away, the advantage was clear. The rifle was fast becoming the favourite weapon of the American frontiersman but it was not yet established as the prime military weapon, and in this campaign it had been largely unavailable even to men described as 'riflemen'. The British had rifles too, but the vast majority of Ross's soldiers were armed with muskets. The British veterans had years of exhaustive experience in fast-loading their muskets. Besides, hundreds of hours of drill and manoeuvre had taught them the rigour of maintaining their lines shoulder to shoulder no matter what was thrown at them. And in close combat a quick flash of steel and a click would signal that every man was fastening a bayonet to the end of his musket. Only the very bravest would stand in their way.

The American army's ill-prepared dispositions were a direct result of the confusion of command at the top. William Winder, who had pleaded for guidance earlier in the day and got short shrift from Armstrong, had turned up too late at Bladensburg to do much to readjust the posture of his forces. They were largely in the positions that General Stansbury and General Walter Smith had chosen for them over the previous twenty-four hours. Stansbury's men, mainly from Baltimore, in the front lines, Smith's men, mainly DC militia, in the third line, a whole mile behind the others at the top of the long slope. There was also a small contingent of regulars in the third line under Lieutenant Colonel William Scott, and at the last minute Joshua Barney and his flotillamen and marines dashed into the line thanks to Madison's acceptance that they'd been wasting their time guarding the Eastern Branch Bridge.

It was James Monroe who was the first on the field that morning. He'd persuaded Madison to let him go ahead and see how things looked. He wasn't happy. He told one commander, 'Although you see that I am active, you will please to bear in mind that this is not my plan.' One cavalry commander, Lieutenant Colonel Jacint Lavall, rode up and told Monroe he'd had no orders and couldn't find Winder. Where should he place his men? Monroe didn't help by ordering Lavall to ride his men into a ravine from which they could see nothing of the battle. Lavall later complained that he was given no idea of where any of the other American troops were on the battlefield. Monroe's dispositions prompted Armstrong to describe him as a 'blundering tactician' – which was pretty rich coming from the man whose own nonchalant attitude that morning had left his colleagues in despair. The most unsettling of the barrage of orders that rang out before the battle began was the last-minute command to Stansbury's troops to move back from their front-line support of the artillery and riflemen to a position no less than 500 yards behind. This left the 'flanks of the artillery and riflemen unprotected', said Stansbury later. 'Whose order this was, I know not; it was not mine, nor did it meet with my approbation; but finding a superior officer on the ground I concluded he had ordered it, consequently did not interfere.' Stansbury then rode up the hill to try and find out who had given the order. He located Winder, who had now appeared on the field, and asked him what was going on. Stansbury's report doesn't make clear what answer he got. Whoever did give this crassly incompetent order – and it's widely accepted it was Monroe – the result was disastrous. The American army now found itself split not into two but into three lines so separated from each other that they could do nothing to support each other. This was the dysfunctional state of the American high command as the first British soldiers appeared in the streets of Bladensburg on the other side of the river marching down towards the bridge.

William Winder's opponent, General Robert Ross, was by contrast driving his men into battle with a headstrong self-assurance that had some of his aides trying to restrain him. Harry Smith, who'd deplored the general's caution two days earlier, now thought him reckless. 'We old Light Division [men]', Smith wrote, 'always took a good look before we struck . . . I was saying to General Ross we should make a feint at least on the enemy's left flank, which rested on the river higher up . . .' But Ross wouldn't listen to him. He was fired up by the ardour of one of his senior commanders, Colonel William Thornton, who was directing his men down the hill towards the bridge. 'To my horror and astonishment,' Smith wrote later, 'General Ross consented to this isolated and premature attack. "Heavens!" says I, "General Ross, neither of the other brigades can be up in time to support this mad attack, and if the enemy fight, Thornton's brigade must be repulsed."'

Neither Ross nor his forward brigade commander was going to be talked out of it. The 85th Light Infantry, with George Gleig among them, marched down the hill and towards the bridge. These were the men who had won Wellington's praise three years earlier for their extraordinary bravery at the Battle of Fuentes d'Oñoro in May 1811. But their enemy here in the USA hadn't yet seen how they could fight. 'The Americans,' recalled Gleig, 'from the instant that our advanced guard came in view, continued to rend the air with shouts. Our men marched on, silent as the grave and orderly as people at a funeral.' Immediately the American guns the other side of the bridge opened up on them. 'A continued fire was kept up, with some exe-cution, from those guns which stood to the left of the road,' reported Gleig; 'but it was not till the bridge was covered with our people that the two-gun battery upon the road itself began to play . . . and with tremendous effect; for at the first discharge almost an entire company was swept down.'

The American fire drove Gleig and his men to seek shelter behind one of the houses in the village. 'Cannon shot after cannon shot continued all the while, to pass through the thin brick walls about us . . . at last a ball struck a soldier between Williams and myself, and carried off his leg. The boy looked at me as much as to ask how, under such circumstances, he ought to behave,' wrote the young subaltern who'd seen far worse when fighting with Wellington in the Peninsula, 'and though I dare say his courage was quite equal to mine, I really could not help laughing at the peculiar expression which passed across his countenance.' Moments later Colonel Thornton rode up and exclaimed, 'Now my lads, forward! – You see the enemy; you know how to serve them.' Gleig and his comrades leapt to their feet and rushed towards the bridge. Seven men were immediately mown down by the guns, and Gleig also noticed a group of riflemen firing at them from the belt of woodland on the other bank. 'These, taking cool and deliberate aim from their lurking places, soon began to gall us with their fire.' Gleig's friend Williams, another young subaltern, had a reckless streak in him and at one particularly exposed point he called out to his men to follow him and

British troops set the White House ablaze on August 24, 1814, as Rear Admiral George Cockburn (in black, bottom left) and Major General Robert Ross discuss what next to burn in Washington. They also torched both houses of Congress, the Treasury, and the War Office.

The White House in flames. This artist's impression shows how efficiently the British incendiaries did their work—after they'd devoured the lavish dinner laid out for the U.S. president and his wife who were now fugitives. Critics said the conflagration was 'barbarous,' but Britain said it was retaliation for U.S. actions in Canada.

Rear Admiral George Cockburn stands in front of a blazing Washington. Blunt and forthright, he was the driving force behind the campaign of destruction. The mere mention of his name struck terror into the Americans, who offered a huge reward for his capture or death.

Major General Robert Ross, the British army commander from County Down, Ireland. His courage and humanity endeared him to his men, but his staff— and George Cockburn—were exasperated by his sometimes excessive caution.

An American artist depicts Admiral Cockburn in the foreground supervising the burning and plundering of Havre de Grace, a Chesapeake Bay town, in 1813. Even a baby's cradle is fair game.

James Madison, U.S. president, 1809–17. A thoughtful undemonstrative man, sombrely attired, he looked like a "schoolmaster dressed for a funeral." He was a founding father of the U.S. constitution but an uninspired wartime leader.

Dolley Madison, the president's wife. Bouncy and sociable with twinkling eyes, her White House parties made her a legend. She and James were unlikely partners but always close, and she showed fierce courage during the crisis.

The U.S. Capitol before the burning: the two houses of Congress were joined by a wooden passage. Broad, tree-lined Pennsylvania Avenue led to the White House one-and-a-half miles away.

Joshua Barney, hero of many naval contests with the British. His gallantry at the battle for Washington did much to make up for the incompetence and cowardice of most of his comrades-in-arms.

Barney's flotilla of flat-bottomed barges was America's main weapon against the might of the Royal Navy in shallow coastal waters. Each barge, powered by oars and sails, mounted two heavy guns—bow and stern.

Vice Admiral Sir Alexander Cochrane, British commander in chief of the expedition. His task was to "give the Americans a good drubbing." His orders were not always obeyed by the willful George Cockburn.

Rear Admiral Edward Codrington, the only admiral in the task force who fought the French at Trafalgar. His job was to manage Cochrane's fleet. He questioned the wisdom of the attacks on Washington and Baltimore.

HMS *Tonnant*, Cochrane's massive eighty-gun flagship, captured from the French at the Battle of the Nile and another veteran of Trafalgar. The plan to invade Washington was devised aboard her when she arrived in the Chesapeake.

Captain Harry Smith, independent-minded Rifles officer who had served Wellington well in the Peninsula. He wrote a frank and often witty critique of Britain's high command, thanks to his job as Ross's staff officer.

Juana Smith, who married Harry at the age of fourteen after he'd rescued her at the siege of Badajoz in Spain in 1812. She was distraught when he was posted to America.

Lieutenant George de Lacy Evans. A junior aide to Robert Ross, he combined deep loyalty to his chief with burning ambition. Like Cockburn, he was constantly urging bolder action.

George Gleig, prolific diarist, aged eighteen in 1814. A discerning eyewitness with a great sense of mischief, he later wrote a biography of the Duke of Wellington and died in 1888, aged ninety-two.

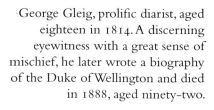

Brigadier General William Winder. Chosen by Madison to defend Washington, he drove himself to distraction trying to muster and then command a force comprised mainly of barely trained militia.

John Armstrong, Madison's secretary of war, overbearing and unloved by his subordinates. He was utterly unsupportive of William Winder, his commander in the field, and refused to take the blame for leaving Washington undefended.

James Monroe, Madison's secretary of state and then war secretary, and bitter rival of John Armstrong. A cool professional, he'd been a colonel in the U.S. War of Independence and went on to succeed Madison as president.

John Pendleton Kennedy. Dashing young Baltimore militiaman who went into battle wearing his dancing pumps, in anticipation of a victory ball at the White House. He became a popular U.S. novelist.

The White House after the burning. A torrential rainstorm the next day helped to douse the flames and leave the outer walls standing. They survive to this day and still show the burn marks. The interior was reduced to ashes.

The two houses of Congress after the burning. The wooden corridor and the lavish interiors were devastated. One outraged British Member of Parliament said British troops had done what the Goths refused to do at Rome.

Save that painting! The portrait of George Washington painted by Gilbert Stuart in 1797 which Dolley Madison insisted on rescuing. She delayed her flight from the White House to supervise its removal on a horse-drawn wagon. The painting is now back in the White House.

then shouted at Gleig: 'Now, who will be the first in the enemy's lines?' Gleig tried hard to restrain him from rushing ahead, but 'at the very moment when I was repeating my entreaties . . . a musket ball struck him on the neck and he fell dead at my feet. The bullet passed through his windpipe and spinal marrow, and he was a corpse in an instant.' One captain in the 85th, John Knox, wrote home that he'd never received such fire. He passed the mangled bodies of three officers and eight or nine men of his regiment sprawling on the ground dead or wounded: 'Thinks I to myself, thinks I, by the time the action is over the devil is in it if I am not either a walking major or a dead captain.'

One thing the American militia could do very well was to fire their weapons accurately. One American observed that what made the sharpshooters such deadly executioners was 'The universal use of firearms in our country in shooting crows and squirrels, deer and pigeons, woodpeckers and bullfrogs . . .'

Harry Smith felt vindicated. 'It happened just as I said. Thornton advanced, under no cloud of sharpshooters such as we Light Division should have had, to make the enemy unsteady and render their fire ill-directed.' Without covering fire Thornton's men, crowding across the bridge and jostling each other for space on the narrow walkway where only three people could move abreast, began to suffer severe casualties. For several minutes the withering rifle and cannon fire had the British at bay. There were cheers from the American side as the head of the British column halted for a time on the bridge. 'As soon as the enemy perceived the head of our column pause to draw breath for a moment,' wrote one 21st Fusilier, who went forward with the 85th, 'they set up three cheers, thinking, I dare say, that we were panic-struck with their appearance.' Thornton's men were, as Harry Smith had forecast, seriously exposed. In his haste to get at the enemy, Ross seems to have ignored the fact that he could have sent some of his men wading across the river in support. In hurrying to despatch his troops unsupported across the bridge he had taken a serious and unnecessary risk.

As Harry Smith watched Thornton's thrust across the bridge, he found himself exclaiming: 'There is the art of war and all we have learned under the Duke [of Wellington] given in full to the enemy!' The struggle to cross the bridge became a desperate one, with officers shouting encouragement and sometimes having to threaten their men to push them on to the narrow walkway. Slowly but surely, drawing on the raw courage that was second nature to them after the struggle through Spain, the redcoats of the 85th stormed across to the other side of the bridge. 'It was not without trampling upon many of their dead and dying comrades that the light brigade established itself on the opposite side of the stream.' At least one American soldier could only admire the discipline and determination that spurred them across. 'The fire I think must have been dreadfully galling, but they took no notice of it; their men moved like clockwork; the instant a part of a platoon was cut down it was filled up by the men in the rear without the least noise and confusion whatever . . .' Ross at last reinforced the crossing by sending some of the new units, who were joining him from behind, across the ford in the river. In the shelter of the banks they were much less exposed than the men on the bridge. The British presence on the west bank built quickly and the balance of the struggle began to shift.

While this bloodletting was taking place on the bridge, the irrepressible George Cockburn and his ADC James Scott were looking for a chance to become involved in the action. Scott recalled the Americans giving a great cheer when the first wave of British troops were forced back across the bridge. He watched a 'gallant soldier of the 85th, a Scotchman, whose arm had been shattered by a roundshot, and was still dangling by a fibre to the stump . . . seating himself on the steps of a house as the clamorous shout was rending the air . . . "Dinna halloo, my fine lads,"' the Scot shouted back, '"you're no' yet out of the wood; wait a wee bit, wait a wee, wie your skirling."' Scott then goes on to claim that he and Cockburn and Ross crossed the bridge at the same time as Thornton. 'The Colonel dashed forward, followed by his gallant regiment, in a manner that elicited enthusiastic applause from the General and his companion the Rear Admiral . . .' Scott watched Thornton leap off his horse, when it fell dead beneath him and draw his sword to lead his men forward against the first American defences.

Cockburn now decided to try his hand at directing the rocket firing, 'mounted on his white charger, his conspicuous gold-laced hat and epaulettes fully exposed within one hundred and thirty or forty yards of his foes'. Scott says he was standing beside him, after 'Jonathan [the Americans] had, I guess, very discourteously unhorsed me by one of his round shot'. 'I trust, Sir,' said Scott, 'you will not unnecessarily expose yourself, for, however the enemy may suffer, they will regard your death as ample compensation.' Scott hoped this would induce the admiral to shift a few yards to his right where he would have been protected by a small stone quarry. 'Pooh! Pooh! Nonsense!' came Cockburn's reply. The admiral was eagerly observing a British lieutenant firing off some rockets at the American lines. The famous Congreve rockets, recently invented by a major general of that name, whose hopeless inaccuracy drove the Duke of Wellington to regard them with contempt, were devastating if they found their target. They rarely did, but the noise they produced and the fiery trail they left behind them were entirely new and terrifying to the Americans. Imagine a modern firework hurling an explosive warhead packed with several pounds of lead shot over a range of up to 3,000 yards. That was way beyond the range of cannon fire. And the rockets the admiral watched were clearly more accurate than most. They 'went directly into the enemy's ranks, creating a fearful gap, and a much more fearful panic in the immediate vicinity. "Capital!" he [Cockburn] exclaimed, "excellent!"' Just at that moment the assistant rocket artilleryman, who was the master's mate from HMS *Tonnant*, fell severely wounded. The admiral comforted him, praised what he had done and promised him promotion. Then a musket shot passed between the admiral's leg and the flap of his saddle, cutting the stirrup leather in two, without doing any damage to him or the horse. He dismounted, and Scott was endeavouring to lash the broken parts together with a piece of twine, assisted by a marine, 'when a round shot came over the saddle and dismissed my assistant to the other world'.

★

William Pinkney was crouching with his riflemen in the American front line beside the guns which had pounded away so successfully at the British on the bridge. But as the minutes went by, he watched the British begin to consolidate their position on the river bank below him. 'A large column of the enemy, which was every moment reinforced, either by the way of the bridge or by the ford immediately above it, was able to form on the Washington side, and to menace the battery and the inadequate force [Pinkney's own] by which it was supported.' Pinkney only had to glance over his shoulder to see that the next line of troops was a long way behind him, moved there by either Monroe or Winder just before the battle began. The troops he had been depending on to support his men and the gunners 'had now, to the great disappointment of my companies and of the artillery, been made to retire to a hill several hundred yards in our rear . . .'.

Suddenly the first American line buckled in the face of the relent-less forward tramp of the redcoats of the 85th. 'The company on our right', recalled Pinkney, 'discharged their pieces and fled, although [their commander] appeared to do all in his power to restrain them, as I myself did.' Pinkney's riflemen were now, as he put it, 'without other known aid than the other company on the left' and they faced 'the whole force of the enemy, which was rapidly accumulating'. Pinkney's men loosed off some more rounds which were 'manifestly destructive and for a short time seemed to produce disorder and hesitation in the enemy's ranks'. But the British were now nearly overrunning the guns next door to Pinkney's men, and the gunners, unable to lower their barrels because of the height of the embrasures, began to haul their guns back. Pinkney's men now decided, without waiting for his approval, to withdraw with the gunners. 'Our small force (somewhat more than one hundred men) could not hope to make an effectual stand against the enemy . . . if they had remained much longer, they must have been taken prisoners or cut to pieces.' Pinkney says he had thought that they should try to hold on and 'venture upon another fire', but he recognised that retreat was actu-ally the only wise option. He was suffering himself from a musket wound that had shattered his elbow.

More British units, seeing the American front line in disarray, now poured across the bridge and the ford. 'They fled precipitately,' wrote John Bluett in his diary, 'very wisely dropping their arms and making the best possible use of their legs.' Captain Peter Bowlby recalled his own 4th Regiment following the 85th across the river and then swinging left. Bowlby was wounded: 'I received a shot in the shin which splintered a bone but did not break it . . . I tied a handkerchief round it.'

Winder now realised far too late that his front line was dangerously exposed, and he ordered one of General Stansbury's three battalions, who had been posted well behind the guns, to move forward and attempt to rescue them. The 5th Baltimore volunteer regiment advanced under Colonel Sterett. For a time they were supported by covering fire from Stansbury's other two battalions, but these units were under heavy fire from the British rockets, which Cockburn and Scott were greatly enjoying helping to launch. They were now being fired more horizontally and, though still pretty inaccurate, the whoosh of the missiles and the trail of flame they left behind struck terror into Ragan's and Schutz's battalions. They turned and fled. Stansbury tried to rally them. 'I rode along the line and gave orders to the officers to cut down those who attempted to fly, and suffer no man to leave the line.' But though some units made a stand, most 'fled in disorder . . . the retreat became general and all attempts to rally them and make a second stand, were fruitless'. Stansbury blamed the exhausting marching and counter-marching of the previous night (largely on his own orders) for his men's collapse on the battlefield. And far from blaming Winder, Stansbury said the Commander in Chief had 'displayed all possible zeal, activity and personal bravery'. Winder did indeed plunge straight into the battle: 'I rode swiftly across the field toward those who had so shamefully fled and exerted my voice to the utmost to arrest them.' They appeared to be ready to fight on, but when next he looked, 'to my astonishment and morti-fication . . . I found the whole of these regiments . . . were flying in the utmost precipitation and disorder'.

Winder still hoped that Colonel Sterett's 5th Regiment would hold out, but the men who had begun by acting so firmly 'evinced the usual incapacity of raw troops to make orderly movements in the face of the enemy, and their retreat in a very few moments became a flight of absolute and total disorder'. Winder probably hadn't helped by ordering them to retreat before it was clear that their position had become impossible. Once they began to withdraw they were quite unable to maintain any kind of order. John Pendleton Kennedy, who had gone into the battle with his head held high, now found himself among those who were 'driven from the field with the bayonet. We made a fine scamper of it. I lost my musket in the melee while bearing off a comrade . . . whose leg was broken by a bullet.'

Any chance that Colonel Lavall's cavalry might ride to the rescue of the collapsing front line were dashed when Lavall felt forced to withdraw too. He could see very little of the battlefield from where he'd been posted by Monroe, and the next thing he knew his horse-men were being swamped by the great mass of infantry in headlong retreat. 'All of a sudden our army seemed routed; a confused retreat appeared to be about in every corner of the battleground and the place we were occupying seemed to have been the one by which it was to be effected.' Within moments Lavall found himself left with only fifty-five troopers facing the oncoming British. He reckoned there was only one course open to him – to follow the infantry off the field.

The cavalry were later criticised by Congress for not having seized the opportunity to counter-attack the enemy who were pressing forward in 'open and scattered order'. Lavall's response was unapolo-getic: 'It has been wondered . . . why I did not cut to pieces four or five thousand of the British veteran troops with fifty-five men, all recruits, and upon raw horses . . . There is a distinction between madness and bravery.' The unfortunate Lavall had had the task of trying to train his force of newly recruited dragoons over the previ-ous few months with far fewer horses than he had men. He had finally managed to build up his stock of horses to full strength only a week earlier. One US officer in the army at the time, who later wrote a history of this episode, remarked that the cavalry were 'mostly without any training or discipline whatever . . . A company of cavalry, formed in the heart of a large commercial city, might choose to assume the name of "Cossacks" . . . but they would remain, in reality, just what they were before – a parcel of ineffective clerks or journeymen mechanics.'

Ross had swept the field in the first phase of the Battle of Bladensburg. The 85th's attack across the bridge had finally broken through – helped by attacks on the American flanks led by Colonel Arthur Brooke. The 44th East Essex Regiment had swept around to the right, and the 4th King's Own to the left. The American front line and the second line 500 yards behind it had vanished. But the battle was not over. A mile ahead of them up a long slope the exhausted British found themselves facing a third American line. And at its centre was a grimly determined Joshua Barney. He and his 500 flotillamen and marines were not going to turn around and run.

8

Barney's last stand

24 August, afternoon

Robert Ross gave his men no time to rest after their successful rout of the American front-line troops. It was early afternoon. The sun was now at its hottest. Men weren't dying only in battle. Many found the heat intolerable and collapsed by the wayside. At least eighteen died of heat exhaustion that day on the British side alone. Without cavalry Ross was unable to deliver a crushing blow to the fleeing American infantry. All he could do was urge his exhausted men to press on and attempt to scatter what was left of the American army, which was strongly posted just short of the top of a slope some thousand yards in front of them.

The main force was General Walter Smith's Washington DC militia. But over to the left, straddling the road to Washington, Ross saw five heavy guns. Two of them were 18-pounders and three 12-pounders. They were manned by Joshua Barney's 400 flotillamen, who had arrived just as the battle was beginning. Also under Barney's command was a company of 100 marines under Colonel Samuel Miller. These 500 men were to be a formidable obstacle. Barney's sailors had been frustrated in their attempts to cause serious damage to Cockburn's navy in the past three months. Now, after being forced to destroy their flotilla, they were aching to get to grips with the British army. On Barney's right there was a battalion of Maryland militia under Colonel William Beall and on his left the main force of Maryland and DC militia as well as some regulars under Colonel William Scott.

Barney watched the Americans retreating in front of him with the British advancing behind them and assumed that when the Americans

94

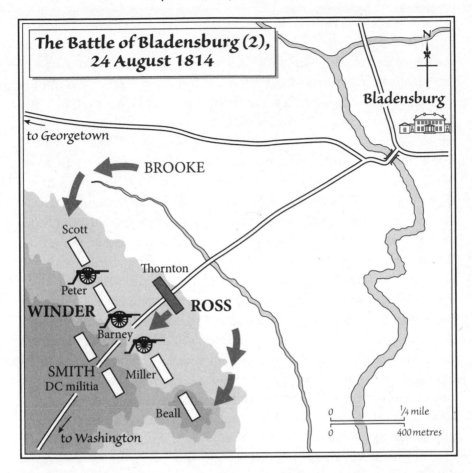

The Battle of Bladensburg (2), 24 August 1814

Bladensburg

to Georgetown

BROOKE

Scott

Thornton

Peter

WINDER

ROSS

Barney

SMITH

Miller

DC militia

Beall

to Washington

0   ¼ mile
0   400 metres

reached his line they would reform and turn and face the enemy – alongside his troops. But nothing of the kind happened. He later described the Americans as 'apparently in much disorder'. They ran in headlong flight past his position and disappeared without making any attempt to reinforce his line. Barney's predicament, with unreliable militia either side of him and Ross's regulars heading straight up the hill towards him, was grim. But he understood what was expected of him. He was now the only credible force that stood between the British and the city of Washington.

Barney knew he could rely on his men not to follow the example of the rest of the US army: they would stand and fight – whatever the odds. President Madison had made a point of reviewing Barney's position before he left the battlefield. He had given his enthusiastic assent to the creation of the flotilla a year earlier and to Barney's leadership of it. He was struck by the number of negroes among the flotillamen – who included the runaway slave Charles Ball. And Madison, a slavemaster himself, asked Barney, 'Won't the negroes run on the approach of the British?' 'No, Sir,' replied Barney. 'They don't know how to run. They will die by their guns first.' Ball was helping to man one of Barney's five guns, and he remarked in his diary what a perfect view they all had of the approaching British army. 'I could not but admire the handsome manner in which the British officers led on their fatigued and worn-out soldiers.'

The British made short work of a small force under Colonel Kramer which failed to delay them at a small ravine, and then moved up on either side of the road. They halted briefly when they saw Barney's men blocking the way ahead of them. Barney waited for them to come within range. 'I reserved our fire,' he later reported. 'In a few minutes the enemy again advanced, when I ordered an 18 pounder to be fired, which completely cleared the road.' Canister and grapeshot with their wide scatter of lethal fire are devastating at close range. Canister is a whole package of musket balls fired from the barrel; grape is a bunch of fewer, larger balls. Barney's gunners made no mistake. It was like firing a gigantic shotgun. Within minutes Colonel Thornton, who'd led the 85th Light Infantry in their charge across the bridge, was again setting the pace. Mounted on horseback, sword in hand, he made a spectacular target for Barney's marksmen as he rode at the head of his men full pelt against Barney's guns. His horse was the first to be hit, collapsing instantly. That didn't stop Thornton who leapt off and continued on foot, charging to within feet of Barney's line. He was stopped by a shower of grape that shredded his jacket and smashed into his thigh. He was instantly thrown to the ground. But his men didn't give up. Sam Davies recalled: 'I had the pleasure of killing a damn rascal who shot a midshipman belonging to the Tonnant through the face; he made the first blow at me with his sword at my head; I parried it like a sailor with my cutlass and then it was my turn so I run him through the guts and killed him, he . . . deprived me of the use of my middle finger on my left hand by cutting the sinues [sic].' The wounded Colonel Thornton's two immediate subordinates, a lieutenant colonel and a major, were also wounded trying to break Barney's line. An American newspaper described Barney's men as opening 'the hottest most destructive fire that, perhaps, ever was seen – they fell before him like the grass before a mower's scythe.'

Seizing the moment, Barney sent Captain Miller and his seventy-eight surviving marines sweeping down the hill straight at the 85th. Yelling 'Board 'em! Board 'em!' the marines crashed in among the British, who, in Barney's words, were 'totally cut up'. Some managed to escape into a wood 200 yards behind them.

Ross himself now made an appearance. He was a fine leader of men in a pitched battle, if a bit foolhardy, never sparing himself and always at the front. The Americans could spot him quite clearly. He certainly impressed Charles Ball: 'I thought then and think yet that General Ross was one the finest looking men that I ever saw on horseback.' He rallied his men and they counter-attacked the marines, seriously wounding Miller himself.

George Gleig of the 85th was in the mêlée throughout and noticed how fatigue was taking its toll of the British. 'Our men were scarce able to walk, far less to run . . . The battle became now little else than an uninterrupted exchange of tremendous volleys. Neither party gained or lost ground but, for a full half hour, stood still, load-ing and firing . . .' Gleig reckoned that the light brigade, of which he was a part, was 'guilty of imprudence. Instead of pausing till the rest of the army came up, the soldiers lightened themselves by throwing away their knapsacks . . . and pushed on to the attack . . . The Americans, however, saw their weakness and stood firm.' Gleig himself was hit. 'One musket ball, hitting the scabbard of my sword, broke it, and another, at the same instant, slightly wounded my arm. Yet I hardly felt the wound, so intent was I on rallying the men.' As soon as Ross appeared, 'Charge, Charge, was the only word of command issued.' But still Barney's men resisted. Gleig admired the way Barney's gunners stood their ground in the face of the British bayonet charge. 'Not only did they serve their guns with a quickness and precision which astonished their assailants, but they stood till some of them were actually bayoneted with fuses still in their hands . . .'

Ross now decided that the way to undermine Barney's men was to concentrate on the weaker-looking militia on either side of Barney's flotillamen. And the strategy worked. Colonel Beall's Maryland militia, who were still recovering from their forced march from Annapolis that morning, suddenly found themselves under attack from a line of British bayonets marching relentlessly up the hill towards them. There was a volley or two of musket fire from Beall's men and then, in Charles Ball's words, 'the militia ran like sheep chased by dogs'.

Moments later Ross threw the 4th and 44th Regiments under Colonel Arthur Brooke against the militia on Barney's other flank. The Americans at first resisted fiercely, but made the mistake of firing at the British at far too great a range. The musket can be lethal at fifty yards but is useless at 150. The militia were loosing off at the advancing British redcoats at a range of 200 yards with negligible effect. Seeing these units under pressure but not yet defeated, General Winder ordered them to retire – a decision that provoked fury from at least one old soldier. 'I have never heard Gen Winder assign any reason for having ordered the retreat at the time he did, it being received by part of our lines before the enemy pressed them.' Colonel Scott's regulars were also ordered back by Winder before they'd even had time to fire a shot.

Barney and his dwindling band of flotillamen and marines now came under intense pressure from three sides. The hill that Beall's men had evacuated was particularly valuable to the British, who could now fire down on Barney. Almost inevitably Barney himself was picked out by a British sharpshooter and severely wounded in the thigh. He concealed his wound for a time in order not to damp his men's spirits. But in order to keep the wound secret he took no steps to staunch the flow of blood. So he soon began 'to feel excessively weak and faint from loss of blood'. To make things worse he discovered that the wagon loaded with cartridges for his cannon and muskets had been carried off in the general confusion. A number of his men and many of his key master sailors, who commanded his smaller units, were also wounded. So he felt he had to order his men to retire, which they achieved in good order, taking many of the wounded with them. John Webster was one of Barney's barge commanders who'd served with him proudly through the whole flotilla campaign. 'Our seamen', he wrote, 'acted nobly and continued to do so until their ammunition gave out and most of us were surrounded.' His horse was shot through the head and he himself was lucky to survive when he had his hat shot off. When Webster and his comrades discovered that the ammunition wagons had gone off, 'We made our escape in double quick time . . . I did not take time to pick up my hat.' But Barney himself was so severely wounded that – even with the help of three of his officers who refused to leave him – he was unable to move back more than a few yards. He ordered them to withdraw, leaving just one man named Huffington to stay with him. One of his less gallant aides sped off on horseback past his commander and ignored Barney's calls to stop and lend him his horse so that he could escape as well. Even the flotillamen had their fainthearts.

The British moved forward to take over the ground the flotillamen had held. And it wasn't long before a British officer, Captain Wainwright, who commanded Cockburn's flagship, came upon the wounded Barney. The moment he identified him he went off in search of George Cockburn, and the two of them were soon back, accompanied by General Ross himself. According to Barney's biographer, Mary Barney, Ross and Cockburn addressed their prisoner 'in the most polite and respectful terms, offering immediate assistance, and the attendance of a surgeon'.

Ross then said, 'I am really very glad to see you, Commodore.' To which Barney replied: 'I am sorry I cannot return the compliment, General.' Ross smiled and turning to the admiral, remarked, 'I told you it was the flotillamen!' 'Yes,' said Cockburn. 'You were right, though I could not believe you – they have given us the only fighting we have had.' Ross and Cockburn then talked quietly to each other and then Ross turned back to Barney. 'Barney, you are paroled, where do you want to be conveyed?' This allowed Barney to go where he wished: he had just to give his parole that he was still technically a British prisoner until an exchange could be made of him. Barney asked to be taken to Bladensburg, the nearest town.

Wainwright noticed Barney wincing in pain as the soldiers picked up the litter he was lying on and promptly directed a young officer who was with him to go and bring a gang of sailors who would make a better job of carrying it. Just as they were about to carry him away, one of Barney's men, badly wounded with an arm hanging down held only by a piece of skin, knelt by his commander and, seizing one of Barney's hands with the only arm he had, kissed it repeatedly with great affection and burst into tears. 'The effect of this action upon the British sailors was electric,' writes Mary Barney, 'and one of them broke out with "Well, damn my eyes! If he wasn't a kind com-mander, that chap wouldn't have done that!"' The sailors apparently 'handled him like a child'. And Barney was so grateful to them that he took fifty dollars out of his wallet and offered it to them, but they wouldn't accept it.

By this time both sides were so exhausted that the battle came to an end. The British could hardly move another step forward. The Americans, fleeing in disorder, were in no condition to be rallied to make a stand further back. Winder, desperately looking for some way to rescue his army – and himself – from total humiliation, made two half-hearted attempts to fight a last-ditch defence of Washington. First he ordered General Walter Smith and his DC militia to turn and make a stand on some high ground. But even as Smith was forming his new line Winder changed his mind and ordered him to fall back into the city itself – to the Capitol. 'I took the liberty of suggesting my impression of the preferable situation we then occupied,' said Smith. Winder insisted he should fall back to where he'd be joined by other retiring troops. But when they got to the Capitol there was no one. Winder then consulted Armstrong, who was near by and who had also favoured making a stand at the Capitol. The only credible force available was that of Colonel Minor's battalion of Virginia militia. They had finally managed to get access to some muskets and ammunition but too late for Bladensburg. Winder reckoned it would be futile to bottle up Minor's men and the few others who had gathered at the Capitol in a gallant attempt to withstand a British siege. The result was another change of mind. Winder said there was 'no reasonable hope . . . that we had any troops who could be relied on to make a resistance as desperate as necessary . . .'. Armstrong and Monroe, who was also there, agreed. Smith was told that 'the whole should retreat through Washington and Georgetown'. The capital city was to be completely abandoned by the army. 'It is impossible', said Smith later, 'to do justice to the anguish evinced by the troops of Washington and Georgetown on the receiving of this order. The idea of leaving their families, their houses, and their homes at the mercy of an enraged enemy, was insupportable.' To the remnant of the army that had been ready to fight with Smith, this was the last straw. They dispersed in disorder and scattered. Many called in briefly at their homes, but all were soon fleeing west of the city. General Smith was burning with resentment. His men, he said, had 'never yielded the ground [to the enemy], but by orders emanating from superior authority'. Smith believed a stand could and should have been made: his superiors, with most of their army fragmenting in panic, felt they had no realistic choice but to quit the city. They may have been right, but their decision earned them enduring contempt.

John Williams, an officer in Smith's brigade who wrote a history of the British invasion of Washington, says he had observed the effect of the final order to retreat: 'Some shed tears, others uttered imprecations and all evinced the utmost astonishment and indignation; for it was impossible for them to comprehend why troops who were willing to risk an encounter with the enemy should be denied the opportunity.'

The British lost sixty-four killed and 185 wounded in the Battle of Bladensburg as a result of the struggle they had had on the bridge and the resistance they had met from Joshua Barney.* A number died of heat exhaustion. Ross was rightly criticised by Harry Smith and others for his conduct of the first phase of the battle. There was no need to expose the 85th to the lethal fire of the American riflemen and artillery for so long. They could have been supported by others crossing the ford sooner than they did. But Ross's impulsiveness and Thornton's enthusiasm prompted them to begin the assault before the whole army was properly assembled and briefed.

Winder reckoned he lost 'more than 30 to 40 killed and 50 or 60 wounded' in a battle in which they were mainly in headlong retreat. Edward Codrington, back with the fleet, remarked wryly when he heard the news: 'I know not yet the probable number of the enemy killed, but they ran away too fast for our hard-fagged people to make prisoners.'

An incompetent, confused and divided high command had led the American army to one of its worst ever defeats. George Gleig remarked that had the Americans 'conducted themselves with coolness and resolution, it is not conceivable how the battle could have been won [by the British] . . . Of the personal courage of the Americans there can be no doubt; they are, individually taken, as brave a nation as any in the world. But they are not soldiers . . .' A more decisive and united American leadership might indeed have saved much of the young republic's self-respect. The unfortunate William Winder, who as the commander in the field had to bear the brunt of the blame for the defeat, later said he regretted not putting Barney and his men in the front line where they might have helped stop the British crossing the bridge. Winder was disgracefully let down by the War Secretary, John Armstrong, and he certainly showed some flashes of determination and courage on the battlefield. Winder had his admirers among those who fought with him in the

* These are the figures Ross reported to London; the American commander Winder reckoned that the British lost at least 400. Gleig estimated that 'upwards of 500 men were killed and wounded' (Gleig, *Fire and Blood*, p. 88).

battle. 'I think it cruel in the extreme to detract from the fame of a man, to whose personal and indefatigable exertions I am a witness, for a failure in a contest with such forces as were hurried by peace meal [sic] under his command, against men long disciplined in the art of war.' But his erratic command at Bladensburg and his unsteady course in the frantic days that led up to the battle proved he should never have been chosen to lead in such a critical campaign. And for that the blame goes higher – to President Madison himself.

The Battle of Bladensburg was to be relegated to comparative obscurity in America's history books. It would be remembered mainly as the 'Bladensburg Races' in which the Americans did more running than fighting. A merciless poem of the same name was soon published, pouring scorn on the US conduct of the battle, but mainly on Madison and Monroe. In this excerpt Madison is speaking on the battlefield:

> 'Where are the British, Winder, where? And Cockburn where is he?
> D'ye think your men will fight or run, when they the British see?
> Armstrong and Rush, stay here in camp I'm sure you're not afraid –
> Ourself will now return, and you Monroe shall be our aid.
> And Winder do not fire your guns, nor let your trumpets play,
> Till we are out of sight – Forsooth my horse will run away.'

And so on.

Joshua Barney and his sailors and marines had been the only real American stalwarts in a disgraceful day on the battlefield. They and the relentless heat of the sun had drained the last ounce of energy from the victorious British army, to which Ross now granted a couple of hours' rest. But with the American militia fled from the field and from all approaches to the capital, the road to Washington was now wide open.

9

Save that painting!

24 August, evening

THE GREAT WAVE of fleeing American soldiers that swept into and then quickly out the other side of Washington that evening caused more than alarm among the civilians waiting anxiously for news. It triggered a surge of resentment. Margaret Bayard Smith was appalled by the American army's abandonment of any defence of the capital. 'Our men were all eager for a fight . . . more than 2000 had not fired their muskets, when Winder and Armstrong gave their order for a retreat . . . The English officers have told some of our citizens that they could not have stood more than 10 minutes longer, that they had marched that day 13 miles, and were exhausted with thirst, heat and fatigue.'

Margaret Bayard Smith had already moved out of the city; others risked staying. One of them was Dr James Ewell, one of the city's few doctors and another pillar of Washington society, close to James and Dolley Madison. James Ewell was a plump, amiable man with a florid complexion and open manner: he had large, expressive blue eyes and a warm smile for everyone. He was also a man of letters and he wrote with immense pride of the young city of Washington, which he compared with 'the noblest cities of the ancient world'. He lived in a very grand house on Capitol Hill. His neighbours were used to the clunk of the large knocker on his front door as anxious patients sought his attention. In recent days many of those neighbours had expressed to him their alarm at the prospect of a British attack on the city, but he'd dismissed their fears: 'What! To make an attack on the metropolis of the United States . . . Will they ever dream of attacking Washington? No never!'

But the British had come, and now Ewell was as frightened as his next-door neighbours. In the hour between twelve and one he and his wife and family, standing on the third floor of their house, had heard the roar of cannon and watched the rockets shooting into the sky. When the firing stopped, 'my feelings were left in fearful fluctuation, fondly hoping that my countrymen had prevailed, then awfully fearing that all was lost'. He wasn't kept in suspense for long. 'I soon discovered the dust beginning to rise above the forests in thick clouds . . . rapidly advancing . . .' He immediately knew the 'dismal fate that awaited us', and the next thing he saw was 'the unfortunate Secretary of War with his suite in full flight followed by crowds of gentlemen on horseback, some of whom loudly bawled out as they came on: "Fly, fly! The ruffians are at hand. If you cannot get away yourselves, for God's sake send off your wives and daughters, for the ruffians are at hand!"' Ewell was well aware of George Cockburn's reputation for wrecking, burning and looting. 'I felt myself palsied with horror, and ... my wife standing by my side with looks wild with terror, as though she beheld the enemy in sight, cried out: "Oh what shall we do? What shall we do? Yonder they are coming!", and fell into convulsions, my daughters shrieking by her side.' The doctor looked around desperately for a cart to transport his family to the country. There was none in sight, so he escorted his wife and daughters down the street to the home of one of his patients, Mrs Orr, who was gravely ill. Her husband and servants had panicked and deserted her, so she'd sent for the doctor's help. Ewell also hoped the British would find her so unwell that they'd leave her house alone.

Ewell was appalled by the conduct of the militia who had, he said, dropped their guns and fled 'like frightened sheep in every direction, except, indeed, towards the enemy'. He said one man had confronted the militia in full flight: '"What," says he, "soldiers, you are not running?" "Oh, no!" exclaimed some of them, "we have done our duty, our ammunition is spent. We gave it to them, boys, didn't we?" "Yes," returned his comrades, "we peppered the rascals; we strewed the damned redcoats ..."' At which the man, suspicious, stole a look at their cartridge boxes and noticed they hadn't used a single one.

Another person who was in no hurry to leave Washington was the intrepid Dolley Madison, the President's wife. She had promised her husband James that she would await his return from a visit to the front two days earlier and she had every intention of doing the same that Wednesday. 'I confess that I was so unfeminine as to be free from fear and willing to remain in the castle. If I could have had a cannon through every window, but alas! those who should have placed them there fled before me. And my heart mourned for my country.' She had received a distraught note from her sister, Anna Cutts: 'Tell me for God's sake where you are and what [you are] going to do ...'

Anna told Dolley that she was packing up her piano and anything else she could fit on a wagon to take off to safety.

Dolley was more concerned about her husband. She spent the Wednesday morning staring out of the White House windows 'turning my spy glass in every direction and watching with unwearied anxiety, hoping to discern the approach of my dear husband and his friends'. But all she could see was 'groups of military wandering in all directions, as if there was a lack of arms, or of spirit to fight for their own firesides'. By three o'clock in the afternoon she was still waiting. 'Mr Madison comes not; may God protect him!' But by now she had heard of the outcome of the Battle of Bladensburg. 'Two messengers, covered with dust, come to bid me fly; but I wait for him.' She told her sister she'd procured a wagon which she would load up with the most precious White House valuables, and as many state papers as she could cram in. Still with her were a group of loyal servants, Sukey, her personal maid, Paul Jennings, James Madison's manservant, and Jean Pierre Sioussat, the White House chief steward, known affectionately as 'French John'. Sioussat had served in the French navy before jumping ship in New York and using his native charm to sweet-talk his way into domestic service. Jennings had served the Madisons since he was fifteen. He was setting out the meal which Dolley and James Madison had ordered to be ready for the President's party when they returned later in the day. He laid a tablecloth, napkins and the full White House dinner service of cutlery, glasses and plates for forty people. The President's White House chef had meat roasting on a spit. Bottles of the President's favourite Madeira wine, a very fashionable drink at the time, were laid on the sideboard. French John suggested to Dolley Madison that he could lay a trail of gunpowder to explode if the British tried to enter the house. She told him not to.

One of the family friends who turned up to help Dolley load the wagon was Daniel Carroll. He lugged a few armfuls out into the waiting vehicle and then told the President's wife it was about time she left. The British were not far away and she should be off in her carriage without delay. But she wasn't leaving yet. She wrote to her sister that Carroll was getting impatient: 'He is in a very bad humor with me because I insist on waiting until the large picture of General Washington is secured . . .' She had suddenly remembered the painting of America's first President on the wall of the Dining Room where Jennings was laying out the meal. The large picture, by Gilbert Stuart, had been bought for the White House back in 1800 and was now a cherished national icon. 'Save that painting! Save that painting!' she exclaimed, ordering it to be unscrewed from the wall. But it proved very difficult to shift the large frame, and it took the resourceful French John to wrench it free. Standing on a ladder held by Paul Jennings, and helped by the White House gardener, Tom Magraw, Sioussat broke the frame and passed down the canvas still stuck on its stretcher. Some accounts suggest that Sioussat, to save time, took a knife out of his pocket and slashed the canvas out of its frame, but an examination of the painting in 1978 could find no sign that the canvas had been cut.

Carroll by this time had left, piqued that Dolley had ignored his advice to escape. One of the picture's new rescuers suggested rolling up the canvas to make it easier to carry, but Sioussat told him not to as it would damage the painting. Dolley Madison now finally swept up a few last belongings including the precious red velvet curtains in the drawing room. Then, grabbing a small handbag, she jumped into her carriage with her devoted maid Sukey and was whisked off out of the city. One way or another the precious painting was then carted away to safety by two passers-by who had made a timely offer of help.

Not long after Dolley had left, James Madison and his attendants returned briefly to the White House, ignored the meal which had been laid out for them and, after a short rest, set off to cross the Potomac into Virginia. Jean Pierre Sioussat was left to shut the place up and carry Dolley Madison's macaw in its cage to the house of the French Ambassador for safe-keeping.

By this time only the bravest families were left in Washington. The Thorntons, Dr William and his wife Anna Maria, waited until the very last moment. 'Almost all our acquaintances gone out of town,'

Anna Maria wrote in her diary for 24 August, 'nearly all the movable property taken away – offices shut up and all business at a stand.' She and William Thornton walked up to the President's House, and 'found that Mrs M— was gone. We sat down to dinner but I couldn't eat nothing and we dilly dally'd till we saw our retreating army come up the avenue. We then hastened away, and were escorted out of town by our defeated troops.' They found themselves travelling out of the city alongside the wagon carrying the Washington picture rescued by Dolley Madison.

Thomas Tingey, the commandant of the US Navy Yard, was facing the gravest crisis of his career. He had faced many in his long naval life. He began as a warrant officer in the Royal Navy in 1771, but when America rebelled against the King he was soon defying his old comrades. In 1799, commanding the US warship *Ganges*, he found himself challenged by a British frigate and ordered to hand over any 'British' sailors on his ship for impressment into the Royal Navy. He retorted that he regarded all sailors on his ship as Americans and would hand none over. What was more, he said, he would resist any effort the British made to search his ship by force. His boldness paid off: the British captain relented and sailed off.

Now a veteran mariner at sixty-one, Tingey had to make a mortifying decision. He was the guardian of an installation that was the pride of the US navy. Washington's Navy Yard was magnificently housed in a precinct that had been custom built by Henry Latrobe, who'd supervised the building of the Capitol. The yard was stacked with vital stores and equipment for US ships, large numbers of heavy guns and small arms, two ropewalks for spinning new ropes, and three brand-new ships near completion – a frigate, *Columbia*, a sloop of war, *Argus*, and a schooner, *Lynx*. At 3 p.m. Tingey heard his name shouted by the Navy Secretary William Jones, who turned up outside his door fresh from his morning of meetings with Madison and his military commanders. 'You will make the necessary preparations', Jones told him, 'for destroying the public shipping and all the naval and military stores and provisions at the Navy Yard including everything that may be valuable and useful to the enemy . . .' He went on: 'Having satisfactorily ascertained that the enemy has driven our army and entered the city you will set fire to the [gunpowder] trains and retire in your gig.'

An hour later Tingey received a message from the Secretary of War John Armstrong, who had witnessed the rout of the US army at Bladensburg. He said he 'could protect me no longer', Tingey recalled. Pressure now built up on Tingey from people who were appalled by the Navy Secretary's order and urged him to ignore it. But Tingey told them there was little he could do unless they could get Jones to rescind his order. He was besieged too by 'a deputation of the most respectable women', many of them no doubt anxious that their houses could be consumed by the flames. Tingey told them he would delay the destruction of the yard as long as he could. He now depended on the punctilious Mordecai Booth, and a naval officer, Captain John Creighton, whom he tasked with reporting on the whereabouts of the British. Creighton had the job of finally blowing up the Eastern Branch Bridge – a quite unnecessary precaution, as the entire British army had already crossed the river at Bladensburg. Booth had been conscientiously trying to move more barrels of powder from the Navy Yard to safety. He was just ordering his team to the magazine when they heard the news of Bladensburg, and 'wagons and men were seen flying in the utmost confusion. Those receiving my orders waited not a moment; but fled with all precipitation.'

Booth and Creighton then set off to see just how close the British were. Both of them were anxious to do anything they could to dissuade Tingey from torching the Navy Yard prematurely. And for a time they lived in hope. 'I saw not the appearance of an Englishman,' Booth wrote in his meticulously detailed report to Tingey. 'But oh! My country – and I blush, Sir, to tell you – I saw the . . . fugitive soldiery of our army – running, hobbling, creeping, and apparently panic-struck.' His hopes were momentarily raised by the fact that he could see no pursuing army. 'I confess I did believe . . . that there had been no general defeat but that some gallant spirits had sustained the action, and had checked our foe.' He was told the army had rallied at

the Capitol, but he found only a few men there, resting. Booth –
determined 'at the hazard of my life to ascertain where the British
army was' – rode on up a ridge on the road from Bladensburg, and as
the sun was setting he spotted the British and was shot at. He then
galloped back to the city centre, checked out the White House
where 'all was silent as a church', and then went back to the Capitol
again, this time with Captain Creighton. They were not left in any
doubt: there was no sign of any Americans but a little further on they
ran into the advancing British. 'I gave reins to my horse and Captain
Creighton followed me.'

It was 8.20 p.m. Tingey had set himself a deadline of 8.30: if there
was no sign of his two men by then, he would carry out his orders to
set light to the Navy Yard. And then with just ten minutes to go
Creighton and Booth arrived. Tingey recalled how the two men
rode up and reported to him that they'd been exposed to enemy fire
and that 'the enemy was in complete possession of the city'. It was an
exaggeration, but within less than an hour it was all too true.

It was nearly dusk when Ross decided that his men were sufficiently
rested for him to take an advance party into Washington. Leaving
most of the troops who had fought at Bladensburg to follow on
behind him, Ross led the 21st Fusiliers and a party of sailors expert
in demolition into the city. By the time they were approaching the
Capitol it was dark. There was no sign of any enemy. Ross and his
staff were in the lead. George Cockburn was at his side, determined
not to miss any action. George de Lacy Evans and Harry Smith were
with them, with James Scott just behind, attending on the admiral,
and a guard of some 100 light infantrymen on either side of them.

What followed was a series of spectacular acts of destruction which
sharply divided opinion not just in the civilised world but within
Ross's own staff. Harry Smith was in no doubt that Ross and
Cockburn 'entered Washington for the barbarous purpose of destroying the city'. Indeed he believed Cockburn would have burned not
just the public buildings but the whole city. Smith believed neither
of them contemplated negotiation. Gleig and others, however, were

convinced that Ross intended 'to lay it [the city] under contribution'. The 'contribution' would be a hefty payment of ransom in return for sparing the city's property. Scott talks of the 'various parleys sounded by the General before our entrance', which suggested to him that Ross would have been ready for some kind of negotiated arrangement. But the prospect of any such deal was swept away by a burst of fire at a crossroads just short of the Capitol. It was directed at Ross personally. His horse, which had carried him through the Peninsular War in Spain and France, was killed instantly. An American eyewitness claimed that one British soldier was killed and three wounded. Scott says the fire came from houses on either side and from the Capitol building itself. 'After this wanton show of hostility the Americans cheered, and retreated down the Capitol hill into the principal avenue leading towards the President's palace.' 'Every thought of accommodation was instantly laid aside,' wrote Gleig. 'They proceeded without a moment's delay to burn and destroy everything in the most distant degree connected with government.'

Both Ross and Cockburn had no doubt that violent resistance would justify them in torching the enemy's public buildings. But would they really have stopped short of that if the Americans had offered some kind of payment? Britain had, after all, also promised to avenge the burning of the parliament buildings at York, the capital of Upper Canada, a year earlier. And there is the blatant threat in Vice Admiral Alexander Cochrane's letter of 18 August to Secretary of State James Monroe, in which Cochrane says his men will 'destroy and lay waste' American towns in retaliation for US depredations in Canada unless the Americans paid compensation. Monroe and Madison were incensed that the letter was not actually handed to them until 31 August, a week after the event, with the clear implication that Cochrane wanted to present a justification for the destruction of Washington but did not want to forewarn them that it would happen. Monroe replied that full reparation had already been made for irresponsible US actions in Canada. But this episode, as some report it, does suggest that Ross might have held back from igniting the devastating conflagration that followed. Whether Cockburn would have been so scrupulous we can only guess. The shots that rang out just after eight o'clock that night removed all doubt. British troops promptly stormed the house from which the shots had been fired and it was burned down. Gleig says some Americans were caught and put to the sword, but Scott, who was there, says all the Americans escaped. Samuel Davies, a midshipman on Cockburn's flagship HMS *Albion*, was the man who led a small squad of four sailors into the house to set light to it. The young firebrand dashed off a quick letter to his mother a week later telling her he was working directly to the orders of George Cockburn. 'We sent a flag of truce to know whether the town had surrendered or not . . . on entering the damn rascals fired out of a most elegant house and hollowed [sic] out here comes the English Buggers . . . I and 4 sailors burnt this house with everything in it by order of Cockburn.'

It was useful practice for what was to follow. The first major candidate for destruction now lay right in front of Ross and Cockburn – the United States Capitol that housed the two chambers of the United States Congress.

10

The barbarous purpose

24 August, evening

JUST A MILE from where Ross and his troops were advancing to the doors of the Capitol, Thomas Tingey listened to a last-minute plea from Captain Creighton not to set fire to the Navy Yard. 'He was', said Tingey, 'extremely averse to the destruction of the property.' But Tingey told him that his orders from the Navy Secretary left no choice. If he neglected to deny the British possession of the Yard, he would be guilty of a crime against the state. He told Creighton, Booth and what was left of his staff to make sure boats were ready for their escape. Then he ordered them to put matches to the powder trains that had been laid to the storehouses and to the ships in the yard, and 'in a few moments the whole was in a state of irretrievable conflagration'.

It was an agonising moment for Thomas Tingey. He'd supervised the construction of the Navy Yard back in 1800 and been its commandant for the last ten years, proudly and meticulously nursing it into the magnificent facility it was by 1814. Now nearly sixty-five years old, he was watching the crowning work of his career going up in flames. Worse, he had been supervising the completion of three warships, vital to the US war effort. The frigate *Columbia* could have been launched within ten days. All that remained to be done was the copper-plating of her hull. Her masts and spars were nearly finished: there was enough timber on the wharf to complete them. Her sails were waiting, folded up in a nearby loft, for her standing rigging to be finished. All *Columbia*'s blocks, dead-eyes and the major parts of her gun carriages were ready to be heaved on board together with a whole stack of water casks and other large storage barrels. One match to the powder trail that led to the new frigate and – as Tingey put it – she was 'immediately enveloped in a sheet of inextinguishable fire'. The sloop of war *Argus* with all her armament and other equipment aboard except her sails, which were still in the loft, was also torched. Most of the Yard's buildings were set alight too, and they burned furiously – the mast shed, the joiners', plumbers', painters', smiths' and boat-builders' shops, the sawmill, and the sheds where the naval gunnery equipment, cordage and sails were stored – all were consumed by the fire. But Tingey allowed himself to make one exception. He hesitated before the brand-new schooner *Lynx*, and 'from a momentary impulse . . . I directed her not to be fired, and have the satisfaction to say that in an almost miraculous escape, she is still "ours".' Miraculous it was, because the next morning the British went into the Yard and destroyed anything that hadn't been burned the night before. But somehow *Lynx* was overlooked.

Mordecai Booth had left Tingey and just reached safety the other side of the Potomac when he looked back and saw the tongues of flame licking the sky above the Yard. He heard an explosion which he thought must be the ordnance store blowing up. But then around fifteen minutes later Booth saw 'a sight, so repugnant to my feelings, so dishonorable, so degrading to the American character, and at the same time so awful – [it] almost palsied my faculties . . .'. The British had set fire to the United States Capitol.

A few minutes earlier Ross's staff officer George Evans had applied himself with typical relish to the task of battering in the doors to Congress. It was the first and only enemy break-in to America's new legislature in its history. Twenty-one years earlier America's first President George Washington had brushed aside the designs of a whole crowd of full-time professionals and chosen one by a close associate of his, Dr William Thornton. This was the same talented William Thornton, also a doctor of medicine, who together with his diarist wife Anna Maria would witness the burning of Washington in 1814. The Capitol stood much as he had designed it in 1793: two great separate sandstone blocks in fine classical Greek style – one, on the north side, housing the Senate, the other the House of Representatives. Between them was a wide gap which Thornton and his successors planned one day to cover with a great dome. But at this early stage the space was filled by a long temporary wooden passageway linking the two houses of Congress.

When the British burst in, they found themselves confronted by an opulence they'd never expected. Thornton's early designs had been adapted and ornamented by another English-born architect, Henry Latrobe. Latrobe had nothing but contempt for his predecessor, whom he described as a 'physician . . . very ignorant of architecture'. Latrobe tasked Italian craftsmen to give the Capitol's interior a lavish flavour of the Renaissance. He was particularly proud of the sumptuous chamber of the House of Representatives. The British could have had no idea of the time and care that he and his team had lavished on it. Latrobe boasted that the twenty-six-foot-high Corinthian columns 'of solid and beautiful freestone' crafted by Giovanni Andrei were the work of 'an artist of first rate excellence'. And over the Speaker's chair Giuseppe Franzoni had carved a 'colossal eagle in the act of rising, with wings spread for flight'. Its head, said Latrobe, was 'a scrupulously correct copy of the head of the bald eagle peculiar to our country'. Beneath it was a marble statue of Liberty holding in her hand the Constitution of the United States.

James Scott conceded that the Capitol building was 'beautifully arranged', but he was scathing of the richness of what he saw. 'The interior accommodations were upon a scale of grandeur and magnificence little suited to pure republican simplicity. We might rather have been led to suspect that nation . . . was somewhat infected with an unseemly bias for monarchical splendour.' Scott described the eagle as 'looking towards the skies, emblematical, it is to be presumed, of the rising greatness of the young nation'. Scott was, as usual, at the side of George Cockburn, who was clearly bent on destroying the building as soon as possible.

One story going the rounds less than a month afterwards was that Cockburn 'in a strain of coarse levity, mounting the speaker's chair, put the question: "Shall this harbour of Yankee democracy be burned? All for it will say Aye," to which loud cries of assent being vociferated, he reversed the question, [and] pronounced it carried unanimously.' Cockburn, with Ross making no objection, then directed the burning of the entire building. They started by firing rockets into the roof, but it was made of iron and wouldn't catch alight. So they piled all the chairs and other furniture, library books and papers on the tables and set light to it all. The entire building was soon being consumed by flames, and the Library of Congress which was packed with thousands of volumes of books – many of them chronicles of political history by British authors – was also burned out. Franzoni's sculptures in the House of Representatives and Andrei's columns were destroyed, as were the rich red silk curtains with their green lining behind the Speaker's Chair. Only the Capitol's outside walls, badly blackened by the fire, survived and some of the more solidly built stonework, like the famous corncob capitals which can still be seen today in the Senate vestibule. Cockburn, wandering into the office used by the President when he visited Congress, helped himself to one memento. It was a slim book, beautifully bound, with the words 'The President of the United States' stamped in gilt on the cover. It was President Madison's personal copy of the government's receipts and payments for the year 1810. Cockburn wrote inside the cover: 'Taken in the President's room in the Capitol, at the destruction of that building by the British, on the capture of Washington 24th August 1814, by Admiral Cockburn, and by him presented to his eldest brother, Sir James Cockburn of Langton Bart, Governor of Bermuda'. It was later discovered by an antiquarian, Dr Rosenbach, who presented it to the Library of Congress in 1940.

It wasn't long before the night sky over Washington was illuminated by the fierce red glow of the two massive fires – at the Capitol and at the Navy Yard. It was just after 9 p.m. George Gleig, who was with the main body of the army outside the city, was awestruck by the scale of the conflagration. 'The sky was brilliantly illumined . . . and a dark red light was thrown upon the road, sufficient to permit each man to view distinctly his comrade's face. Except the burning of St Sebastian's [after the British storming of the city in Spain which Gleig watched in 1813], I do not recollect to have witnessed at any period of my life a scene more striking or more sublime.' All the same, when Gleig later heard the extent of the destruction that Cockburn and Ross had set their hands to, he couldn't help observing that the burning had, in his judgement, gone too far. 'Unfortunately . . . a noble library, several printing presses and all the national archives were likewise committed to the flames, which, although no doubt the property of the government, might better have been spared.' Harry Smith was at Ross's side throughout and he wrote later that he found it all too much for his sensitivities. He deplored the way his commanders went about destroying the city.

Americans looked on in horror and shame as the British began to burn their capital city. Anna Maria Thornton and her husband William watched from a distance as the buildings to which he had devoted so much energy and devotion were engulfed by flames. Like their friends the Madisons and the Bayard Smiths, they'd decided not to risk staying at their home in the city. They were in Georgetown and heading west, fearful that the British might chase US forces even beyond Washington. Others had opted to stay, like Dr James Ewell, who clung to the hope that the British would spare his family because they'd moved down the street to care for a desperately ill Mrs Orr. It was from her house that Ewell and his family watched the Capitol burn. 'Never shall I forget my tortured feelings,' Ewell recalled, 'when I beheld that noble edifice wrapt in flames, which, bursting through the windows and mounting far above its summits, with a noise like thunder, filled all the saddened night with a dismal gloom.' As if this sight and their harrowing day wasn't enough for the Ewell family and the invalid who was now their hostess, there was suddenly a great rapping at Mrs Orr's front door. On the doorstep were five or six British soldiers, 'asking politely for something to eat'. The Ewells immediately set a cold ham, a loaf of bread and butter and wine in front of the men, who were obviously ravenous but were, according to Ewell, 'conducting themselves with the utmost good behaviour'.

James Ewell glanced across at his own house down the street and his heart sank when he saw what looked like a light in every room. In the reflected flames of the Capitol it almost looked as if it too was on fire. Fearing for his property, in particular his precious library of medical books, he asked the soldiers who were still tucking into their supper if they could help. The sergeant in charge of the men said he doubted that the doctor's house was on fire but he and his men would certainly do what they could. It turned out that his house had not been burned but plundered. One of Ewell's servants came back to report that the culprits were British soldiers.

A friend, a local priest, then appeared and asked if he would like to meet the two British commanders, Ross and Cockburn, with whom he'd been talking. They were, he said, 'perfect gentlemen'. Ewell readily assented, hoping to secure his house and what was left of his belongings. The priest led him to the admiral whom he introduced mistakenly as 'General Ross'. 'My name is Cockburn, Sir,' said the admiral in a brisk and piercing tone of voice. Ewell was face to face with the man whose reputation for vandalism and terror was legendary. Nothing daunted, Ewell told Cockburn that he understood that private property was to be held sacred. 'It will be so deemed,' replied Cockburn. To which Ewell replied: 'Some of my furniture, apparel and plate has been plundered.' When Cockburn asked him whom he had left in charge of his property, he replied his servants. To which Cockburn retorted, 'Well, Sir, let me tell you it was very ill confidence to repose your property in the care of servants.' Ewell says he was then spared further conversation with the abrasive Cockburn by the arrival of General Robert Ross, who'd overheard enough of Ewell's talk with Cockburn to know that his house had been robbed. 'In a tone that will forever endear him to me as a "perfect gentleman" indeed, he observed that he was very sorry to hear that my house had been disturbed, and begged that I would tell him which it was, and he would order a sentinel to guard it.' When the doctor pointed out his house, Ross exclaimed – with what Ewell described as 'an amiable embarrassment' – that it was the house that he'd chosen as his head-quarters. Ewell said he was glad to hear it and that he was sorry the general hadn't taken the place earlier as that would have protected it. Ross replied that he 'could never think of trespassing on the repose of a private family, and would order his baggage out of my house immediately'. Ewell would hear none of it and pressed Ross to remain in his house. Ross politely agreed, promising to cause 'as little trouble as possible'.

The doctor then took Ross up to his own bedroom, which was the best furnished in the house with a large mattress on the bed. Ross was reluctant to accept the offer of the bed but in the end graciously accepted. He told Ewell that he should go and bring his family home. 'I am myself', said Ross, 'a married man, have several sweet children and venerate the sanctities of conjugal and domestic relations.' Ewell decided to leave the house to Ross and Cockburn, but, writing this account after the departure of the British, he paid particular tribute to Ross's 'consummate modesty and politeness'. The image of a victorious commander in chief treating his defeated enemies in such a way was 'a spectacle too honourable to human nature and too conducive to the general good to give offence'. Ewell went on to write that he hoped his full narrative of his remarkable encounter with Ross would – after the war – 'rekindle the pleasant flame of former friendship'. There were many Americans who thought Ewell a traitor for his dealings with the British. He came in for some scathing comment in the press, but he remained unrepentant.

Mary Hunter was another who stayed in the city. Her husband, the Reverend Dr Andrew Hunter, was Chaplain at the Navy Yard. They had no illusions about the kind of destruction to expect from the British army. The family's estate in New Jersey had been devastated during the Revolutionary War. But the two of them agreed that Mary should remain at home to try to protect the house with her housekeeper and one black servant while Andrew went off to safety with their children and other servants. 'I will leave you to conjecture', she wrote to her sister Susan six days later, 'what our feelings must have been when we saw the British flag flying on Capitol Hill, and the rockets brandished for the destruction of our Capitol and for what other property we knew not.'

That evening Mrs Hunter was confronted at her front door by a horseman she described as a 'grim looking officer' who asked where her husband was. She told him he wasn't at home. The officer asked where he was. Not at home, she replied; he'd left that morning. Why? asked the man. 'I then looked at him full in the face and very deliberately told him that my husband was gone to take a family of young children from witnessing such a horrid scene.' When, asked the man, would he be back? She replied that under the existing circumstances she hardly expected him to return home. Deciding that generosity was the better part of valour, she then invited the British officer to help himself to whatever he wanted from her sideboard. 'While he was regaling himself, I asked in my turn what they were going to do; whether to burn the city generally, or confine themselves to the public buildings?' He replied that that would depend. If people remained in their houses and offered no resistance, private property would be safe. But houses where arms were found or where anyone resisted, would be burned down.

Mary Hunter then crossed the road to a neighbour's house to get a better look at the Capitol. She and her servants found a group of British officers there helping themselves to some food they'd found. 'Seeing us alarmed they said everything that could be said to quiet us.' And Hunter herself told them she had seen 'a lot of British officers who were gentlemen, and that I could not bring myself to be afraid'. They talked of burning the Washington Bank, but when they were told that the fire would quickly spread to other nearby private houses, they agreed to spare it. They then told her they wanted to do all in their power to mitigate the distress of the citizens of Washington 'against whom they had no enmity . . . Their war was with the government and not with the people. All this relieved our fears concerning the city and ourselves.' Back in their own house, Mary Hunter and her two attendants watched the destruction of the Navy Yard from the top of the house. 'No pen can describe the appalling sound that our ears heard and the sight that our eyes saw.' It was 'an awful scene . . . the most suicidal act ever committed'. They saw warships in flames and the immense quantity of dry timber 'produced an almost meridian brightness. You never saw a drawing room so brilliantly lighted as the whole city was that night.'

It was now after 10 p.m. Leaving the blazing Capitol behind them, Ross, Cockburn and their escorting units proceeded up the great wide expanse of Pennsylvania Avenue. They marched along, two abreast, some of them carrying lanterns. Their pace was fast, and every now and again, when the officer in front heard men talking to each other, he shouted back, 'Silence! If any man speaks in the ranks, I'll put him to death.' The avenue they marched along would have looked primitive to a modern eye, surrounded as it was by only a few mainly timbered houses, but it was every bit as ambitious in scope as George Washington's visionary architect, the French-born Pierre L'Enfant, had planned it. The grandest stretch was the mile between the Capitol and the White House. James Scott called it a 'fine and spacious causeway'. There was a dual carriageway in the centre for horse riders and horse-drawn vehicles with a row of trees and generous footways for pedestrians at either side. L'Enfant had set himself the task of designing a city 'proportioned to the greatness which . . . the capital of a powerful empire ought to manifest'. When he began, Washington was little more than a village in a marsh: two decades later, in 1814, the nation's capital was beginning to show signs of matching up to those early pretensions.

In the interval between the flight of the US army and the British advance, American looters had moved into the vacuum and snatched what they could find in places like the White House and the Navy Yard. As the British approached, the looters vanished, and Ross sought to exert a measure of control. He appeared determined to prevent his men being accused of plundering private houses, and he issued orders that looting should be outlawed. We know of at least one British officer who later won the respect and gratitude of the Americans for carrying out Ross's orders. Major Norman Pringle was detailed with his company of grenadiers to protect private property on Pennsylvania Avenue. One American old soldier who talked to the local community after the British had left noted that Pringle carried out his task 'faithfully and successfully'. There were even accounts of British soldiers, who were caught looting, being lashed or shot.*

One Washington resident, William Gardner, leant out of his window as the British were passing and addressed Cockburn. 'I hope, Sir, that individuals and private property will be respected.' 'Yes, Sir,' replied Cockburn, 'we pledge our sacred honour that the citizens and private property shall be respected. Be under no apprehension. Our advice to you is to remain at home. Do not quit your houses.' Cockburn then went on to ask where President Madison was. Gardner replied that he was probably a long way off. 'We have got your Commodore Barney prisoner with us,' said Cockburn. 'So I have heard, Sir, and that he is badly wounded.' 'Yes, Sir, he is badly wounded but I am happy to say not mortally. He is a brave man and depend upon it, he shall be treated with the greatest humanity and kindness.' At which Ross, who was riding beside Cockburn, added: 'Yes, Sir, he shall be taken good care of.'

Ross stopped at a street corner just 200 yards short of the White House, where a boarding house overlooked the Presidential mansion. It was owned by Barbara Suter, an elderly lady who had two sons serving with the American forces, one a soldier, the other a sailor who'd fought with Joshua Barney and been wounded at Bladensburg. 'It was', said Mrs Suter, 'a whole week of great trouble.' She said she remembered 'hardly sleeping at night, and all the day time spent in fright'. She was alone in the house with just a servant when suddenly it was surrounded by soldiers whom she first mistook for Americans. But then an officer walked in and introduced himself as General Ross saying he had 'come, madam, to sup with you'. She told him she hadn't any food in the house and that he'd do better to go across to Macleod's Tavern where they'd be able to look after him. Ross replied that Macleod's Tavern wouldn't do because it didn't overlook the public buildings as her house did. He told her he'd like her

* See below pp. 142 and 170.

to prepare supper for himself and a few other officers who'd come back later. Trembling with fear, Barbara Suter and her servant reckoned they had no choice but to warm up some bread and go out and kill the chickens in the yard.

I I

The dreadful majesty of the flames

24 August, night

IT WAS AROUND an hour before midnight on Wednesday 24 August. A small detachment of British soldiers led by George Cockburn and Robert Ross, accompanied by their staff officers, crossed the road and approached the supreme sanctum of American power. The White House was dark, deserted and unprotected. Arthur Brooke, one of Ross's brigade commanders, wrote later that he found it hard to believe the Americans 'would tamely allow a handful of British soldiers to advance into the heart of their country and burn and destroy the capital of the United States'. Allen McLane, a senior military aide to William Winder, was just one of many American participants who felt that the British could have been stopped before they reached this far. 'I could see many opportunities lost,' he was to write later. Proper use of Winder's and Barney's forces earlier should have crippled the enemy's advance. 'A legion of . . . troops . . . could have entered Washington and have routed Ross, Cockburn and as many of the incendiaries, drunk on the night of the conflagration, as they pleased to select . . .' but just about every chance had been missed. 'Such reflections', said McLane, 'are too mortifying to dwell on.'

Ross and Cockburn entered the mansion of the fourth President of the United States as easily as if they'd been invited guests. It was by far the finest and most elegant building in Washington. If Presidents like Madison and Jefferson had had their way, it would have been a much more modest home in line with their view that the American republic and its leaders should have no pretensions to all the pomp and opulence of the old British monarchy. But the White House was the brainchild of George Washington, America's first President, who wanted to see a residence that would be the centrepiece of his new city – matching the grandeur of the Capitol at the far end of Pennsylvania Avenue. And Washington decreed that the President's House would be built of stone not of brick, the material used in nearly every other fashionable dwelling in the republic. Washington's chosen architect, James Hoban, an Irishman from Kilkenny, designed him the fine Anglo-Palladian building with its ornate stonework decoration that is still – with the exception of the later porticoes, north and south – the essence of today's White House. Hoban's work was overseen by three commissioners including William Thornton, whose enthusiasm and persistence helped ensure that it was completed in time for America's second President, John Adams, to take up residence there in 1800. It required a team of specially imported Scottish stonemasons to craft the intricate detail of Hoban's decorative stonework. And it wasn't just the ornamentation that was built to last, it was the very fabric of the building itself. The sandstone from the Aquia quarries in Virginia formed the outer layer sixteen inches thick. Inside that would be an inner lining of clay bricks around twenty-four inches thick. And the insides of the walls were lathed and plastered. To seal the porous sandstone, the exterior was coated with several layers of whitewash. Washington didn't live to see the building completed. The cornerstone was laid in October 1792; Washington died in 1799, a year before his successor, President Adams, moved into the finished building in November 1800. March 1801

This was the magnificent mansion, fourteen years old by this time and lovingly furnished by Dolley Madison, that Cockburn, Ross and their staff now explored by torchlight. And they were immediately struck by the smell of cooked food emanating from the Dining Room in the south-west corner of the ground floor and the kitchen near by. None of them had eaten properly since an early breakfast around five or six that morning. None of them imagined they would be treated to a feast prepared for a President.

'We found the cloth laid for the expected victorious generals, and all the appliances and means to form a feast worthy of the resolute champions of republican freedom,' wrote James Scott. The table was laid for forty. Paul Jennings, Madison's manservant, had done his job well. He had set the table with a damask tablecloth, matching napkins, silver and delicate wineglasses. 'Several kinds of wine in handsome cut glass decanters were cooling on the sideboard; plate holders stood by the fireplace, filled with dishes and plates; knives, forks and spoons were arranged for immediate use . . .' – Gleig, who wasn't an eyewitness himself, had the scene described to him in great detail. In the kitchen, he tells us, 'spits loaded with joints of various sorts turned before the fire; pots, saucepans and other culinary utensils stood upon the grate; and all the other requirements for an elegant and substantial repast were in the exact state which indicated they had been lately and precipitately abandoned'. Harry Smith, who was there, recalled, 'We found supper all ready, which was sufficiently cooked . . . and which many of us speedily consumed unaided by the fiery elements and drank some very good wine also.'

Scott walked over to where he saw the wines cooling in ice together with what he described as 'a large store of super excellent Madeira'. He helped himself to at least one generous glassful. 'Fagged nearly to death, dusty, feverish, and thirsty, in my extremity I absolutely blessed them for their erring providence. Never was nectar more grateful to the palates of the gods, than the crystal goblet of Madeira and water I quaffed at Mr Madison's expense.' Someone, possibly Cockburn, then proposed a toast to 'peace with America and down with Madison'.

Robert Ross himself relished the irony of America's successful invaders enjoying the defeated President's hospitality. 'The fare . . . intended for Jonathan was voraciously devoured by John Bull, and the health of the Prince Regent, and success to his Majesty's arms by sea and land, was drunk in the best wines, Madison having taken to his heels . . .'

Cockburn had met a young American bookseller, Roger Weightman, in the street and insisted on the man accompanying the British party into the White House. There Cockburn teased him mercilessly and made him drink the health of 'Jemmy' Madison.

Then the British party explored the White House to look for a few souvenirs. In the President's dressing room upstairs they noticed a lot of drawers half opened with contents spilling on the floor: they reckoned it was either the work of local pilferers earlier or the results of Dolley's rush to grab what she could before she escaped. Cockburn told Weightman that he could take something 'to remember the day'. The terrified and baffled bookseller reached for something that was obviously valuable, no doubt hoping to save it. But Cockburn, whether to avoid being accused of looting or just to taunt the young man further, said, 'No No . . . that I must give to the flames.' Weightman had to settle for an armful of trinkets Cockburn gave him from the mantelpiece. Cockburn then helped himself to one of Madison's hats and snatched a cushion from Dolley Madison's chair, saying with a smirk that it would remind him of 'her seat'.

James Scott went off on his own private scavenge. He went upstairs and tried on one of Madison's shirts. 'I accordingly doffed my inner garment, and thrust my unworthy person into a shirt belonging to no less a personage than the chief magistrate of the United States: the operation equalled in luxury and benefit the draught in the banqueting room.' One contemporary letter writer, Phoebe Morris, claimed that the British 'ruffians tore down' a portrait of Dolley Madison in her private sitting room 'and swore that they would "keep Dolley safe and exhibit her in London"'. A twenty-three-year-old lieutenant in the 85th Light Infantry, glorying in the name of Beauchamp Colclough Urquhart, had a lucky find. He spotted James Madison's very smart dress sword and reckoned it would make a fine addition to his collection. Twenty-one years later Urquhart would inherit the Scottish estate of Meldrum, and the sword no doubt had pride of place among the family treasures. George Chesterton, who didn't take part in the advance into the city, said there was a lot of 'idle gossip' among those who claimed to have walked off with White House treasures. 'Almost everyone you met had some relic to produce snatched from the possession of "Maddison" . . . I examined with nice curiosity a pair of "diamond" shoe-buckles (unmistakingly paste) which came from that inexhaustible source.'

Ross and Cockburn appear to have had no difference of opinion about what was to happen next. Ross had been in two minds about the wisdom of proceeding as far inland as Washington, but there is no evidence that he opposed the torching of the chief public offices of American state power. He had been scrupulous – as had Cockburn, to the surprise of many Americans – about opposing the destruction of private property. If a house offered no resistance, it was not to be burned down. But the object of the raid on Washington was to deliver President Madison and his country a devastating blow and to make him pay a price for starting and con- tinuing a war which the British government regarded as a deeply damaging and infuriating distraction. It was no part of this strategy to seize and hold on to the enemy's capital permanently, but to have occupied the city and moved on without exacting some kind of spectacular retribution would have been seen as half hearted. Besides there was that outstanding score to settle – revenge for the American burning of the capital of Upper Canada. Robert Ross may have been a man of much gentler sensibilities than the hard-bitten Cockburn. But he now readily gave his assent to the act that was to echo down the ages as one of the most humiliating moments in American history.

Once his men had finished devouring the President's supper, Ross ordered the chairs to be piled on the tables, and the furniture in all the rooms stacked up so that the fire would devour as much as pos- sible. One soldier helped himself to as many of the plates, knives and forks as he could wrap up in the tablecloth. Ross lent a hand collect- ing the furniture and was distracted only by a messenger from the French Ambassador begging him to spare the French embassy. Ross replied that the French embassy would 'be protected as much as though his Majesty [the King of France] himself was there in person'. It was again Cockburn's men, the team of sailors under Samuel Davies, who went about the business of setting light to all the chairs, tables, curtains and upholstery that Dolley Madison had taken such pride in introducing to the White House in the six years she and her husband had been there. 'I shall never forget the destructive majesty of the flames as the torches were applied to beds, curtains, etc. Our sailors were artists at their work,' wrote Harry Smith.

Margaret Bayard Smith's account suggests that, once the place had been made ready, as many as fifty sailors and marines 'were marched by an officer . . . each carrying a long pole to which was fixed a ball about the circumference of a large plate'. These 'balls', presumably of a highly inflammable material, were set alight. Each man was then stationed by a window 'with his pole and machine of wild fire against it', and then 'at the word of command, at the same instant the windows were broken and this wild fire thrown in, so that an instantaneous conflagration took place and the whole building was wrapt in flames and smoke'.

All stood and watched as the flames took hold of the White House. To save time during the construction of the President's House, the floors had been fashioned not of marble, as intended, but of wood. Everything inside was combustible. Within minutes the interior was a raging inferno. In seconds the flames swept through the main reception rooms on the ground floor and devoured all the furniture and soft furnishings that Dolley Madison hadn't managed to rescue. Only the great stone walls would withstand the destructive force of the conflagration. 'I never saw a scene at once more terrible or more magnificent,' reported the French Ambassador to his government.

William Gardner watched from the window of his house in Pennsylvania Avenue. First he saw the smoke belching out of the windows of the White House, 'and in a short time, that splendid and elegant edifice, reared at the expense of so much cost and labour, inferior to none that I have observed in the different parts of Europe, where I have been, was wrapt in one entire flame'.

The British officers who'd been instrumental in preparing the White House for destruction had mixed feelings about their handiwork. Harry Smith reckoned his old boss the Duke of Wellington would never have behaved like this. 'Well do I recollect that, fresh from the Duke's humane warfare in the south of France, we were horrified at the order to burn the elegant Houses of Parliament and the President's house.' Charles Furlong, one of the party from the

21st Fusiliers who had eaten at the President's table before helping set fire to the place, had his doubts too. 'I must confess', he wrote in his diary, 'I felt sorrow when witnessing such magnificent buildings demolished.'

When the news of the burning of the White House reached the rest of the army and the fleet, opinions were divided too. The midshipman Robert Barrett said he believed the Americans had escaped lightly. The British action, he said, fell far short of the 'stern severity' that would have been justified after Ross was fired on as he entered Washington. This was enough reason for Ross and his army to subject the city to 'a merciless and indiscriminate plunder'. George Chesterton had no doubt that the Americans deserved retribution, but he remarked: 'on reflection even the victors grieved over the summary and cruel havoc they had made ... The whole scene of explosion, spoliation, and ruin, combined to stamp such fierce and indiscriminate excess with a barbarian character.'

The fires at the White House and Congress raged on, and it was only when the heavens opened later that the rain brought merciful relief to the stone outer walls that still stood in both buildings. They survive to this day – though they have been massively enlarged, strengthened and restored – and the White House still bears the scars, the burn marks, of the fire of 24 August 1814. All the interior fittings were destroyed. The only modest piece of furniture that someone managed to rescue was a small walnut, brass and ivory medicine chest. It emerged in the possession of a Canadian, Archibald Kains, in 1939, who gave it to President Franklin Roosevelt. It remained in the Roosevelt Library until 1961 when it was restored on loan to the White House – where it has remained ever since.

It was midnight but Ross and Cockburn had not finished yet. From the upper dormitory of the Catholic seminary of Georgetown University two of the staff watched the buildings blazing away in the city to the east. 'The flames from those buildings were so great that a person could read at the college,' wrote the Reverend John McElroy, the university's bookkeeper. He and Father Grassi watched the British move on to burn the Treasury Building. They hoped that the enemy occupation would stop short of the university in Georgetown where a large number of local families had stored their plate and other valuables for safe keeping before fleeing the city.

The Treasury Building Grassi and McElroy saw wrapped in flames was only just across the road from the White House. Cockburn and Ross were by this time so impatient to get the job done that they ordered the firing of the Treasury before they'd properly examined it. The flames had already taken hold when someone discovered a great iron door which they tried but failed to break open in the con-flagration. In the end an officer managed to smash a window and scramble into what looked like a strongroom and the men contrived to help him manhandle some heavy chests out of it and on to the street. There was a flutter of excitement that they might have set hands on a stock of bullion, but it turned out their effort was in vain. The boxes contained nothing of interest, the Americans having taken care to remove all the gold and silver in their retreat. Scott wrote of the men's frustration 'on finding that the contents would by no means compensate us for our exertions and possible suffocation'.

The two commanders, who'd already tasted a few of the delicacies on the President's table, now hurried back to Mrs Suter's. They must have had some appetite left, because they now attacked the supper she had prepared for them. After they'd eaten, Ross went off to catch up on sleep in the bed he'd been offered by Dr Ewell, leaving Cockburn to settle one more score. He and Scott had spotted the offices of the *National Intelligencer*, the newspaper that had, said Scott, 'for ever taken the lead and given the keynote to the Republican press in vilifying England and the English'. Scott described the editor, Joseph Gales, as 'an Irish renegade'. He and his paper had often used colourful language to describe Cockburn's depredations of the last few months.

Cockburn was just ordering the place to be burned down when a bevy of local women appeared to plead with him not to start a fire that would threaten their houses. He agreed and ordered the building pulled down with ropes passed through one window and out of another: this allowed the men to heave down the wooden-framed building. All the papers inside were piled into a large bonfire and the printing press itself was smashed to pieces in the street. Cockburn took particular delight in watching all the letter Cs being destroyed. 'The rascals can have no further means of abusing my name,' he said gleefully. It was, said Scott, 'a fitting purification of the instruments of corruption and falsehood emanating from a traitorous proprietor'. Cockburn explained to the women: 'Good people, I do not wish to injure you, but I am really afraid my friend Josey [Gales] will be affronted with me, if after burning Jemmy's palace, I do not pay him the same compliment.' He told some others: 'you may thank old Madison for this [destruction], it is he who has got you into this scrape . . . we want to catch and carry him to England for a curiosity'. Scott reports that the women asked him for the name of this chivalrous British officer who had granted their request to spare their houses. 'Why, that is the vile monster, Cock-Burn,' replied Scott, pronouncing the middle consonants as the Americans always did. 'A half uttered shriek of terror escaped from the lips of some of them as the dreaded name tingled on their ears. The announcement was electrifying . . . they had absolutely stood in the presence of and amiably conversed with that most venomous of all "British sarpents" and for whose head a reward of one thousand dollars had been publicly offered.' They parted on the best of terms.

A number of Americans commented on how Cockburn's restraint and respect for the citizenry of Washington contrasted with his barbaric reputation. The normally vehement *Niles' Register* newspaper commented on 27 August that apart from burning the public buildings the British had 'otherwise behaved much better than expected'. The *National Intelligencer* newspaper wrote that, when it came to looting, the Americans were guiltier than the British: 'No houses were half as much plundered by the enemy as by the knavish wretches about the town who profited of the general distress.' Margaret Bayard Smith, as patriotic as any Washingtonian, observed in a letter she wrote six days later that Cockburn 'deserves praise and commendation for his own good conduct and the discipline of his sailors and marines'. She noted that Cockburn and his men were 'perfectly polite to the citizens. He bade them complain of any soldier that committed the least disorder and had several severely punished, for very slight offences. All provisions were paid for.' She generously omitted to mention the President's dinner that the British had wolfed down at the White House. Bayard Smith, who wasn't there at the time, but got the story from her neighbours a day or two later, said Cockburn was seen a number of times riding his white mare up and down the avenue. He stopped at one house and asked a young lady: 'Were you prepared to see a savage, a ferocious creature, such as Josey represented me? But you see I'm quite harmless, don't be afraid. I will take better care of you than Jemmy did!' The admiral's manner, Bayard Smith remarked, 'was that of a common sailor, not of a dignified commander . . .'. But she went on, 'I must praise his moderation, indeed his conduct was such as to disarm the prejudices that existed.' Well pleased with his reception and the work he'd done that night, George Cockburn finally returned to headquarters at the Capitol for a few hours' sleep.

12

Damn you! You shan't stay in my house
25 August

JAMES MADISON WAS the only US President in history to be a fugitive in his own country other than George Bush Jr who, nearly two centuries later, retreated to the US strategic command bunker at Offutt Air Force Base in Bellevue, Nebraska on 11 September 2001 when terrorists struck Washington. Madison's flight was far less efficiently organised. He crossed the Potomac at 6 p.m. on Wednesday 24 August 1814, accompanied by Richard Rush, the Attorney General, and the Navy Secretary William Jones. They had no idea where Dolley or the rest of the Jones family were, and so Madison sent off a note which he hoped would find her, suggesting they meet at Wiley's Tavern near the Great Falls of the Potomac. Madison and his companions rode on horseback about six miles up the west bank of the river safely inside Virginia. Every now and then they'd pause on a piece of high ground and glance back at the fires in the capital. It was, recalled Rush, 'a dismal sight . . . columns of flames and smoke ascending throughout the night . . . from the Capitol, the President's House and other public edifices . . . some burning slowly, others with bursts of flame, and sparks mounting high up in the dark horizon'. It was getting late and the group decided to stop short of Wiley's at the house of a churchman called John Maffitt in the village of Salona.

By coincidence Dolley was only a mile away. She had not made it to Wiley's either but had stopped at the house of a friend, Matilda Love. Sofas and other substitutes for beds were rapidly made ready for the unexpected guests. The women spent what one contemporary chronicler described as a 'frightful, miserable night, all disconsolate, several in tears, Mrs. Madison sitting at an open window gazing on

the lurid flames and listening to the hoarse murmurs of the smouldering city'. The next day, after a nervous journey through groups of
refugees, Dolley Madison and her friends and attendants reached
Wiley's Tavern, the appointed meeting place. She was in for a shock.
The inn was full of fugitive women whose husbands were still with
the army and the moment they recognised Dolley they vented their
anger on her for all their misfortunes. Some of them had even
enjoyed her hospitality at White House parties. The wife of the
President who had landed the country in such a catastrophe had no
right to shelter in the same house as them, they said. According to the
Madisons' servant Paul Jennings, Dolley was unceremoniously
shouted out of one house – perhaps it was the tavern – after she'd
gone upstairs for a moment. 'The lady of the house, learning who she
was, became furious and went to the stairs and screamed out "Miss
Madison, if that's you, come down and go out! Your husband has got
mine out fighting, and damn you, you shan't stay in my house, so get
out!"' Jennings says he learned all this from Dolley's servant Sukey
who travelled with her. Madison himself came in for some catcalls
when he reached the tavern later on, exhausted and soaked to the
skin by driving rain. 'He was insulted by some of the refugees, who
held him responsible for their misfortune.' In spite of this humiliation, both James and Dolley Madison managed to arrange to stay at
the tavern that night. She had even contrived to persuade the staff to
set aside some food for him and his famished companions. But they
were to spend another restless night. At midnight the rumour went
around that the British were coming, and one story has it that
Madison's aides hurried him out of bed and into hiding in a small
hovel in the woods. Before he left, he told Dolley to disguise herself
and leave the tavern at dawn.

Little did the President and his wife know it, but far from advancing beyond Washington that night of 25 August, the British had
already left.

Cockburn and Ross had spent their first night in Washington, on the
24th, sleeping soundly as the city's public buildings blazed around

them. They were with their troops near the Capitol, Ross in the bedroom he'd been lent by the benevolent Dr James Ewell. The doctor returned there around breakfast time and immediately made himself useful attending to the soldier who had been guarding Ross's horse. The man 'suddenly fell down in a fit. I hastened to the poor fellow and opened a vein, which gave him immediate relief.' But then a file of British soldiers marched up led by a sergeant and one of them 'desired me rather roughly, to give him some water'. Ewell promptly called to his servant to bring out 'a pitcher' of water, not suspecting for a moment that this would cause the soldier any offence. 'You damned rebel,' the man shouted at him, 'do you think I am a beast, to drink out of a pitcher?' Luckily for Ewell Robert Ross heard the soldier's insolent language and walked out of the house to see what was going on. The man rapidly tried to shrink back among his mates, but the general, with a furious look, jerked him by the collar and exclaimed: 'Villain, is this the way you speak to a gentleman, and in this moment too, that he is doing a kindness to a sick fellow-soldier of your own? . . . This conduct shall not pass unnoticed.' Ross then turned to the doctor and said that every army had its scoundrels and he was sorry to say there were too many of them in his own army.

Ross was then introduced to the doctor's wife, who'd made no secret of her fear for herself and her family. 'The general shook her hand with every mark of undissembled friendship,' Ewell wrote in his diary, 'expressed his deep regret to learn that she had been so seriously frightened, and lamented sincerely the necessity that had given cause to these tragedies, namely, the burning of the British capital in Canada.' Ewell thought to himself that Ross's case for burning Washington as an act of revenge was wearing a bit thin. And he had a point. York was burned in April 1813 by American troops who had lost all discipline: it was not a deliberate act ordered by the US government. Besides, towards the end of 1813, British troops had burned Lewiston, Blackrock and Buffalo. That, to many, looked like fair recompense for York.

Ewell decided not to engage in heated debate with Ross about this, but he did say what a pity it was that the British had burned the library in the Capitol. At which Ross in his disarming way replied: 'I lament most sincerely I was not apprised of the circumstances, for had I known it in time the books would most certainly have been saved.' 'Neither do I suppose, General,' said the doctor, 'you would have burnt the President's house had Mrs Madison remained at home.' 'No, Sir,' replied the general, 'I make war neither against letters nor ladies, and I have heard so much in praise of Mrs Madison that I would rather protect than burn a house which sheltered such an excellent lady.' This was more than a bit rich coming from the man who had a few hours earlier given the orders to burn the place down. Ross even went on to express his regret that Britain and America were fighting each other. It was, he said, a 'war between two nations so nearly allied by consanguinity and interest'.

Ross had particular praise too for Joshua Barney's gallant stand at Bladensburg. 'I am sorry he was wounded,' he told Ewell. 'Had half your army been composed of such men as this commodore . . . we should never have got to your city.' Ewell noted that, unlike the sharp-tongued George Cockburn, Robert Ross did not publicly mock Madison or any other American official. Nor had Ross the brash outgoing personality of his naval counterpart. 'His countenance', reported Ewell, 'seemed constantly shrouded in the close shades of a thoughtful mind.' In spite of Ross's obviously honourable and generous attitude, Ewell said, 'I never saw the sunbeam of one cheerful smile on General Ross all the time he was in Washington.'

Ewell saw some humanity in Cockburn too. He recognised that this would startle some of his readers: 'What! Magnanimous traits in Admiral Cockburn! Impossible!' But, Ewell went on to say, he did have an example or two. The admiral heard the Bank of Washington had not been burned down the night before in order to protect nearby private houses. 'Well then, pull it down,' he said. 'Admiral Cockburn,' said Ewell, 'you do not want to injure private property.' 'I do not,' replied Cockburn, 'but this is public property'. 'No Sir,' went on Ewell, 'the United States have no bank here now; this is altogether private property.' 'Well then,' said the admiral, 'let it alone.'

Ewell had to fight for another building as well. His neighbour Elias Caldwell, commander of a company of volunteers, nearly lost his house when the British found some cartridges and cartridge boxes stacked there. When Ewell argued that Caldwell was a brave man who had only been doing his duty, Cockburn, after a word with Ross, spared the place.

All that morning, Thursday 25 August, the burning and destruction went on. The light infantry replaced the fusiliers as the core of the occupying force. Captain Wainwright of HMS *Tonnant* led a naval demolition party to the Navy Yard first thing in the morning and set about completing the work that Tingey, the Yard's own commandant, had started the night before. A few more store sheds were set alight, and James Scott and another group – at Cockburn's instigation – saw to the torching of the main ropewalk, a long shed used for spinning the great hemp warps, sheets, braces and other ropes for the warships. 'The beautiful government ropewalk, with its adjoining ample stores of cordage, hemp and tar, filled to the roofs, was next visited under my orders.' Scott told his men to spread the materials along the middle of the place and then, 'knocking out the heads of some dozens of tar barrels, their contents were spread over the train. The whole was speedily in a state of ignition; black dense volumes of smoke, obscuring the heavens . . .' Scott said the fire ran so rapidly along the 600-yard building that it was all ablaze within thirty minutes. 'The red flames flashing forth from the lower part of the mass of heavy vapour gave it the appearance of a Tartarus upon earth. It was quickly reduced to a heap of smouldering rubble.'

Remarkably, only minutes after the British incendiary teams had moved on, Tingey himself crept back to the Yard in his gig to see what had happened. It was 8.45 a.m. when he landed at the main wharf and was amazed to find – amid all the destruction – that the schooner *Lynx* had survived. He got his men to haul her out of harm's way as best they could. Tingey was also delighted to see that his house had been spared, on the ground that it was a private residence, although local neighbours had looted it and other parts of the Yard.

As the British teams headed towards their next target – the War Office – shots suddenly rang out. A horseman appeared from nowhere and charged down the street firing off his two pistols at the British troops. He was an American seaman, John Lewis, on a suicidal mission of revenge. Lewis was George Washington's nephew. He had been seized from an American ship and forcibly impressed by the Royal Navy to fight in a British ship against his own country. He'd now escaped and was bent on retribution. Seething with resentment he galloped straight at the head of the British column and ran into a hail of fire from the troops. He fell mortally wounded in the middle of the road and his body lay there for hours.

Harry Smith and James Scott were chatting outside their commanders' headquarters when an American prisoner who'd been led past them suddenly made a dash for it. He snatched a British horse, leapt on its back and raced off. Quick as a flash Harry Smith was in the saddle chasing after him. Scott was then treated to the sight of Smith slashing at the man, missing him, but bringing both of them crashing to the ground. Smith came away with only a scratch but the American broke his thigh and Smith promptly found him a doctor.

The British team went on to burn down the War Office. Some precious relics, such as the flags and other regimental trophies they'd managed to grab from the British in the War of Independence thirty years earlier, had already been rescued, but huge quantities of furniture, documents and accounts were consumed by the flames. The next building identified for destruction was the Patent Office. This was the pride and joy of Dr William Thornton, the erudite physician who had designed the Capitol and was now the Patent Office's superintendent. It was the home of a whole host of models of machines and gadgets submitted for patenting by inventors. Thornton saw it as a treasure house, a testament to the creative and innovative talents of Americans. The inventor Eli Whitney, for example, had patented his famous cotton gin, the labour-saving machine that extracted the seeds from cotton and transformed the American economy. 'Hearing . . . while at breakfast in Georgetown, that the British were about to burn the War Office and the public buildings containing the models of the arts, I was desirous not only of saving an instrument that had cost me great labour, but of preserving the building and all the models.'

He left his breakfast and cannily made sure he found someone – 'one of the most respectable gentlemen of the district' – to accompany him, 'lest the malevolent should insinuate that I had in any manner held an improper communication with the invaders of the country'. Thornton and his comrade watched helplessly as the War Office was burned by a team of soldiers under the command of a Colonel Jones. He then asked the colonel if he could remove a musical instrument, a violin he was designing, from the Patent Office. The colonel promptly accepted, saying that it was not the army's intention to burn any private property. Thornton then headed for the Patent Office but was delayed as he had some difficulty finding a replacement for his travelling companion who said he had had enough. Colonel Jones meanwhile was marching his men in two columns for the Patent Office backed up by a squad of blacks carrying a quantity of gunpowder to help with its destruction.

When Thornton arrived at the Patent Office he was told that he could remove anything in the building that was private. He replied that there was nothing in the building that was public property. Inside, he said, were hundreds of models, which it would be impossible to remove. 'To burn what would be useful to all humanity', he told the British, 'would be as barbarous as formerly to burn the Alexandrian library, for which the Turks have been ever since condemned by all enlightened nations.' His plea was successful. The Patent Office was left undisturbed, and William Thornton, hugely relieved, returned to his family in Georgetown. He was home in time for lunch, and in her diary that day his wife Anna Maria wrote that her husband had, 'by his exertions, saved the Patent Office from destruction'. She described some of the fires the British had lit and wrote: 'It appears almost miraculous that the whole place was not consumed. But great pains were taken by the English not to injure private property.'

William Gardner, who'd talked to Cockburn from his window in

Pennsylvania Avenue the evening before, was particularly impressed by the conduct of one British officer that morning. He was, recalled Gardner, 'a young man of age 26 or 27, remarkably handsome in his person and of very intelligent mind'. Gardner reported to him that a man he knew had been robbed by a British soldier. The officer promptly told him to run with him to the man's house, which Gardner did – without pausing to put on his jacket. And as they rushed up, they found the same soldier looting someone else's house. 'You villain,' shouted the officer, 'you have turned thief and are disgracing your country.' The soldier protested his innocence, but the officer 'closing his fist gave the soldier a most violent blow, which staggered him considerably and his hat fell to the ground. I took it up,' wrote Gardner, 'and found it filled with silk shawls and silver articles of value which I pulled out and showed to the officer.' The officer then struck the soldier with the butt of his pistol and told him to follow him immediately to the army headquarters. 'I was later informed that he was taken out on parade the same day and shot.'

Ross and Cockburn spent much of the day – in between their bouts of burning and destruction – in the company of Dr Ewell. He made no secret of his fellow feeling with them, which many of his countrymen later classed as collaboration. At one moment a woman dashed up shrieking: 'O I am killed, I am killed! A British sailor has killed me!' Cockburn furiously ordered the perpetrator to be rooted out and shot, but Ewell took one look at the woman, whom he described as 'a common strumpet', and pronounced that she had only slight wounds and was far too drunk to identify her attacker.

Ewell was in his dining room with Cockburn when a delegation from the town of Alexandria, just seven miles down the Potomac River, knocked on the door. It was only natural that the people of Alexandria, like the people of the even closer settlement of Georgetown, were terrified for their safety with the British causing mayhem on their doorstep. The town council of Alexandria had made earnest pleas to Winder in the presence of James Madison himself to apprise him 'of the necessity of providing some adequate defence against an attack by water'. They warned that, unless defences were provided, the town would 'be compelled to make the best terms in its power' with the enemy. Both communities preferred to forestall a British rampage by offering to negotiate. They had watched with horror the botched and hopeless fight for Washington, and were determined not to suffer the same fate. James Ewell wrote, 'The terror struck into our people . . . rolled on in such conglomerating floods to Alexandria that it acquired a swell of mountainous horrors, that appear to have entirely prostrated the spirits of the Alexandrians. Men, women and children saw nothing in their frightened fancies but the sudden and total destruction of their city . . .'

It wasn't just the British army threatening the people of Alexandria: they'd also heard news of a major naval squadron heading up the Potomac towards them under the command of Captain James Alexander Gordon clearly bent on creating further destruction. Gordon was still a day or two short of Alexandria, but the prospect of their town being stormed by land and sea was enough to prompt the Alexandrians to send a four-man delegation to talk to Cockburn. The admiral replied that he was ready to talk about some arrangement with them but they would have to agree to supply his army with provisions. And according to Ewell, who witnessed the encounter, Cockburn added: 'Let me tell you that for every article we take you shall be allowed a fair price.'

The biggest death toll by far that day was the result not of enemy action but of what looks like a clumsy accident. In the early afternoon a British captain led his company of soldiers to a spot called Greenleaf Point where he'd been told to destroy an American gunpowder magazine. They found the magazine empty. The powder had been removed earlier and dumped in a disused well. By an appalling coincidence the British soldiers were relaxing by the well and one of them threw a lighted match or a cigar end into it. There was a gigantic explosion. James Scott's account suggests that it was the British team's fault. He says they were the ones who removed the powder and threw it down the well. But they dropped the casks down carelessly making no allowance for sparks flying around as they caught on the well's stone walls. However the accident was caused, around thirty soldiers died instantly. Body parts were thrown far and wide, and an immense pile of rubble from the crater made by the blast crashed down and buried many others alive. The survivors were – in the words of Dr Ewell, who saw them carried to lodgings next door to his house – 'horribly mangled'. An American officer who visited the site a day later wrote that he witnessed 'the horrible spectacle of legs, arms and heads protruding from the mounds of earth thrown up by the explosion'.

Ewell counted forty-seven men who would need their wounds urgently attended to. He remembers Ross being particularly moved by their plight. 'He observed, looking at me with an eye of searching anxiety: "I am much distressed at leaving these poor fellows behind me. I do not know who is to mitigate their sufferings." "The Americans, General Ross," I replied, "are of the same origin as yourself. We have, I trust, given you many splendid instances of our humanity in the course of this unfortunate war; and you may rely on it, Sir, no attentions in my power shall be withheld from them." He gave me a look of gratitude which I shall never forget.' It would be easy to dismiss the behaviour of men like Ewell, Thornton and Gardner as cowardly collaboration with their country's enemy. But the evidence suggests that they were men of dignity and honour who behaved as they believed civilised men should.

Later that afternoon a storm of wind and rain struck the city and the area around it. It was so violent many called it a hurricane. One eyewitness said early growls of thunder suddenly turned into a 'terrific tornado . . . The sky changed from the peculiar leaden hue portending a wind storm, into almost midnight blackness. Then came the crash and glare of incessant thunder and lightning, and the wild beating of the rain, mingled with the sound of roofs tearing from their supports, and the whir of heavy bodies flying through the air and falling upon the ground beneath.' George Gleig saw 'roofs of houses [being] torn off by it, and whirled into the air like sheets of paper whilst the rain which accompanied it resembled the rushing of a mighty cataract . . . The darkness was as great as if the sun had long set.' The storm reached the fleet too – where the ships' crews waited anxiously for news of the invasion of Washington. Harry Smith said the storm lasted twenty minutes. 'It resembled the storm in Belshazzar's feast, and we learned that even in the river, sheltered by the woods, several of our ships at anchor had been cast on their beam ends.' Harry Smith allowed himself a generous dollop of poetic licence here. The Bible makes no mention of a storm at Belshazzar's feast. Robert Barrett called it a 'hurricane of the most tremendous description. It drove both the *Severn* and our own ship on shore, close to the village [of Benedict] and lashed the smooth and placid waters of the Patuxent into a vast sheet of foam.'

Ross now decided that the time had come to abandon Washington and return to the ships. Cockburn didn't disagree. The mission had been successfully accomplished. The rainstorm had stopped the fire spreading and devouring more of the city: it had even doused the flames at the White House and Congress leaving much of their walls intact. But within the limits the British had set themselves – no permanent occupation, no unbridled plunder, no wild destruction of private property – the raid on Washington had achieved its purpose: decisive defeat and utter humiliation of the enemy, the proudest monuments of America's capital devastated. The question now was what effect the victory would have on the war, and whether there was anything more the British task force could do to hasten its end. Lord Liverpool's Tory government in Britain, battered and impoverished by two decades of war in Europe, was daily more anxious to find an honourable end to the contest with America. As the war dragged on, both sides came to appreciate that while they were each winning tactical victories here and there, strategically they were gaining nothing. Neither side had managed to inflict a decisive blow on the other. But now there was an opportunity for the British to do just that. If the army that had destroyed Washington could swiftly destroy another major American city, Britain could be close to landing a knockout blow.

Only thirty-five miles up the road from Washington lay a no less tempting target. Washington was the heart of America's state power, but in population, wealth and commercial dynamism it was a mere village compared to Baltimore. Maryland's big city was one of the busiest, richest and most ambitious of the burgeoning cities on America's east coast. Its population of some 50,000 was six times the size of Washington's. Before America's trade was deadened by the Royal Navy's blockade, Baltimore was an exuberant mercantile centre, its harbour bustling with ships loading tobacco and wheat from Maryland and fertile neighbouring states and unloading sugar from the Caribbean and luxuries from Europe. It offered Atlantic traders a shorter route to Ohio and the expanding midwest than Philadelphia or New York. But most provocatively Baltimore was the home of the scores of American privateering skippers who often managed to evade the Royal Navy and cause havoc to British commercial shipping. The British called Baltimore 'that nest of pirates'. Joshua Barney had been the city's most renowned maritime hero before Madison lured him away to harry the British. His flotilla was built in Baltimore shipyards.

There were some – like his aide George Evans – who urged Ross to march straight for Baltimore. It would fall easily. Its face was to the sea: it was hardly defensible against a land attack. The fleet could sail up Chesapeake Bay and join the army at Baltimore. The navy would bombard from the east, the army would attack from the west. 'Before the retreat was decided upon,' wrote Evans in his official memorandum, 'the propriety of a movement on Baltimore was agitated . . . the army was provided with an abundance of guides capable of affording the most ample information, a thousand horses could have been supplied in two days and the brilliant result of the late enterprise, the disorganization of the enemy's public departments, the confusion and disarray of the country seemed to justify the attempt.' Cockburn too, in typical gung-ho fashion, recorded that he believed if they moved on Baltimore 'without loss of time' they would 'get possession also of that place without any very great loss or difficulty'.

The people of Baltimore themselves had no doubt they were next in line. One Baltimore soldier wrote to his brother, 'To my sorrow it is not to end here. We expect every minute to hear that they have taken up the line of march for this place, and if they do we are gone.'

If Ross saw the force of the argument for an immediate attack on Baltimore, he knew it wouldn't be accepted. He'd allowed the dogged Cockburn to needle him into flouting the wishes of his Commander in Chief Sir Alexander Cochrane once. He wasn't going to do it again. As Evans noted, Cochrane had disapproved of the advance on Washington. He would certainly disapprove of extending it to Baltimore. The idea was one that 'No one would have ventured to propose'. James Scott, Cockburn's ADC, concluded his brief account of the flurry of excitement for Baltimore with the mournful words: 'The favourable moment was suffered to pass unheeded.'

That night Ross gave the order for the army to march. In total secrecy, they would march off – not towards Baltimore but the way they had come, leaving a wall of burning campfires to deceive the Americans into believing they were spending another night in Washington. Harry Smith was away briefly when the order was given, and when he returned and the general told him the army was to move out, Smith exclaimed: 'Tonight? I hope not, sir.' He pleaded with Ross to allow the men a night's sleep and then proceed early the next morning, but Ross was adamant: 'I have made the arrangement with Evans, and we must march.' Smith no doubt bridled at the thought of Evans, his junior, having more apparent influence with Ross than he did, and he writes that he 'muttered to himself' that he wished he was serving under another commander.

Ross had no doubt that he was right. Delay, he reckoned, could allow the Americans time to assemble a force that would make the retreat very uncomfortable. At nine that night the army was on the move back towards the ships. The British would not march direct from Washington to Baltimore. But Baltimore would not escape a British assault: it would just be postponed for three weeks.

13

Into the Potomac

26–27 August

'MY DEAREST,' WROTE President James Madison to Dolley on the morning of Saturday 27 August, 'I have just read a line from Colonel Monroe saying that the enemy were out of Washington and on the retreat to their ships. We shall accordingly set out thither immediately, you will of course take the same resolution.' Madison told his wife he didn't know where they would 'hide their heads' in the city once they arrived, but he'd sort something out. As suddenly as the dark hand of destruction and defeat had battered the capital and its people, it appeared to have vanished. Madison's Secretary of State, the energetic James Monroe, sent a message from the army, which was now cautiously returning to the city, that the President could return and that he would come and help escort him back.

James Madison had just spent a quiet night with a family at Brookville back on the east bank of the Potomac. He was grateful for the rest after a harrowing three days riding from one place of refuge to another. He was reported to be calm and, 'though much distressed by the dreadful event which had taken place, not dispirited'.

Once Monroe had arrived, Madison and the faithful Rush, his Attorney General, who'd been at his side throughout, saddled up and set out for home. It was noon. Five hours later they were riding into Washington and getting their first glimpse of the damage. Over the next twenty-four hours, avoiding the bodies of dead horses scattered outside, they inspected the Capitol's two houses of Congress. Both were burned out, along with the central wooden structure that had bound them together. Rush wrote that they were 'the most magnificent and melancholy ruin you ever beheld'. The marble floors of the chambers were littered with the smashed glass of the chandeliers that had lit them. When Margaret Bayard Smith and her family ventured back into the city the next day they found the shell of the House of Representatives still smoking, its 'beautiful pillars . . . cracked and broken, the roof, that noble dome, painted and carved with such beauty and skill, lay in ashes in the cellar beneath the smouldering ruins . . .'. In the White House 'not an inch, but its cracked and blackened wall remained'. Only days earlier Mrs Smith had seen it 'splendid, thronged with the great, the gay and the ambitious'. Now it was 'nothing but ashes'. It would take years to rebuild it – too long to allow the Madisons to return to it. 'Who would have thought that this mass so solid, so magnificent,' she wrote in her diary, 'should by the hands of a few men and in the space of a few hours, be thus irreparably damaged.'

America had however been spared one horror that America's slave-owners had long feared. There was no rising by the black slave population. Margaret Bayard Smith wrote that they 'have behaved well, been quiet and in general appear to dread the enemy as much as we do. Thus we are spared one evil and the one I had most dread of.'

The two formidable doctors, James Ewell and William Thornton, and the handful of citizens who had braved the occupation had arranged the burial of the dead, almost all of them British, and the treatment of the enemy wounded. Thornton, who had spent twenty-four hours trying to persuade the British not to plunder and burn, found himself trying to curb ordinary Americans from looting their fellow citizens' property. But at least the British had left, and Rush offered Madison lodging at his house, which still stood and could comfortably accommodate the President and his wife.

If Madison did have a few minutes that evening to sit back and hope that his city and its people could now look forward to a quick recovery, he was soon rudely jolted back to reality. Before it was dark, the noise of naval guns boomed across the waters of the Potomac. At eight o'clock the President and his colleagues were shaken by a mighty explosion from the fort that guarded the southern approaches to the city. Its powder magazine had detonated. The squadron of British warships that had been spotted days earlier moving up the Potomac had penetrated the upper reaches of the river and started shelling Fort Washington, which was evacuated without a fight. The capital, which only three days earlier had been invaded and devastated by an assault from the east, was suddenly wide open to attack from the south.

It was one of the most startling and daring naval exploits in British history. Unlike most of the great waterway inlets on America's east coast, the Potomac was regarded as impenetrable to large ships. It wound for more than seventy-five miles from its estuary in Chesapeake Bay over a series of shoals that made long stretches treacherously shallow. Even American warships helmed by expert pilots used to offload their guns to reduce the draught before attempting it. To a sizeable flotilla from a foreign power with no local help and hostile banks on either side, it was a death trap.

Back on 17 August when Admiral Cochrane had first despatched his main naval force up the Patuxent to destroy Joshua Barney's American flotilla and deliver Ross's invasion force on to the road to Washington, he ordered two diversionary naval thrusts to confuse the enemy about the Royal Navy's main target. One under Captain Peter Parker was to cause trouble in the northern waters of Chesapeake. It was abandoned when Parker himself was killed leading a disastrous attack on a coastal settlement. The other was the Potomac expedition.

Two of Britain's toughest seadogs, both Scotsmen, were put in charge of the squadron of warships which headed up the river that led direct to Washington. The overall commander, temporarily appointed commodore, was Captain James Alexander Gordon. His grandfather had fought with Bonnie Prince Charlie against King George II at Culloden, and James himself had a wild childhood in Aberdeenshire in which he enjoyed leaping out of the upper windows of his home, Kildrummy Castle. He grew up to be a giant of a man for those days – at well over six feet. He joined the navy at the age of eleven and was a master's mate helping steer HMS *Goliath* into the anchored

French line at the Battle of the Nile in 1798 when he was only seventeen. He fought the French in several ships and lost his leg to a 30-pound cannonball in 1811. By the time he joined Cochrane's expedition Captain Gordon's wooden leg could be heard clumping its way back and forth on the quarterdeck of his frigate *Seahorse*. He and his wife Lydia had eight children.

Seahorse had thirty-eight guns. Her partner in this ambitious enterprise, HMS *Euryalus*, had thirty-six. *Euryalus* was commanded by an equally single-minded character, Captain Charles John Napier, who was – in contrast to Gordon – a stout and swarthy figure of a man. He'd been nicknamed Black Charlie ever since he joined the navy against the stern opposition of his father. The young lad was an unusual mixture. At fifteen he was so homesick when he served on the seventy-four-gun HMS *Renown* that he was seen to burst into tears. But he showed early signs of pluck as well. When a zoo keeper told him that one of the lions was so tame you could put your hand in its mouth, Charles Napier did just that – and got away with it. Thirteen years and several bitterly fought battles later, Black Charlie joined Cochrane as Captain of *Euryalus*, and was made second in command of the expedition up the Potomac. Cochrane knew Napier well: seven years earlier he had been instrumental in promoting the inspired young officer to the rank of commander. It was not surprising that Cochrane now chose Charles Napier for this challenging mission up the Potomac.*

Between them Gordon and Napier had six warships, the two frigates, *Seahorse* and *Euryalus*, three bomb vessels and a rocket ship. They were accompanied by a small tender and despatch boat, the

---

* Napier was so hungry for experience of battle that during one slack period in his career he went to visit his brother, a junior army officer, and three cousins, all colonels, fighting with Wellington in the Peninsula. He managed to get himself slightly wounded at the Battle of Bussaco in 1810, when one of the colonels, Charles James Napier, actually fell severely wounded into the arms of the other Charles, his naval cousin. Colonel Charles James Napier was to go on to command a brigade under Admiral George Cockburn when he was conducting raids on the American coast in 1813. He was heartily critical of Cockburn and his methods. See above p. 12.

schooner *Anna Maria*. The rocket ship, *Erebus*, had sixteen guns on her upper deck and below a stack of 32-pound Congreve rockets. These newly concocted but hopelessly inaccurate weapons had done their bit to surprise and terrify the American army at Bladensburg. They packed a deadly punch of explosive. The bombships, *Aetna*, *Devastation* and *Meteor*, carried two mortars each, as well as between eight and ten guns. Naval guns fired solid shot: the advantage of the mortar was that it propelled 10-inch and 13-inch explosive shells over a considerable distance. Shells scattered their lethal fragments over a much wider area than a single ball.

It was an incredibly arduous voyage up the Potomac. As Charles Napier observed: 'the navigation is extremely intricate . . . the charts gave us mostly very bad directions and no pilots could be procured'. On the second day they reached the notorious Kettle Bottom shoals. These were a random group of shallows with narrow passages between them, so narrow that even if the ship in front appeared to pass through one, the ship behind could easily ground – as Napier found to his cost. *Seahorse* led the way, taking regular soundings and managed to find a channel, but *Euryalus* following carefully behind suddenly stopped. Even the lead line cast over the side of the frigate showed plenty of water right beside the ship. 'A diver went down', wrote Napier, 'and found, to the astonishment of all on board, that an oyster bank, not bigger than a boat, was under her bilge. After some hard heaving, we floated.' But no sooner was *Euryalus* free than *Seahorse* grounded. And Gordon had to unload up to ten of her thirty-eight guns and much of her stores before she could be refloated. One after another the ships grounded and were refloated until they finally cleared the shallows.

But then the wind turned against them. For five whole days the only way they could move the vessels upriver was to heave them forward on their anchors. It was a laborious process known as 'warping', unimaginable to today's ships' crews who don't have to depend on wind-power. Two small boats were lowered overboard and each in turn rowed some distance forward to dump one of the ship's anchors. The ship's crew would then heave on the anchor's hawser and haul the ship up to the anchor before the second small boat took its turn to carry another anchor forward and repeat the exercise. For five whole days Gordon's crews bent their shoulders to the capstans. By the evening of 24 August they'd clawed their way just fifty miles upriver and anchored off Maryland Point, still thirty miles short of Washington. And what they saw that evening made their hearts sink. They watched the sky light up as Washington burned. 'The reflection of the fire on the heavens was plainly seen from the ships, much to our mortification and disappointment,' Napier remembered, 'as we concluded that that act was committed at the moment of evacuating the town.' Ross and his army did indeed leave the city twenty-four hours later, but Gordon and Napier had come too far to think of turning back. Besides, by pressing ahead and threatening Washington from the south, they believed they could distract American attention and help Ross's withdrawal. So on they went, stopping only on 25 August to repair severe damage to the ships' rigging when they were hit by the same whirlwind that hit Washington.

Throughout the long trip Gordon strictly forbade any landing for looting or any other mischief. But Napier couldn't resist going ashore when he spotted one 'agreeable-looking residence – the first indeed we had observed on the banks of the river'. There Napier found an American farmer who was 'not the most polished man in the world', with two daughters 'rather homely, and as uncouth as himself'. They offered Napier a glass of punch brandy and told him they hoped the 'Britishers' would not carry off their slaves, 'which appeared to be their only apprehension'.

On the evening of 27 August Gordon's squadron found itself confronted by the only real obstacle that lay between them and their goal. On a hill on the east bank of the river guarding the final approach to the capital was the heavily fortified stronghold of Fort Washington. It had a garrison of sixty men, twenty-seven mainly heavy guns inside and outside its walls, and 3,500 pounds of gunpowder in its magazine. Gordon and his men were exhausted. They had had only two nights' real sleep since they left Chesapeake Bay and Gordon said he believed that 'each of the ships was not less than twenty different times aground and each time we were obliged to haul off by main strength'. But he immediately began the bombardment of the fort. He was then astonished to see that the garrison promptly abandoned the place. 'Supposing some concealed design I directed the fire to be continued. At 8 o'clock however my doubt was removed by the explosion of the powder magazine.' It was the massive blast that also startled Madison in Washington. The commander of the American garrison, Captain Samuel Dyson, had decided to spike all his guns and then destroy the place rather than fight it out. He claimed in a letter to the War Secretary John Armstrong, who was by this time already beleaguered and utterly discredited by what had happened in Washington, that he had been authorised to abandon his post. Dyson said that Winder had sent him oral orders 'in case I was oppressed by, or heard of, an enemy in my rear, to spike our guns and make my escape'. He wrote that when he saw Gordon's ships approaching and heard that the British were also marching on the fort from Benedict (which they weren't), he and his officers agreed that 'the force under my command was not equal to the defence of the place'. Dyson was later court-martialled and sacked from the army for conduct unbecoming an officer. He was acquitted on a further charge that he'd been drunk at the time.

Gordon and Napier were delighted. They reckoned the capture of the fort by force could have cost them up to fifty men. Gordon had now more than accomplished his mission. But there was another tempting target just an hour or two's sail up the river. Four miles short of Washington, which Ross's army had already devastated, was the prosperous town of Alexandria. Its mercantile trade had once rivalled New York and Boston. Rich Virginian planters and political leaders like George Washington had bought fashionable clothes and furniture imported by its traders. With the war in its third year, many of them were as deprived and disaffected as the merchants and shippers of New England, whose congressmen had voted against the war in the first place. And now their livelihoods and homes faced the very real threat of destruction from an enemy flotilla on their doorstep. The Mayor, Charles Simms, who was a leading attorney and merchant, and other prominent Alexandrians decided they had no choice but to surrender. The town was more or less undefended: there were one or two militia units within reach, but after the Battle of Bladensburg the idea of attempting to resist appeared futile. They sent a deputation in a small boat to meet the British squadron under a flag of truce and offered to surrender the town if the British would promise to respect private property as they had in Washington. Gordon politely told the men that he would deliver his terms once his squadron had anchored off the town. That way the Alexandrians would be in no doubt that, if they rejected his terms, he could enforce them. A hundred British guns could destroy the town in minutes.

14

A tempest of dissatisfaction

28–29 August

BY THE MORNING of 29 August Captain James Alexander Gordon was ready. His ships were at anchor on the seafront of Alexandria. He wrote down his terms for the town's surrender and had the document delivered to the town council. The deal would guarantee their lives and homes but it would cost them dear. All military stores should be handed over. All vessels and all merchandise 'must be delivered up' and 'possession will be immediately taken of all the shipping'. Gordon even insisted that a number of ships, which had been sunk in the harbour to avoid capture, should be refloated and reloaded with their cargoes. Gordon's final demand was that refreshments should be delivered to his ships; these would be 'paid for at the market price by bills on the British government'. It had long been a custom, rigorously enforced by Wellington in the Peninsula, that food supplies raised from local people should be paid for. It was a fine principle, sometimes ignored: Gordon was going to insist that his men respected it on this occasion.

It didn't take the town council long to agree to the terms – with one or two minor concessions that they persuaded Gordon to accept. The British promptly spent three days raising the sunken ships, and loading them and many others – twenty-one ships in all – with a massive cargo of booty. They amassed around 1,000 hogsheads of tobacco, some 15,000 barrels of flour, together with scores of bales of cotton, stocks of wine and other useful stores. Alexandria's merchants stood mournfully watching their warehouses being emptied. The British sailors made a thorough job of it, but they cast an occasional glance over their shoulders in case they were attacked.

Alexandria's leaders came in for scathing censure afterwards for surrendering to the British. They said the criticism was 'cruel and unfounded'. A group of indignant citizens of the town wrote a public letter to both houses of Congress: 'What alternative had we to tell the enemy we could not resist, because we had not the means? We yielded to superior power. Our weakness has been no crime. Our reliance upon the protection of our government has been our misfortune.' The Mayor himself wrote a revealing letter to his wife, Nancy, on 3 September expressing his admiration for the way the British navy had conducted itself. 'It is impossible that men could behave better than the British behaved while the town was in their power. Not a single inhabitant was insulted or injured by them in their person or houses.' Charles Simms even went on to deplore the 'outrage' committed against a lone British midshipman who was assaulted by three American naval officers on the quayside. He was seized by his neck scarf and was being dragged away struggling when, luckily for him, the neck scarf came undone and he escaped. Simms found himself having to explain to a furious British captain that the townspeople had had nothing to do with the attack and ought not to be held responsible for it. There was general panic in the streets as people expected the British to react violently. Women and children ran about screaming and there was widespread alarm, but, mercifully for the town, the British captain's 'fury seemed to abate and he went off'. Simms very wisely apologised to Gordon for this bizarre incident, which Gordon took with good humour as a young officers' prank. But he warned the Mayor to make sure it didn't happen again. British gunners had been on the point of firing their carronades: another such incident could lead to the destruction of the town. Gordon's deputy, Charles Napier, described the affair as 'neither more nor less than an American midshipman's lark – and it appears they have larking mids [midshipmen] as well as us – but it had well nigh put the town in a blaze'.

All this enemy activity in Alexandria and the spectre of another attack on Washington from this alarming new enemy force caused consternation in the capital. Anna Maria Thornton, who had stayed in the city with her redoubtable husband, wrote in her diary that there was 'a general alarm in the city as it is expected the fleet will come up, and the sailors be let loose to plunder and destroy'. Margaret Bayard Smith came back with her family on the Sunday afternoon, 28 August. She was glad to find their house exactly as they'd left it. But the news that the British were helping themselves to ships and supplies in Alexandria was deeply unsettling. 'What will be our fate, I know not. The citizens who remained are now moving out, and all seem more alarmed than before . . .' Smith, who was also a bit of a poet and novelist, occasionally lets her emotions carry her away: 'Oh that I, a feeble woman, could do something! . . . Rome was reduced still lower by the Goths of old than we are . . . May a Roman spirit animate our people . . .' She had nothing but contempt for John Armstrong, the War Secretary: 'Universal execration follows Armstrong, who it is believed never wished to defend the city, and I was assured that had he passed through the city the day after the engagement, he would have been torn to pieces.' She said the city was beset with rumours: 'we know not what to believe and scarcely what to hope. We are determined however not again to quit the house, but to run all risks here, as we find the enemy not so ferocious as we expected . . .'

President Madison, who had returned in the hope that the worst of the crisis was over, was having second thoughts. On the Saturday morning he'd written to Dolley suggesting she should return. Reports the next morning that Fort Washington had fallen made Madison change his mind. 'Should the fort have been taken,' he wrote to her on the Sunday, 'the British ships will be able to throw the city again into alarm . . . it will be best for you to remain in your present quarters.' Confident that this would keep her safe and sound well away from Washington, Madison then set about trying to regain some kind of grip on his utterly disorganised administration. It wasn't only in disarray; it was deeply discredited and resented. Most people were now blaming him and his cabinet for the humiliation of Bladensburg and the burning of Washington. The Federalist opposition, many of whom had opposed the war from the start, heaped contempt on Madison and his government. Maryland Senator Robert Henry Goldsborough said that Washington 'once very beautiful . . . is the dreadful monument of an unfortunate and ill-timed war, and the unerring evidence of a weak, incompetent and disgraced administration'.

Newspapers, never at a loss for colourful language, poured out a torrent of invective against the country's leaders. The leading opposition newspaper, the *Federal Republican*, accused Madison's whole cabinet of being 'completely panic struck'. The *Portsmouth Oracle* called it 'an imbecile administration'. 'Poor contemptible, pitiful, dastardly wretches!' exclaimed the *Virginia Gazette*. 'Their heads would be but a poor price of the degradation into which they have plunged our bleeding country.' The humiliation and shame of what had happened weighed heavily on all. The ups and downs of the fighting were most powerfully felt by the men on both sides attempting to find ways to end the war at peace negotiations in Europe. Richard Rush, Madison's Attorney General and close companion in those dark days, described the sense of national despondency in a letter to America's chief peace negotiator in Europe – and future President – John Quincy Adams: 'What a dreadful time we have had of it here lately: and yet not dreadful, were it not for the national disgrace. We cannot mince the matter; there is, I fear, no other view to take of it.' Washington might be a meagre place, added Rush, but it was 'the capital of the nation, and six thousand troops have laid its best parts in ashes'.

Monroe recognized that 'A tempest of dissatisfaction at the late events rages here with great fever.' Worse than that, many people were persuaded that any further military action against the British would be disastrous.'The people are violently irritated at the thought of our attempting to make any more futile resistance,' wrote Anna Maria Thornton. Her husband went further. William Thornton sought out the President to inform him that the people of the devastated capital – like the people of Alexandria – wanted to send a deputation to meet the British and discuss terms. As the news of the

Washington catastrophe spread, Americans as far away as New York were bewildered and angry. 'Where are our commanders?' asked the *New York Evening Post*. 'Why have we nothing to satisfy the public mind, in such a disastrous crisis? It is a fact that to this hour we know not where our army is, or whether we have any. Our president and his secretaries are also missing, and no one knows where to look for them! Was there ever such a thing before in a civilized nation? A country invaded – battles fought – and yet no official account of the movements of either friend or foe.' Graffiti were scrawled on what was left of the walls of public buildings in Washington: 'James Madison is a rascal, a coward and a fool.'

It was in this atmosphere of growing demoralisation and despair that Madison suddenly began to pick himself up and restore his severely damaged authority. He was encouraged by James Monroe and the Navy Secretary William Jones, who were appalled and ashamed by the news from Alexandria. Alexandria, said Jones, had been presented with such 'degrading and humiliating terms as to excite the indignation of all classes of people'. The President was galvanised. He gave his Secretary of State, Monroe, full authority – for the time being – to do whatever was needed to oversee the city's and the country's defence. And when Thornton broached the idea of a mission to talk to the British, Madison and Monroe acted with a new resolve. 'The President forbade the measure,' Monroe stated in a memorandum recording events at the height of the crisis. He added that 'if any deputation moved towards the enemy it should be repelled by the bayonet'. An awareness of the depth to which the nation had sunk somehow reanimated Madison's leadership. Margaret Bayard Smith alluded to Madison's ability to lose his normal appearance of 'calm serenity' if the 'powers of his mind were called into action. His brow was knit – deep and strong lines gathered on his forehead . . . and to the deep lines of thought thus developed was added that air of unyielding determination . . .'

Madison's resolve may have been further strengthened by the sudden arrival of his wife Dolley. She had left her country retreat that morning before receiving his message telling her to stay away from Washington. Her two close friends, Anna Maria Thornton and Margaret Bayard Smith, met her that evening and said that although she 'seemed much depressed and ... could scarcely speak without tears' she was 'very violent against the English – and wished we had 10,000 such men as were passing (a few troopers) to sink our enemy to the bottomless pit'. When she heard of the surrender of Alexandria she said the people ought to have allowed their town to be burned rather than submit to such terms.

William Thornton, who, like James Ewell, had raised suspicions that he had been close to collaborating with the enemy, was quick to demonstrate that he was an enthusiastic patriot as well as a realist. When his idea of a deputation to the British was rejected out of hand by the President and Monroe, he immediately went home and fastened on his sword – much to the distress of his wife – and went round energetically supporting the President's call to arms. He went out of his way – in a letter to the city's leading newspaper – to reject 'several misrepresentations' which he said were being made about his conduct. When the President asked him to help defend the city once the British had left, he said he immediately rose to the occasion: 'I went to the different quarters and gave, as far as I could, every assistance in my power to fulfil the wishes of the government.'

Army units began to return to Washington, ordered back by the President and Monroe. They were told that their duty was to defend the city and not let the enemy break into it again. Three senior naval officers were despatched to intercept and attempt to destroy Captain Gordon's British squadron as it made its way back down the Potomac with any prizes it had seized in Alexandria. They would establish shore batteries on the river to cause what damage they could and also attempt to destroy the British squadron with fireships.

While all this was going on, the man who still officially held the office of War Secretary chose to return to the capital. John Armstrong's name was on everyone's lips as the man who had failed to provide for the defence of Washington, and some people had been heard saying they 'were disposed to hang him'. He finally returned from Virginia on Monday morning, 29 August. With the British at Alexandria, Armstrong went to inspect defences on the Potomac, and he was soon being met by men who openly denounced him. One prominent citizen told him he was the cause of all the disasters that had befallen the city. Shortly afterwards General Walter Smith, commander of the Washington militia, was confronted by a group of officers who told him: 'There, Sir, are our swords. We will not employ them, if General Armstrong is to command us, in his capacity as Secretary of War. But we will obey the orders of any other member of the cabinet.' The general immediately sent two of his top aides, Major John Williams and Major Thomas McKenney, to find the President and tell him that 'every officer would tear off his epaulets if General Armstrong was to have anything to do with them'. Smith told McKenney: 'Say to the President that under the orders of any other member of the Cabinet, what can be done will be done.' They sped off on horseback and tracked down Madison, who told McKenney to go back and assure General Smith that Armstrong would be giving no more orders.

That evening the President rode in person to John Armstrong's lodgings. He wrote his own account of the confrontation that then took place. They were meeting, said Madison, 'under apprehensions of an immediate visit from the force of the enemy at Alexandria'. The President told his War Secretary that 'violent prejudices were known to exist . . . particularly against me and himself as head of the war department; that threats of personal violence had . . . been thrown out against us both, but more especially against him'. Madison told Armstrong what General Smith had reported about the refusal of the troops to take any more orders from him. Armstrong replied that 'he had been aware of the excitement against him; that it was altogether artificial, and that he knew the sources of it and the intrigues by which it had been effected'. Madison said that what made people resentful was their belief that Armstrong had not done enough to defend the city. 'I added that it would not be easy to satisfy the nation that the event was without blame somewhere, and I could not in candour say that all that ought to have been done had been done and in proper time.' When Armstrong answered that he had 'omitted no preparations or steps whatever for the safety of the place', the atmosphere began to heat up. 'I replied', recorded Madison, 'that as the conversation was a frank one, I could not admit this justification, that it was the duty of the Secretary of War not only to execute plans, or orders committed to him, but to devise and propose such as would in his opinion be necessary and proper.' Madison added 'that it was due to truth and to myself to say, that he [Armstrong] had never appeared to enter into a just view . . . of the danger to the city; that he had never himself proposed or suggested a single precaution or arrangement for its safety, everything on that subject having been brought forward by myself'. 'I remarked', Madison recalled, 'that it was not agreeable thus to speak' and that he had always treated Armstrong with friendliness and confidence. Armstrong must have suspected that Madison would then formally fire him, but the President was too subtle for that. 'The conversation was closed', wrote Madison, 'by my referring to the idea of his setting out in the morning on a visit to his family . . .'

Whether or not Madison actually wanted Armstrong to resign, it was only a few days before the War Secretary did so, bitterly blaming everyone but himself. He wrote a snarling piece in the *Baltimore Patriot* accusing Madison of yielding 'to an impulse so vile and profligate, so injurious to truth and so destructive of order . . .'. He went on to complain, 'It became a system to load me with all the faults and misfortunes which occurred.' As for the defeat at Bladensburg, Armstrong asserted: 'If all the troops . . . had been faithful to themselves and to their country, the enemy would have been beaten and the capital saved.' Armstrong also blamed Monroe, whose 'lust for power is insatiable', for the defeat at Bladensburg. He wrote, 'It is a well known fact that to this man's interference in the arrangements [on the field] much of our misfortune on that day was owing . . . With men of such imbecility I cannot longer connect myself.' It was Madison – not Monroe – who was instrumental in securing Armstrong's departure, but Monroe had long abhorred Armstrong and had advised Madison not to promote him. Monroe also had every interest in further discrediting a man he had seen as a possible rival in a future contest for the US presidency. Now, with Armstrong gone, Monroe became incontestably the second most powerful man in Washington. Madison asked his Secretary of State to take over the duties of War Secretary as well.*

---

* Monroe was haunted for the rest of his life by the charge that he had engineered the resignation of John Armstrong. Long after his Presidency – he was to succeed Madison – Monroe begged Thomas McKenney, who was at his bedside as he approached his death, to use his knowledge of what had happened that weekend in August 1814 to absolve him of all responsibility for Armstrong's departure.

15

Do not attack Baltimore!
End of August

ROBERT ROSS, GEORGE Cockburn and their victorious soldiers and sailors, who had stolen away from Washington on the night of 25 August, took four days to return to their ships. They were back at Benedict on 29 August ready to embark. It had been an astonishing achievement. Many years later, George Gleig, by then a budding historian looking back over the legacy of the Napoleonic Wars, remarked that among all the other events:

> the campaign at Washington was, I believe . . . but little spoken of; and even now, it is overwhelmed in the recollections of the all-engrossing Waterloo; but the time will probably come when he who . . . penetrated upwards of sixty miles into an enemy's country, over-threw an army more than double his own . . . took possession of the capital of a great nation and . . . returned in triumph to his fleet, will be ranked . . . among . . . those who have most successfully contributed to elevate Great Britain to the height of military glory . . .

The Americans allowed the British army to retire without any interference. Their sharpshooters and cavalry skirmishers could have caused the British no end of trouble in some of the wooded country on the way. But they were glad enough to see them go without provoking further fighting. Ross halted his army briefly, around midnight, at Bladensburg where 'the dead were still unburied, and lay about in every direction completely naked. They had been stripped even of their shirts and . . . the smell which arose upon the night air was horrible.' Any wounded who could be safely removed were heaved gently on to a dozen wagons for transport to the ships. But the most severe cases would have to be left behind. Gleig made his way into one house which had been converted into a hospital for the worst casualties and 'found them in great pain, and some of them deeply affected at the thought of being abandoned by their comrades, and left to the mercy of their enemies'. But Gleig was able to add that in the event such fears did an injustice to the Americans, 'who were found to possess at least one generous trait in their character, namely that of behaving kindly and attentively to their prisoners'. Before he left the makeshift hospital Gleig shook hands with one of his own company's sergeants, who burst into tears when he saw him. The man was too badly wounded to be moved: a musket ball had passed through both of his thighs.

Harry Smith had been correct to warn his chief, General Ross, that the night march would be an ordeal for the troops. There were constant delays as the head of the column lost its way in the darkness. Many men were so exhausted after several sleepless nights that they collapsed on the roadside. Ross had no choice but to allow a six-hour rest at eight o'clock the following morning. 'No bed of down could have proved half so luxurious', recalled James Scott, 'as the green sward on which I stretched myself. In less than five minutes I was wrapped in forgetfulness.'

There was only one curious exception to the Americans' failure to molest Ross's withdrawal. A seemingly minor incident at the time, it led to one of America's proudest moments – the unfurling of the star-spangled banner over a fort in Baltimore which inspired the US national anthem. The story of how this happened is one of the most intriguing in Anglo-American history and reveals much about how national myths are created. It began during the British retreat – on 27 August – with the arrest of Dr William Beanes. Beanes was the respected local doctor in Upper Marlborough who had made a point of being gracious and hospitable to Robert Ross on his way through the town a week earlier.* The doctor and two friends were enjoying a drink in Beanes's garden after the British army had passed back

* See above p. 53.

through the town on its way to the ships. The three men heard that some British stragglers had stayed on in the town after the rest had passed through and were now bent on robbery and looting. One report says three of the stragglers burst into the doctor's garden and insolently demanded a drink. The elderly doctor, who was effectively the town's patriarch, briskly set about rounding up the stragglers and locking them up. But one of them managed to escape. He dashed off, rejoined the British army and reported the arrest of his mates.

That night, 27 August, a troop of mounted British soldiers raced back to Upper Marlborough, released the detained stragglers and burst into William Beanes's bedroom in the small hours. The doctor was unceremoniously dragged out of bed and forced to ride the thirty-five miles to Benedict together with his two house guests. They were quickly released but the doctor was kept in detention. He was treated not as a prisoner of war but as a civilian who had won the respect and gratitude of the British commanders for his sympathetic attitude a week earlier but had now betrayed that trust.

William Beanes would no doubt have spent the rest of the war in an obscure British prison if it hadn't been for a young Washington lawyer who took up his case. Francis Scott Key, the thirty-five-year-old son of a prosperous Maryland plantation-owner and judge, lived with his wife Polly and eight children in Georgetown next to Washington. He was slight, with brown hair and blue eyes. He was deeply religious and had toyed with the idea of entering the Church. He opposed slavery and thought the war unnecessary and unwise. But he was a patriot and had made a name for himself as an articulate advocate with a passion for words: he wrote a poem about America's action against the Barbary pirates from North Africa whose corsairs were a menace to international trade. Key's poem mentioned the 'star spangled flag of our nation, where each radiant star gleamed a meteor of war'. Key knew William Beanes, and when he heard that the old doctor had been captured he called on President Madison after he'd returned to Washington. He asked the President to give his sanction to him joining a special mission to the British. He would go together with the official prisoner exchange commissioner, John Skinner, and they'd appeal personally to General Ross.

Madison agreed and the two men sailed off in a small vessel under a flag of truce to rendezvous with Ross on HMS *Tonnant* at the mouth of the Potomac. They were greeted with civility and had the strange experience of being invited to sit down to dinner with the men who'd burned their capital. Skinner sat next to Ross, 'the most reserved gentleman at the table', and noticed a scar, still not properly healed, on the left side of his neck – the wound he'd suffered months earlier fighting with Wellington in the south of France. Key's and Skinner's hopes of freeing Beanes faded sharply when Cockburn launched an attack on the old doctor, saying that he'd betrayed his trust. But then Skinner handed Ross a bundle of letters written by British officers captured at Bladensburg who praised the way they'd been treated by the Americans. It was enough to make Ross relent and to persuade the naval commanders to agree that Beanes should be set free. Ross wrote in an official letter he gave to Skinner that he was agreeing to the release of Beanes 'not from an opinion of his not being justly detained, nor from any favourable sentiment of his merit . . . but purely in proof of the obligation which I feel for the attention with which the wounded have been treated'. Key and Skinner were then allowed to give Beanes the happy news, but they were not for the moment permitted to leave the ship. They had seen and heard too much to be allowed to go home.

It had taken Ross's army some time to re-embark after its successful attack on Washington. When the footsore marchers finally came within sight of the ships' crews awaiting them in the Patuxent River a great roar of applause went up, and the men happily began embarking. Gleig could hardly wait for a clean shirt, a proper wash and his old bunk to sleep in. George Chesterton, whose job was to support the artillery, which consisted, he says, of just one 6-pounder, spent most of his time in the rear and missed the raid on Washington. But that allowed him to get up to more mischief on the river banks in what he called 'foraging expeditions' which clearly infringed the rules of proper military conduct. Some days they would merely fill the ships' water casks from the wells dug on either side of the Patuxent. But on other occasions 'we literally scoured the country . . .'. They knocked up farmhouses as late as midnight, woke up inmates and insisted upon the 'pick of the pantry, yards or pigsty, upon our own terms . . . I am afraid we sadly lacked consideration for the harassed inhabitants of this war-girt coast.' Chesterton added: 'We paid where payment was practicable, but were not over-scrupulous in helping ourselves. We ran many serious risks, for patrolling parties of the Americans were abroad.'

One night their shouts woke a sleeping farmer. He appeared at his bedroom window and 'solemnly protested that he had not a fowl or a pig upon his premises and employed such singular oaths to fortify his words, that we laughed . . . loudly proclaimed our disbelief and commanded him to descend . . .'. The half-dressed farmer, carrying his lantern, was then made to open the door to his outhouse. And 'there arose such a cackling of fowls of various species, that our host stood convicted of something near akin to perjury, and we made uncommonly free with his stock'.

On another occasion Chesterton and some mischievous comrades tried to trap a runaway calf in a farmer's field. When they couldn't catch it, much to the farmer's mirth, one of the party made a noose as if to hang the farmer if *he* didn't catch the calf. The wife was so terrified that the men relented – 'We found the joke had gone too far' – and did a whip-round to compensate the terrified wife. They often sat and chatted with American families. 'I remember on one occasion, sitting in the richest imaginable rural parlour and enjoying a lively chat with a pretty, interesting, well educated girl, about twenty years of age, and with her respectable father.' Chesterton and his mates enjoyed an hour of 'agreeable conversation, and we parted with tokens of mutual cordiality, and moralised upon the painfulness of national enmities'.

George Chesterton and his comrades were lucky that their some-times rascally conduct escaped the notice of Edward Codrington, the admiral responsible for discipline in the fleet. In a series of letters to his ships' captains he declared that 'plunder and robbery has been committed on shore . . . and that even women from some of the Transports have been guilty of enormities shocking to humanity'. He said 'great outrages' had been committed 'upon the houses and property of inhabitants . . .' and that only senior officers or people in their company would be allowed ashore. He made an example of one group of men who'd robbed a family in a village. He had them taken ashore and there in the presence of the people whose house they'd robbed, and watched by the boys who'd been part of their raiding party, the ringleader would be given four dozen lashes and his henchman three dozen. A surgeon would be on hand 'to see that no more of this punishment be inflicted at one period than the parties could bear'.

When the Commander in Chief, Vice Admiral Sir Alexander Cochrane, heard the news of Ross's successful assault on Washington, he sent a fast vessel to recall Captain Gordon's squadron from its diversionary attack up the Potomac. Early on 1 September the eighteen-gun sloop HMS *Fairy* arrived off Alexandria ordering them back to join the main fleet. Gordon and Napier mustered their large flotilla of twenty-one prize ships loaded with produce taken from the town and set off down the river on 2 September. If their voyage up the river had been a navigational nightmare, their voyage down it was at risk of being suicidal. The Americans had prepared two sets of shore batteries, one of them with a furnace that could heat up the roundshot and convert it into balls of fire that could set light to a wooden ship. Furthermore they sent flaming fireships floating towards the English fleet in order to set it ablaze. And as if all this wasn't enough, one after another Gordon's vessels again grounded and had to work their way free, sometimes under heavy fire. In the event, brave small boat crews towed the fireships away, the squadron's broadsides outgunned the shore batteries, and all the ships that took the ground were pulled free.

The squadron rejoined Cochrane's fleet in Chesapeake Bay after twenty-three days and many sleepless nights. They had suffered forty-two casualties – seven killed and thirty-five wounded including

Captain Charles Napier, who was wounded in the neck by a stray musket ball. His boss, James Alexander Gordon, was more than generous in his report to Cochrane: 'To Captain Napier I owe more obligations than I have words to express.' Gordon's Potomac operation had been as successful as that of Ross and Cockburn in penetrating deep into enemy territory. It had caused a few more days of anxiety in Washington, and the surrender of Alexandria amplified America's humiliation. The twenty-one captured ships and their cargoes earned the crews and their officers a tidy sum in prize money. 'It was', Edward Codrington wrote, 'nothing less brilliant than the capture of Washington.' Theodore Roosevelt, US President and naval historian nearly a century later, called it 'a most venturesome feat reflecting great honour on the Captains and crews . . .'. Even the disgraced John Armstrong commended Gordon for his 'skill, diligence and good fortune'.

While waiting for Gordon and his squadron to return to Chesapeake Bay, Cochrane and his commanders had continued their debate about what to do next. Ross's objections had – for the moment – removed the immediate prospect of an attack on Baltimore. Cochrane and Ross sent accounts of their successful campaign back to London. The news would take a month to reach Britain. Ross modestly reported to the Secretary of State for War, Lord Bathurst, that 'the troops under my command entered and took possession of the city of Washington'. He left it to Cochrane to boast – in his report to the Admiralty – of 'a series of successes in the centre of the enemy's country surrounded by a numerous population'. But Ross didn't conceal his pride in letters to his wife and sister-in-law. 'Our little operation here', he wrote to Maria Suter, 'will no doubt appear brilliant and so, not to speak too partially of our own feats, it ought.' To his wife Elizabeth, he wrote: 'My Ly will surely be pleased to find that our arms have been . . . crowned with a success that I had no reason to expect . . . Fortune favoured us and we succeeded beyond our most sanguine expectations . . .' Ross paid particular tribute to George Cockburn, saying the attack on Washington was the admiral's 'original suggestion', and he went on: 'I trust that all our differences with the Yankees will shortly be settled. That wish is, I believe, very prevalent with them, they feel strongly the disgrace of having lost their capital, taken by a handful of men, and blame very generally a government which went to war without the means or the abilities to carry it on . . . The injury sustained by the city of Washington in the destruction of its public buildings has been immense and must disgust the country with a government that has left the capital unprotected.' Ross was right about the immediate effect on Madison's government, but his burning of the new nation's proudest monuments was in a matter of days to put new heart into Americans and determination never to let such a thing happen again. A country divided about the wisdom of going to war would find a new unity in its fury at what had happened to its capital.

But Robert Ross had a personal concern that went far deeper than his pride in what he had achieved in the field. His wife's depression and loneliness, which must have been distressingly conveyed in her correspondence to him, now sadly lost, was constantly on his mind. He began his letter to her not with the story of his exploits but with the words 'It is, my best loved Ly, with feelings of the most acute misery that I take my pen to write to you.' He told his wife that the letters he received from her 'completely overwhelmed' him. 'I declare to you if it was in my power to leave the army I would without hesitation fly to you.' He begged her to try and be cheerful at the prospect of their meeting soon, and asked her to put the 'care of our dear children' before anything else. 'The war cannot last long. We then meet, my Ly, never again to separate.'

Harry Smith was a happy man. He was chosen by Ross to carry his despatch bearing the good tidings to the government at home. Smith was one of Ross's aides but hardly his closest. He may have had his doubts about his commander's competence, but he never doubted his humanity: 'Kind-hearted General Ross, whom I loved as a brother . . . there never was a more kind or gallant soldier,' wrote Smith. 'I had not been to England for seven years. Wife, home, country, all rushed in my mind at once.' Smith was overjoyed at the prospect of seeing his wife, Juana. He had left her in France three months earlier. Before that, the couple had been inseparable from the day Smith married the fourteen-year-old Spanish girl at Badajoz until the end of the Peninsular campaign.

As he prepared to leave, Smith worried about the pressures that would now be brought to bear on Ross in his absence. He was particularly concerned about the influence of George de Lacy Evans, another of Ross's aides for whom Smith clearly felt a competitive dislike and even a pang of jealousy. 'Sir Alexander Cochrane, Admiral Cockburn and Evans, burning with ambition, had urged General Ross to move on Baltimore. The General was against it, and kindly asked my opinion. I opposed it, not by opinion or argument, but by a simple statement of facts.' Evans was junior to Smith, but Smith knew that Ross liked and respected Evans and might be persuaded by him once he, Smith, was away. Ross was indeed so delighted with Evans that he wrote to the War Secretary requesting Evans's double promotion from lieutenant to major, skipping the rank of captain. It was a preposterously ambitious suggestion, and was rejected by Lord Bathurst.

Smith's case against attacking Baltimore was that the enemy was now concentrated there in strength, its harbour could be seriously obstructed by sunken ships, and British troops, now ravaged by a spreading epidemic of dysentery, would be unlikely to repeat the kind of triumph they'd achieved at Washington. Smith says he ended by telling Ross that success at Baltimore would add little to the effect of Washington, but that a reverse 'would restore the Americans' confidence in their own power and wipe away the stain of their previous discomfiture'. Ross listened and then said, 'I agree with you. Such is my decided opinion.' 'Then, Sir, may I tell Lord Bathurst [the War Secretary] that you will not go to Baltimore?' When the general said yes, his aide recorded, 'I was delighted, for I had a presentiment of disaster, founded on what I have stated.' It is only fair to observe that Smith does have a habit of trying to ensure that he is on the right side of history. He wrote his autobiography long after all these events, and with Ross long dead and no one else to gainsay him, he could happily invent conversations that never took place. Which is not, of course, to say that he did.

As Smith set off in the thirty-eight-gun frigate *Iphigenia*, Ross bid him a very warm farewell. The general asked him to call on Elizabeth, the wife he was so concerned about, and Smith promised he would. 'A pleasant voyage, dear Smith, and thank you heartily for all your exertions and the assistance you have afforded me. I can ill spare you.' 'Dear friend,' replied Smith, 'I will soon be back to you.' Smith then writes that he ended by asking Ross a question he had asked before: 'And may I assure Lord Bathurst you will not attempt Baltimore?' 'You may.' 'These', wrote Smith, 'were the last words I ever heard that gallant soul utter.'

16

Is my wife alive and well?

End of August

FAVOURABLE WINDS BLEW Harry Smith – accompanied by a naval counterpart, Captain Wainwright – across the Atlantic to Portsmouth in southern England in a brisk twenty-one days. As he rode up to London on horseback, feeling hugely important as the bearer of a vital despatch, he felt 'a maddening sensation of doubt, anxiety, hope and dread, all summed up in this – "Does your young wife live? Is she well?"' He delivered his despatch safely to Downing Street, then rushed off and found an army friend who would know where Juana was staying at the time. 'Is my wife alive and well?' he asked. 'Harry, in every respect as you would wish. I was with her yesterday,' the friend replied. Smith burst into tears. 'O thank almighty God,' he gasped. He asked her address and was there within minutes. As his coach drove along, there was a yell. His wife had recognised the hand he pressed to the coach window as he peered through trying to read the street numbers. 'Oh Dios, la mano de mi Enrique!' she exclaimed. 'Never shall I forget that shriek,' he wrote later, 'never shall I forget the effusion of gratitude to God, as we held each other in an embrace of love few can ever have known, cemented by the peculiarity of our union and the eventful scenes of our lives.' Their dog, Pug, was 'in her way as delighted to see me as her more happy mistress'. Juana told him that Pug had often comforted her by moaning pitifully when she was grieving.

After this joyful reunion Harry Smith went to Downing Street and met Lord Bathurst, the Secretary of State for War, who told him: 'The intelligence you bring is of such importance, the Prince Regent desires to see you. We will go immediately.' George III's son, later

George IV, was effectively running the country while his father was incapacitated. As Smith waited to see him, he was a bit nervous. But then he said to himself: 'I never quailed before the dear Duke of Wellington, with his piercing eye, nor will I now.' 'Call him "Sir" and do not turn your back at him,' advised Bathurst helpfully. 'In we went to the Prince's dressing room, full of every sort of article of dress, perfumes, snuff boxes, wigs, every variety of article, I do believe, that London could produce. His Highness rose in the most gracious manner, and welcomed me to his presence saying: "General Ross strongly recommended you to my notice as an officer who can afford me every information . . . the importance of which is marked by the firing of the Parliament and Tower guns you now hear."' Smith 'could not refrain from smiling within myself' that 'all London was in an uproar' at the news he had brought.

Smith was 'thunderstruck' by the quality of military questions the Prince asked him. He looked at the plan of Washington Smith had brought with him – 'with the public buildings burnt marked in red. He asked the name of each, and in his heart I fancied I saw he thought it a barbarian act.' Smith told him he regretted there hadn't been enough troops to hold Washington: that would have taken three times the number Ross had with him. The questions went on for a while and then the audience ended with the Prince Regent telling Smith he and the country were obliged to him. As Smith backed out of the room as instructed, the Prince told Bathurst, 'Don't forget this officer's promotion.' Smith was to make himself popular with another eminent family that very evening. Lord Bathurst invited him to dinner, and among the guests were Wellington's ADC Lord Fitzroy Somerset, who was to lose his arm at the Battle of Waterloo the following year. Smith spoke rapturously about the Duke of Wellington, whom he regarded as 'something elevated beyond any human being'. 'I am glad,' said a man sitting beside him. 'He is my brother.'

Harry Smith's sensational news from America provoked an immediate outburst of national rejoicing. The big guns fired their salutes, church bells rang, hearts everywhere leapt at the prospect of another enemy humiliated and perhaps now hungry for peace. Britain was a country deeply fatigued by the long struggle with France, which now seemed to be concluded – with Napoleon apparently securely contained on the small island of Elba. The thankless and unproductive war with America had so far got nowhere after years of inconclusive clashes in the Niagara peninsula and tit-for-tat sparring at sea. The fighting had yielded no advantage for either side and had damaged trade. Now, suddenly, came the heartening news that Britain had delivered what must surely be a crushing blow to America.

The newspapers published dramatic 'stop press' headlines on 27 September announcing the 'brilliant' achievement of British forces in the United States. 'Washington, the proud seat of that nest of traitors,' trumpeted *The Times* the following morning, 'whose accursed arts involved us in war with our brethren beyond the Atlantic – Washington captured, its dock, its arsenal and all its public buildings destroyed – the heads of the faction beaten, disgraced and flying for their lives.' The paper reminded its readers that it had been the Americans who'd started the war: its leaders had 'deluded' their people 'into a war with her most natural friend and ally, Great Britain'. The US army, 'drawn together to protect the seat of government under the eye of Mr Madison and his most notorious accomplices', had been 'put to flight'. The *Morning Post* called America's defeat 'an example of pusillanimity hitherto unknown in the long course of ages'. The Americans had 'yielded an almost bloodless triumph' to an enemy much smaller in numbers. 'The deeper their shame, the higher must our exultation soar. But a few months have elapsed since the . . . downfall of the European tyrant. A similar blow has now wounded the power of his transatlantic imitator.'

British opinion, however, was divided over the burning of Washington. The doubts Harry Smith himself had felt in the White House and which he detected in the Prince Regent were soon reflected in the press and parliament. The *London Statesman* said, 'Willingly would we throw a veil of oblivion over our transactions at Washington. The Cossacks spared Paris, but we spared not the capital of America.' The *Liverpool Mercury* said that actions like the burning of Washington only heightened the violence of the conflict, and 'a war of this kind will, even with success, reflect very little glorious on the victors'. The *Annual Register* condemned such action as a return to 'the times of barbarism . . . the extent of devastation practised by the victors brought a heavy censure upon the British character, not only in America, but on the continent of Europe'. In Paris the Duke of Wellington, no great enthusiast himself for Britain's war in America, felt he had to 'silence' his volatile French lady friend, Madame de Staël, when she launched into a tirade against the burning of Washington. A leading critic of government in the House of Commons, Samuel Whitbread, deplored an action 'so detested and abhorred by all who respected the character of this country and the civil rights of the world'. Whitbread said Britain had done 'what the Goths refused to do at Rome'. The invaders of the Holy City had been persuaded that 'to preserve works of elevated art was an act of wisdom but that to destroy them was to erect a monument to the folly of the destroyer . . . After sullying the British name,' declaimed Whitbread, what had we gained?

There were no such doubts in the reactions of British government ministers. If any of the more liberal of them shivered privately at the torching of the shrines of US democracy, they showed not a sign of it publicly. Quite the reverse. 'Nothing could have been more complete and brilliant than the success of the combined operations on the Potomac and Patuxent,' the Prime Minister, Lord Liverpool, wrote to Cochrane. 'The capture of Washington cannot fail to make a lasting impression upon the American people and I trust its first effect will be to induce them to withdraw their confidence from a government who have wantonly led them on this unnatural war . . .' Lord Bathurst went further. He praised Ross for the discipline he and his troops had shown in Washington. 'It was prudent as well as merciful to show . . . such forbearance.' But he went on to encourage him to pull no punches in inflicting more pain on the Americans. He urged Ross, if he now went on to attack Baltimore, to 'make its inhabitants feel a little more the effects of your visit than what has been experienced at Washington . . .' Bathurst, like Liverpool, had his eye on the paramount imperative of British policy. This expensive and pointless war should be brought to an end as quickly as possible. They now looked to their commanders in America to deliver a crippling blow to Madison's administration. Only then would the Americans be persuaded to sign up to peace in the negotiations which were under way in the town of Ghent in the Netherlands. Madison had already told his negotiators they could quietly drop their demands for Britain to stop impressing sailors. The end of the Napoleonic Wars had removed Britain's need for extra naval manpower. But the news of the success at Washington encouraged the British to stick to their demand that any territory seized by either side in the war should be retained. That would give Britain half of the land area of Maine. And a tough line should persuade America to renounce its designs on Canada and respect the rights of North American Indians who relied on British protection.

Liverpool and Bathurst were ready to back up their ambitious demands with reinforcements. The victory at Washington prompted the government to go for a major expansion of Ross's army. It would be more than doubled to a total of some 10,000 men. Ross and Cochrane would then be free to attack the United States 'at your discretion' and to ramp up their already laid plans to use the approach of winter to seize America's deep south. If Cochrane and Ross could capture New Orleans, it would 'reserve the whole province of Louisiana from the United States'. Seizure of Louisiana, the huge slab of territory sold to Madison's predecessor by Napoleon Bonaparte for the princely sum of $15 million* a decade earlier, would give Britain access to the Mississippi and a potential stranglehold on the young American republic.

It was Harry Smith's wife, Juana, who noticed Harry's promotion to major in the newspaper. 'The reward', she told him, 'of our separation.' She was no longer the fourteen-year-old girl he had rescued from the marauding British soldiers after the siege of Badajoz two years earlier. 'She was', wrote Smith, 'a woman – not a girl . . . with

---

* The equivalent of less than $300 million today.

a pair of dark eyes possessing all the fire of a vivid imagination, and an expression which required not the use of speech. Her figure was beautiful . . . and she would sing the melancholy airs and songs of constancy of her country (so celebrated for them) with a power and depth of voice and feeling peculiar to Spain.' Harry was the fifth of the eleven children of John Smith, a surgeon who lived in Whittlesea (now Whittlesey) near Peterborough, and he was delighted when his father and Juana met for the first time and became inseparable friends. Harry and Juana just had time to go home to Whittlesea and meet the family, and pay a call on Elizabeth Ross in Bath – who was 'in the highest spirits at the achievement of our arms under her husband' – before Harry was summoned to London and told he had a new posting to America. He was to sail with a fleet to reinforce Cochrane's assault on New Orleans. He had to tear himself away from Juana yet again. 'I can see her now with her head resting on the chimney piece . . . in a state bordering on despair. My father, too, was awfully over- come.' The army contingent would be commanded by someone Smith knew well – Major General Sir Edward Pakenham, the Duke of Wellington's brother-in-law. His division's opening attack on the French at the Battle of Salamanca had played a decisive role in one of Wellington's greatest victories. Smith was now thrilled to be appointed Pakenham's Assistant Adjutant General.

All these preparations raised hopes across the nation of a quick end to the war. And the view of British ministers that one more blow might make Madison and his discredited administration see sense would have been even more forthright had they known of the des- perate state of American finances after the burning of the US capital. There had been an immediate run on the banks in Baltimore and Philadelphia. Deposits, mainly in coin, were withdrawn by nervous depositors. And this came on top of the already devastating effects of Cochrane's blockade of American east coast ports. Total US foreign trade, which had been $119 million in 1811 before the war, was to slump to $19 million by the end of 1814. The tonnage of US ship- ping engaged in foreign trade was one-twenty-sixth of its pre-war level.

But, near bankrupt though America was, its army humiliated and James Madison's administration ridiculed, an important change was taking place. Liverpool had said he hoped that the capture of Washington would induce the Americans to reject their government. But one of his predecessors as Prime Minister, Lord Greville, a parliamentary critic of the invasion, was nearer the mark. He was admittedly speaking with the benefit of much more hindsight: he made his speech, like Whitbread, in early November, ten weeks after Washington had been burned. He said he deplored the burning of Washington's monuments because they were non-military. And he went on: 'There is in truth too much reason to believe that the destruction of public buildings has tended to unite against us the American people.' He was right. It wasn't that the American people rallied enthusiastically to their beleaguered President. It was more of a sudden realisation that there was now no alternative but to throw all their resources and manpower into the struggle to defend the United States. It was an upsurge of national feeling against the 'British vandals' and a robust determination to avenge the destruction of Washington. Far from America caving in, as the British government hoped, the next few weeks would see Americans rallying to the flag and rebuffing the rampant British drive for outright victory.

17

The star-shaped fort and its banner

1–11 September

ALEXANDER COCHRANE, VICE admiral and Commander in Chief of the American station, faced an agony of indecision in the aftermath of the burning of Washington. He was already deeply depressed, as he admitted himself in a letter to the First Lord of the Admiralty, 'over the shameful conduct of some of my near relatives'. His brother and his nephew had been involved in a Stock Exchange scandal in London. And now his own judgement was in question.

Cochrane's immediate problem was that his subordinate commanders had achieved a runaway victory over US forces and the occupation of the country's capital against his advice. The Royal Navy officer directly responsible to him, Rear Admiral George Cockburn, had pointedly disobeyed his orders. If the invasion had failed, Cochrane could have sent a despatch to Whitehall saying 'I told them not to go' and Cockburn's court martial would have followed. But the operation had been, embarrassingly for Cochrane, a stunning success. He had no alternative but to claim it as his own, while praising Cockburn and Ross. Once he'd swallowed his pride, this would be no problem. No one would know he'd made the wrong call except Cockburn, Ross and a handful of others. The real dilemma for him was deciding what to do next. He had Cockburn and Evans pressing him to go straight for Baltimore. He was reluctant to move against that much better-defended city without reinforcement. Besides Ross, in line with Harry Smith's advice, was arguing against it. Should he abandon the Chesapeake and move south and wait for reinforcements before launching his attack on New Orleans, or should he first head north-east and make a surprise assault on

America's flourishing maritime state of Rhode Island? He was torn. The strategic caution that had dulled his enthusiasm for the advance on Washington urged him to hold his hand. But that ruthless streak in him, his visceral hatred of the Americans who had killed his brother at the Battle of Yorktown back in 1781, and his hunger for prize money,* made him look for a quick success.

Cochrane tries to juggle these options as best he can in his letter of 3 September 1814 to the First Lord. He confirms that his primary long-term goal is to subdue New Orleans and 'thereby hold the key to the Mississippi'. But first he would go north-east and 'if possible try to surprise Rhode Island'. After that, 'if the reinforcements arrive, I propose an attack upon Baltimore, the most democratic town and I believe the richest in the country'. But he then highlights the fact that Ross too has his doubts about Baltimore. 'As this town ought to be laid in ashes, if the same opinion holds with his Majesty's ministers, some hint ought to be given to General Ross as he does not seem inclined to visit this state.' Cochrane makes it clear that Ross, who, he says, could not be 'a better man nor a more zealous officer', has to be induced to take drastic action. 'When he is better acquainted with the American character he will possibly see as I do that like spaniels they must be treated with great severity before you ever make them tractable.' As for the attack on Washington which he had tried to call off, Cochrane barefacedly boasts of the 'brilliant success that has attended all our efforts'. Ten days after Ross's victory in Washington, Cochrane was now asserting that only Ross and his need for reinforcements stood between him and Baltimore.

For the next few days there was a fierce debate between Cochrane and his commanders. Admiral Codrington, canny veteran of Trafalgar,

---

* The Duke of Wellington made a revealing and caustic comment on Cochrane's character in a letter to Lord Longford, his wife Kitty Pakenham's brother. Referring to the mission of another brother-in-law, Major General Sir Edward Pakenham, to serve under Cochrane at New Orleans a year later, Wellington wrote: 'I cannot but regret that he was ever employed . . . with such a colleague.' The object of Cochrane's expedition, asserted the Duke, was 'plunder' (Wellington to Longford, 22/5/1815, in Pakenham, p. 37).

lent his weight to the argument for at least postponing an attack on Baltimore. By 6 September it appeared that it would indeed be put off: Cockburn set off out of the Chesapeake towards the south, but then he was suddenly recalled. Ross had apparently withdrawn his objections to Baltimore and believed he had enough men to do the job without reinforcements. George Evans, who'd long been pressing Ross to ride the wave of American panic and strike swiftly at Baltimore, wrote that it was the newspapers which 'depict in such strong colours the general alarm and defenceless state of Baltimore' that 'induced the Vice Admiral . . . to resolve on the attack of that place'. The army that had burned America's capital would now do the same to one of its richest cities, unless it paid up a massive 'contribution', as Alexandria had done. The dithering was over. Baltimore was on. On 9 September, while Harry Smith was still on his way to London, the British fleet headed north – past the mouth of the Patuxent. It was making for the waters of the Patapsco, which led up to Baltimore's harbour.

Edward Codrington wrote to his wife Jane: 'We were going out of the Chesapeake directly, but the Chief has assented to another operation here at the wish of the General and Cockburn, which I think would have been much better deferred until our return from the northward . . .' Codrington added that he hoped it would succeed, 'because we are determined it shall; but it would have been better insured by postponement'. James Scott, Cockburn's devoted ADC, who was with him as he headed back into Chesapeake Bay, reckoned 'this unfortunate delay' offered the Americans a huge advantage. 'The lapse of eighteen days gave the enemy an opportunity of perfecting their defences and collecting a large body of troops from the surrounding country.' Scott reflected Cockburn's exasperation at what he saw as another show of half-heartedness by Cochrane and Ross. If they had moved on Baltimore immediately after taking Washington, 'there existed a well-grounded hope that it would have fallen an easy conquest to our arms'. But now, instead of pursuing a defeated enemy, they were going to have to 'take the bull by the horns'. Scott had been rather miffed that he hadn't been sent home with Harry Smith to carry the Royal Navy's account of the sack of Washington. Such missions usually ended in promotion, as Harry Smith's did, and, as Cockburn's right-hand man, Scott was an obvious candidate. But at least the naval officer who did get the job had the grace to tell Scott he was sorry: 'He was sensible he was taking the bread out of my mouth.'

Another note of alarm was sounded by a local Methodist preacher, the Reverend Joshua Thomas, who had become friendly with the invaders. Somehow he persuaded the British commanders to let him deliver a sermon to the assembled troops as they completed their preparations to sail off to Baltimore. Thomas recalls that he perched on a little platform facing the troops, who stood with their hats off and held in their right hands. 'I felt determined to give them a faithful warning, even if those officers with their keen glittering swords, would cut me in pieces for speaking the truth. I told them it was given me by the Almighty that they could not take Baltimore, and would not succeed in their expedition. I exhorted them to prepare for death, for many of them would in all likelihood die soon . . .'

The moment the people of Baltimore saw their southern night sky lit up by the flames of Washington, they were convinced that it was their turn next. The news of the army's defeat at Bladensburg and the destruction of Washington 'came upon us like an avalanche causing the spirits of many to sink within them', wrote one Baltimorean. He and his neighbours were horrified by the prospect of what would happen to their homes and livelihoods. Many resigned themselves to inevitable defeat and destruction. All children and valuable goods were being evacuated from the city. 'You may be sure this is the most awful moment of my life,' wrote David Winchester from Baltimore to his brother, 'not because, if the place is defended, I shall put my life at hazard in common with my fellow citizens but because I am positively sure we shall not succeed.' He reckoned that, if the British did march on the city, 'we are gone'.

But Baltimore was not Washington. Maryland's big city was a thriving commercial metropolis, passionately proud of its prosperity

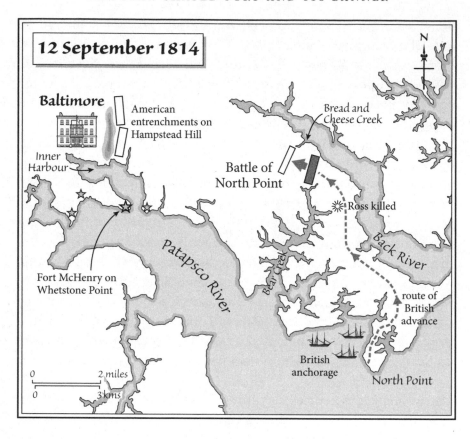

and blessed with a citizenry that had had the foresight to make some serious provisions for its defence. Baltimore stood at the head of another river that flowed into Chesapeake Bay – the Patapsco. The river's North-West Branch made a fine natural harbour protected by a headland, Whetstone Point, and the early American revolutionaries had built a primitive fort there in 1776. When Britain went to war with Napoleon, the fort was upgraded under the keen eye of the then US War Secretary, James McHenry, himself a citizen of Baltimore. It was in the shape of a star, designed by French architects in the tradition of Louis XIV's fortress-builder Vauban to give it maximum all-round protection. It had the distinctive low profile of the Vaubanesque fortress. Its walls and ramparts presented hardly any exposed vertical face to direct cannon fire. Even a lucky hit would do little damage as the great stone walls were reinforced by vast mounds of earth behind them.

Another of Baltimore's citizens, Sam Smith, a tough-spoken Maryland congressman, had in the late 1790s been a powerful advocate of the fort's modernisation. He had fought with distinction in the American Revolutionary War of Independence. He'd been garrison commander of Fort Mifflin, an island in the Delaware River, in 1777, and his dogged defence had kept the British at bay for weeks. Sam Smith became a byword for robust leadership during the siege. When one of his aides ducked an incoming shot, he said: 'What are you dodging for, sir? The King of Prussia had thirty aides de camp killed in one day!' Thirty-five years later, in 1812, when war broke out with Britain, the fifty-nine-year-old Smith was a US senator and major general commanding Baltimore's militia. When Maryland's Governor, Levin Winder, looked around for a prestigious commander to superintend the city's defences in case of a British attack, Smith was the natural choice. He was appointed on 13 March 1813, and only five days later he was complaining to the War Secretary John Armstrong that Fort McHenry's pinewood gates could be 'knocked down by a few strokes of the axe'. Four weeks later Smith was demanding the replacement of the fort's veteran commander, Major Beal. 'Do you really believe', he wrote to Armstrong, 'that a gentleman of nearly 60 years of age sorely affected with gout . . . is equal to the defence of such a post?' Smith was delighted when Beal was replaced two months later by Major George Armistead, who'd distinguished himself in the capture of Fort George on the Niagara River sixteen months earlier. Armistead wasted no time in greatly improving Fort McHenry's firepower with more big guns, and helping to supervise the construction of more batteries to guard the harbour mouth. Over the next year three new gun positions sprang up: the Lazaretto battery on the opposite side of the entrance to Fort McHenry, and two further west at Fort Babcock and Fort Covington. Some of the best gunners were seamen, and the city's leaders posted a call for them to volunteer for service in the city's batteries. 'The cloud gathers fast and heavy in the east and all hands are called.' Woe betide anyone who tried to be excused service: 'If he cannot sponge and ram as well as his messmates, he can pass a cartridge. It is well known by tars the just stigma that is fixed by the ship's crew on the man that skulks . . .'

But this wasn't enough for George Armistead. He wanted a spectacular emblem that would raise Baltimore's morale, a huge flag that would wave over his fort and be seen by an enemy many miles away. The city's leaders* eagerly agreed. Mary Pickersgill, a local widow whose mother had made flags during the Revolutionary War, was commissioned to make two new flags for the fort. One was to be a storm flag, of modest dimensions, but the other would be a giant banner forty-two feet by thirty. Each of its fifteen stars, like its fifteen stripes, would be two feet wide. An act of 1795 provided for fifteen stripes and fifteen stars – one for each of the thirteen original states plus Kentucky and Vermont, which joined the Union later.† It would require no less than 400 yards of strong bunting. Pickersgill and her thirteen-year-old daughter Caroline borrowed the ample floor of a nearby alehouse for the work. They laboured till midnight for several weeks, and by August 1813 Armistead had his flag.

All this was achieved before the British invasion of Washington. When Ross and Cockburn landed their forces at Benedict and began their march inland, the leaders of Baltimore's city council acted swiftly. They ordered the election of a special Committee of Vigilance and Safety. Thirty-one members were elected by the city's wards on 23 August and met every day from then on. They were given extraordinary powers to fortify and police the city in the face of the British threat. And on 25 August, the day after the burning of Washington, furious at the incompetent leadership that had led to the

---

* Commodore Joshua Barney and General John Stricker, a militia commander at Bladensburg, were two members of the special three-man committee appointed to superintend the making of the flag.

† Although eighteen states had joined the Union by 1814, the stars and stripes remained limited to fifteen until 1818. From then a new act reduced the stripes back to thirteen but added a new star for each state. So today's US flag has thirteen stripes and fifty stars.

capital's destruction, they demanded that Baltimore's defence force should be commanded not by the discredited William Winder but by Sam Smith. Smith was at the meeting. He heard one member, Colonel John Howard, say that all that he owned was in the city of Baltimore, 'my wife, my children, my friends . . . but I had sooner see them all buried in ruins, and myself among them, than see Baltimore make a last and disgraceful surrender to the enemies of our beloved country'. Smith was then called in and asked to add to his existing supervision of the city's defences the command of all the armed forces that would come to its assistance. 'I willingly obey the call,' replied Smith. Anticipating a row with William Winder, he insisted on the appointment being sanctioned by Winder's uncle, Maryland's Governor Levin Winder. The Governor, struggling to be fair to his nephew but helpful to Smith, wrote a rather cryptic reply, saying that Smith was indeed the state's major general, and had therefore 'been selected'. Smith then promptly wrote to William Winder, who was on his way to Baltimore to take charge, saying that he, Smith, was assuming command. Winder, no doubt inwardly aware of his own shattered reputation after Bladensburg, still forthrightly asserted his authority. After all, the 10th Military District, which he'd been appointed by Madison to command two months earlier, included Baltimore. But Sam Smith would have none of it: when Winder arrived in Baltimore, he found Smith riding around busily boosting the city's defences and clearly being recognised as its commander. Winder didn't give up: he wrote to Armstrong and then to Monroe, when he took over as Secretary of War, expressing his astonishment at Smith's conduct and demanding a ruling that he, Winder, was in command. It was only after a flurry of increasingly petulant letters from Winder that Monroe finally sent back a definitive verdict – after seventeen days. 'There can be but one commander,' he wrote, and that had to be Sam Smith.

Smith had been blandly ignoring all this. Backed enthusiastically by Baltimore's increasingly confident committee, he was throwing all his energy into ensuring that Baltimore would learn the lessons of Washington. He believed that, if he was to save his city, he had to ignore federal incompetence and rely on local enterprise and enthusiasm. Earthworks had to be constructed, reinforcements summoned from other states, weapons of all types procured, forward medical posts established. While older men stuffed cartridges with powder, women could wrap bandages. The all-powerful committee ordered 'all wheelbarrows, pick-axes, spades and shovels' to be assembled in special places so that those who were not on militia duty and 'the free people of colour' could help build up ramparts of earth to defend the city. 'The owners of slaves are requested to send them to work,' said the committee. Few failed to rally to the call. Sam Smith's twelve-year-old nephew was reported missing from home by his parents and was found digging trenches with a family shovel. The committee ordered 'All those houses where spirituous liquors are retailed to be closed at 9 o'clock every night and to remain closed during the night.' And the committee had the power to order the arrest of people who were 'in the constant habit of making use of very improper and intemperate expressions calculated to produce disunion'.

Letters written by Smith in early September are bursting with impatience over the lack of equipment for troops arriving from neighbouring states. He managed to assemble a very substantial force of militia from Pennsylvania and Virginia, but he told James Monroe, 'They have muskets, but they don't have cartridges, ammunition, tents or camp kettles.' He wrote to the military authorities in Philadelphia that 2,000 of their men had arrived without cartridge boxes. 'You will therefore without a moment's delay forward that number to this post.'

Smith had the valuable support of the American naval commodore John Rodgers, who commanded 1,000 seamen from various ships and units. His flotillamen, who had fought so well with Joshua Barney at Bladensburg, and other marine gunners helped to man the forts guarding the harbour mouth. Rodgers had fired many a broadside from the warships he'd commanded at sea. He would now be based on the eastern heights of Baltimore with many of his naval guns guarding the likely land approach to the city. He had his own bitter personal reasons for wanting to see the British crushed. His home town and his own house had been burned down in a raid by George Cockburn, and his wife and family had had to shelter elsewhere. His wife now wrote to him: 'Oh my husband! Dearest of men! . . . When I think of the perils to which your courage will expose you, I am half distracted, yet I would not have you different from what you are . . .'

Smith and his fast-growing army could hardly believe their luck in having more than two weeks to build up their strength before the British arrived. Cochrane's dithering allowed him to muster a force of up to 15,000 men. Many of them were new to the ranks, and they came from all walks of life. Edgar Allan Poe's seventy-one-year-old grandfather was there. He had responded to a call to the elderly who were capable of carrying a gun. There were butchers, carpenters, customs officers, clerks – all with the same intent: to stop Baltimore suffering the fate of Washington. One of them recalled how 'every heart [was] bursting with shame . . . the horrible mismanagement at Washington has taught us a useful lesson and we must be worse than stupid if we do not make proper use of it'. George Douglas was a merchant with the rank of private on the now well-fortified eastern heights on Hampstead Hill. He could see 'an extensive and beautiful prospect of a multitude of tents, baggage, and cannon in every direction . . . at least a mile of entrenchments with suitable batteries were raised as if by magic . . .'. All sorts of people had been working on them, 'old and young, white and black . . . All hearts and hands have cordially united in the common cause.'

A Baltimore judge, Joseph Nicholson, was a militia captain. He now commanded a motley group of artisans in the gun emplacements of Fort McHenry, and was one of the few Baltimoreans who had his doubts about Sam Smith. Smith, he wrote, had assumed command 'without authority at the request of some of our citizens'. The British would have found Baltimore 'an easy prize' if they had marched directly from Washington. 'If they come now . . . they will have a fight, but I am not quite sure that it will be a hard one.' And he went on: 'Our militia are so raw, and so totally undisciplined, and our commanding general so entirely unqualified to organise them, that I have very little confidence of our success.'

More than two weeks after the disaster at Washington, there was no sign of any British approach to Baltimore, and Nicholson and his men were given leave to take time off in the city. It was noon on Saturday 10 September. British ships were apparently heading south – down the bay. But by Saturday evening they had tacked around and were heading back with a fair wind behind them. Up to fifty ships approached the mouth of the Patapsco in driving rain. Nicholson and his men were back in the fort by midnight. 'On our arrival,' recalled one of his men, Isaac Munroe, 'we found the matches burning, the furnaces heated and vomiting red shot, and everything ready for a gallant defence.'

At noon the following day, Sunday 11 September, the gun on Federal Hill overlooking Baltimore harbour sounded the alarm. The bells of Christ's Church, cast in a foundry in Britain, clanged out their warning that the British enemy were at hand. Cochrane's fleet was anchoring off North Point, just thirteen miles down the road. The army that had burned the White House was preparing to land and march on Baltimore.

18

Many heads will be broken tonight

12 September

GeORGE COCKBURN RELISHED the prospect of a new battle as the fleet came to anchor off North Point. He was glad Ross and Cochrane had swallowed their doubts about Baltimore, but he was exasperated by the loss of momentum. 'Ample time had now been afforded to the Americans to call in the troops from all around,' he noted in his ship's log. He guessed, rightly, that the people of Baltimore had used every moment of the past two weeks to bolster their defences. But none of that was going to dissuade him from accompanying Ross's army to Baltimore, and he had no trouble persuading Cochrane to allow him to ride alongside the troops again. He would stick close by Ross and give him 'every assistance within my power'. The two men were now close brothers-in-arms: Ross had spoken warmly of Cockburn's encouragement in the attack on Washington. They might have to fight harder at Baltimore than at Bladensburg, but the outcome would not be in doubt. The city would be a far richer prize than Washington or Alexandria.

George Gleig had been scanning the Maryland coast with mounting excitement as the fleet drew nearer to North Point. It sailed past a number of watchtowers and signal stations, and, as the warships approached each of them, horsemen would leap into the saddle and gallop off. 'Beacon after beacon burst into a blaze; guns were fired from every tower; and telegraphic communication carried on without intermission.' Gleig watched panic-stricken villagers abandoning their homes with their belongings strapped on wagons. As they neared the elegant state capital, Annapolis, Gleig thought it a tempting target, but 'we passed it by . . . hugging ourselves in the idea that another, and no less valuable one, was before us'.

As the sun went down on 11 September, the water around the anchored ships was flat calm. A bright moon rose, and Gleig found himself captivated by the light it cast on the beach, the green fields and the woods behind. The only sounds were the calls of the sentries every half-hour: 'All's well!' But he was quickly snatched from his reverie by the bustle and noise of the army preparing for a mass landing in the early hours. He and the other officers supervised the handing out of three days of provisions for each man. Because Baltimore was reckoned to be only a day's march away, the men would travel light. They would need only a spare shirt and a blanket. But because it might be hard to rush more ammunition forward, they were each made to stash away twenty extra musket balls and cartridges in their ammunition pouches – eighty rounds a man.

By 3 a.m. the moon had gone. The night was pitch dark. In total silence the men climbed down into small boats and rowed ashore under the guns of a specially anchored brig just 200 yards off the beach. Every precaution was taken in case the landing was opposed. Gleig's boat was the second to run up the beach. 'We leaped from the bow, one after another, and collecting close to the water's edge, proceeded at a quick pace, to ascend a sloping sandbank.' They lay flat on their bellies and waited for the signal to move. Then they ran forty more yards inland and dropped to the ground again. 'We held our very breath, in anxious expectation of what the next moment might bring forth.' But as the day dawned it became clear that there were no enemy guarding the shoreline, and the army was able to muster in the fields behind the beach and prepare to advance on Baltimore. By seven o'clock the entire army was ready to march off.

Rear Admiral Edward Codrington, still aboard, wrote to his wife: 'The work of destruction is now about to begin, and there will probably be many broken heads tonight . . . the army with as many seamen and marines as could possibly be spared were landed this morning and are now on their march to the town of Baltimore, distant about 15 miles by land and 12 by water.'

It was Captain James Alexander Gordon's task to make the approach to Baltimore by water. His legendary passage through the shoals of the Potomac made him Cochrane's natural choice to lead the squadron of frigates and bomb ships which now braved the shallows of the Patapsco to take up a position off Fort McHenry and prepare to support the army's attack on the city. The problem was that the river was only just deep enough for a frigate to pass through. One of Gordon's most experienced officers, who'd fought with Nelson at Trafalgar, recalled: 'The labour of getting up to Baltimore without pilots, feeling our way with the lead, whilst boats on each bow and one ahead were sounding also, gave little time for respite. The heat of the weather too was very great, the thermometer varying only from 79 to 82 in the shade . . . which added much to the exhaustion.' Cochrane himself had shifted his flag to a frigate to accompany Gordon up the river. Gleig writes that Gordon was directed 'clapping a press of canvas upon his ship, to drive her, in case of any sudden obstruction, through the mud; and to break, at all hazards, such booms or other impediments as might be laid across the channel'.

Robert Barrett was in the frigate HMS *Hebrus* as she and the other ships struggled up the river. 'Well do I remember the scene. Our boats were ahead sounding: I was in our launch, with the stream and kedge anchors, and cables coiled away in her ready to heave the ship off if necessary . . .' The midshipman watched as a measured line of spun yarn, marked off in three-, four- and five-fathom lengths (eighteen, twenty-four and thirty feet), was dropped in the water, weighted down by marlinspikes, to test the depth. And he recalled the sailors chanting 'And half – three! By the mark – three!' and so on. 'Notwithstanding all these precautions we frequently grounded on the numerous shoals which abound in this channel.' Barrett himself was busy casting out the anchors whenever they had to pull the ship free, 'until I was literally covered with mud from head to foot in the process'. 'The bomb vessels, brigs, and frigates', reported Codrington, 'are all pushing up the river with an eagerness which must annoy the enemy, I presume, as much as it delights me . . . my heart is deeply interested in the coercion of these Baltimore heroes, who are perhaps the most inveterate against us of all the Yankees.'

Codrington was right. The citizens of Baltimore had every reason to stop British invaders from ruining their prosperity, and they'd had more than a fortnight since Bladensburg to prepare. And by now humiliation had given way to anger and a thirst for vengeance across much of the nation. James Madison had sensed the opportunity a week after the burning of Washington and had issued a proclamation on 1 September. He said that what British forces had done in Washington was a 'deliberate disregard of the principles of humanity and the rules of civilised warfare . . . I therefore, James Madison, president of the United States, do issue this my proclamation, exhorting all the good people thereof to unite their hearts and hands . . .' in order to 'expel the invader'. A number of newspapers took up the call: it was time for patriotism to replace recrimination against the government. 'The spirit of the nation is roused . . .' trumpeted *Niles' Weekly Register.* 'War is a new business to us, but we must teach our fingers to fight — and Wellington's invincibles shall be beaten.' A Baltimore militiaman wrote to a friend, 'We have recovered from our consternation. All hearts and hands have cordially united in the common cause . . . the horrible mismanagement at Washington has taught us a useful lesson, and we must be worse than stupid if we do not make proper use of it.'

With the arrival of the first intelligence that the British were anchoring at North Point General Sam Smith summoned his commanders and revealed his plan to defend the city. He would not send his whole army forward to meet Ross. He would keep his main force back behind the fortifications they'd erected over the previous three weeks on the city's fringe. He couldn't risk another Bladensburg – his army defeated in the open and his city at the mercy of the victors. Besides, there wasn't much time: the British were less than a day's march away. He would send his most trusty commander forward with just over 3,000 of his best men. The man he chose was Brigadier General John Stricker. Stricker, now aged fifty-five, had made his mark as a young officer in the Revolutionary War, and since then had advanced to command a brigade of militia. He was Joshua Barney's brother-in-law, and like Barney he ran a thriving commercial firm in Baltimore and was one of the leading citizens who had pressed for Sam Smith to take command. Stricker's 3rd Brigade was widely recognised as the best trained of Baltimore's units, and he was now chosen by Smith to lead his men forward in the evening of Sunday 11 September and take up a blocking position on the road from North Point.

While the British ships worked their way up the Patapsco, Ross's army tramped on towards Baltimore through quite dense woodland on the North Point peninsula. By breakfast time the leading troops had reached the Gorsuch Farm about two miles inland. The farmer, Robert Gorsuch, whether out of fear or a sneaking sympathy for the invaders, provided Ross, Cockburn and their staff with breakfast and enquired whether they'd be back to dinner that night. 'No,' said Ross, 'I shall sup in Baltimore tonight – or hell.'

Not far away George Gleig and his light infantrymen spotted three American cavalrymen on a small mound watching the British advance. Gleig's party began stealing through the trees hoping to catch the men by surprise. But Gleig and his men were in bright red uniforms, and that, as Gleig admitted, was 'an inconvenient colour, in cases where concealment happens to be desirable'. The Americans saw them approaching, clapped spurs to their horses and galloped off. They didn't go far. Minutes later, to Gleig's surprise and delight, the three Americans were spotted again. This time Gleig and his squad were nearly upon them when they again raced off not on horseback but in a canoe. 'They were paddling, as fast as they could, to the opposite shore. There was no time to lose. I called out to them to surrender . . . and commanded the whole of my people to level their pieces.' This was too much for the Americans, who were young volunteers. They waved a white handkerchief and paddled back to hand themselves over. Gleig then took the three men to the farm where he found Ross and Cockburn laughing heartily at the antics of

a few soldiers who'd thrown discipline to the winds and were frantically chasing after the farmer's livestock.* The arrival of Gleig's three
prisoners soon had Ross earnestly asking them questions about the
strength and quality of the American forces. They left him in no
doubt that the city was well defended, by several batteries of guns on
the heights manned by experienced seamen, and by a force of some
20,000 men – five times the size of Ross's force. But the general
showed no sign of hesitation: when someone observed that most of
the American defenders were militia, he is said to have exclaimed: 'I
don't care if it rains militia.' Gone was the diffidence he had shown
on the way to Washington when Cockburn had had to revitalise
him. Robert Ross was now all confidence and bravado. And that
recklessness which had sometimes characterised his leadership led
him to take a risk that would change the course of the campaign.

The officer who had led the army's advance party to Bladensburg
had been badly wounded in the battle. So Ross had had to appoint
someone else. He wasn't entirely confident that the replacement
would be so reliable, and so, as his troops advanced on Baltimore,
Ross himself was never far behind the men at the very front of his
army. Soon after they left the Gorsuch Farm they ran into territory
where the Americans for the first time mounted a dangerous threat.

John Stricker, the American 3rd Brigade commander, had halted
his main force at a spot where the North Point peninsula was at its
narrowest, about midway between Baltimore and the British anchor-
age. The neck of land here was as little as a mile wide: Bear Creek cut
into the peninsula from the Patapsco on the south side, and Bread and
Cheese Creek from the Back River to the north. Across this isthmus
Stricker established his main position. But he sent 200 of his best
men, including a number of riflemen, forward to do what damage
they could to the advancing British.

The ground was wooded. The riflemen, working as they did best,

* The only other reported lapse of discipline at this stage was the story that a girl had
to leap out of an upstairs window of the Shaw family's house to escape a British
lieutenant who was trying to kiss her. Ross had the young officer sent back to his
ship (Eshelman, Sheads and Hickey, p. 167).

as individuals with weapons with which they were as skilled as any in the world, picked their way through the undergrowth and soon spotted the approaching redcoats. Shots rang out: some British soldiers fell, but their weight of numbers ensured that they had no trouble pushing the Americans back. Gleig was one of those near the front: 'we drove them from thicket to thicket, and tree to tree, not, indeed, with any heavy loss, for they were no less expert in finding shelter than in taking aim . . .'. The heat was stifling and progress was slow, but the Americans were being pushed back. There was no need for Ross to do what he did next. Not satisfied with the speed of the advance, he chose to ride right forward to see for himself what the opposition amounted to. 'How bitterly had the whole expedition cause to lament that step,' wrote Gleig. Ross took one good look at the ground ahead, decided he needed more men up front and turned to Cockburn, who, typically, had accompanied him to this exposed spot right at the front line. Ross just had time to shout to the admiral, 'I'll bring up the column,' and turn his horse around, when a shot rang out. 'An American rifleman singled him out,' says Gleig, 'he fired, and the ball, true to its mark, pierced his side.' The fatal shot is reputed to have been fired by either Private Daniel Wells or Private Henry McComas. They were hiding in trees when they saw Ross approaching on horseback. Both were shot dead by the British moments later – even before they'd had time to reload their weapons. The ball passed through Ross's left arm and into his chest. 'I chanced to be standing at no great distance from him; I saw that he was struck, for the reins dropped instantly from his hand, and he leaned forward upon the pommel of his saddle . . . His horse making a move forward, he lost his seat, and but for the intervention of his aide de camp's arm, must have fallen to the ground.' The first the troops following up knew was when the ADC raced past them 'with horror and dismay on his countenance and calling loudly for a surgeon'.

Cockburn watched as the general's wounds – in his arm and chest – were bandaged up. 'He assured me that the wounds he had received in the performance of his duty to his country caused him not a pang; but he felt a lone anxiety for a wife and family dearer to him than life . . .' Ross handed Cockburn a locket saying, 'Give that to my dear wife and tell her I commend her to my king and my country.' The admiral then watched Ross's aides racing to carry him back towards the ships, but they knew he was dying. 'My impression', Cockburn later recalled, 'is that if he could have been borne easily on a good litter to the boat instead of being jolted down to it in a cart, he might possibly have been saved. Although', he added, 'I would not like his friends to know that such was my impression, as it would now avail to no good purpose.' One of Ross's aides, Captain Edward Crofton, escorted the cart and was with Ross when he died before they reached the shore. A small rowing boat carried his body back to the fleet wrapped in the Union Jack. Crofton wrote to Ross's mother-in-law and told her of the 'impressive lesson which I received in viewing the dying moments of a Christian hero. His last words were "O! My beloved wife and family . . ."' Admiral Codrington wrote: 'he is a most severe loss to his country and to us at this most important juncture; and to his wife, with whom, after long experience, he lived in the sincerest affection, the loss of all her earthly bliss!'

When Sir Alexander Cochrane, the Commander in Chief, passed on the news to the War Secretary in London, he expressed the hope that 'a grateful country will provide' support for Ross's wife and family.

No one doubted the effect that news of Ross's death would have on morale. When they carried him back they kept him covered in the hope that no one would know who the wounded man was, and George de Lacy Evans, his devoted aide, said that his death was 'concealed from the troops'. But it was a vain hope. 'The sad and mournful glances of the men as he passed by betrayed their knowledge of the fatal truth and the estimation in which he was held by the army.' As the columns of men passed his body, Gleig recalls, 'No language can convey any adequate idea of the sensation which this melancholy event produced in the bosoms of all who were aware of it. It may with truth be asserted that a general, young in command, has rarely obtained the confidence of his troops in the degree in which General Ross had obtained it.' 'I cannot mention or depict the sorrow every soldier in the army felt,' wrote a corporal in the Scots Fusiliers; 'he was well beloved by every man in the army.' George Chesterton was struck by the extraordinary intensity of the despair that he witnessed everywhere that morning: 'Every face betokened grief, and many hundreds were constrained to give vent to their tears.'

Ross was a huge loss to the British army in America at this particular moment. He always led his men from the front. He was excessively brave – to an extent that was to prove fatal. His impulse to take personal risks in battle may have influenced him to expose his men to excessive danger on the bridge at Bladensburg. Many have questioned his judgement in ordering them across it in such haste at the start of the battle. In contrast, his occasional diffidence and caution had exasperated Cockburn and had led some to question the consistency of his leadership. But he was immensely popular with the men who witnessed his courtesy and gentleness of character – rare qualities in those tough times when the iron rule of discipline left little room for sensitivity in a commander.

The man who now suddenly found himself propelled into command was Colonel Arthur Brooke. He was a veteran forty-two-year-old battalion commander, who had led his 44th Regiment through many a Mediterranean battle with the French. He used to enjoy wearing the Sultan's gold medal which he'd been awarded for helping to throw Napoleon out of Egypt. He was another Anglo-Irishman like Robert Ross – and the Duke of Wellington. His family were landed gentry with a vast estate at Colebrooke in Northern Ireland. Brooke's family was later to give Northern Ireland a prime minister, Lord Brookeborough, and Winston Churchill his most valuable military aide, Field Marshal Alan Brooke. Unlike Ross, Arthur Brooke had a wife who did not yearn mournfully for his return. While Elizabeth Ross languished in tortured loneliness, Marianne Brooke was left in the care of Lord Belmore, who seems to have made the most of Arthur Brooke's absence by having an affair with her.* Brooke was a competent commander – he had led the pincer movement that helped scatter the Americans at Bladensburg. But he was never to enjoy the depth of respect and affection Robert Ross did. To George Gleig, Brooke was 'an officer of decided personal courage, but, perhaps, better suited to lead a battalion than to guide an army'.

Brooke had no time to be troubled by any self-doubt. The moment he heard Ross was wounded, he spurred his horse to the front: 'I rode as fast as I could . . . and found our advanced light troops halted, who informed me that the enemy were drawn up in an opposite wood . . . and on my going to a rising ground in order to reconnoitre I found him strongly posted.' The American advance guard, which had been sent forward to skirmish with the approaching British, had withdrawn to where Colonel Stricker had formed his line. Brooke found himself looking at a row of guns flanked by thousands of American troops apparently determined to fight. Within an hour of taking command he faced what looked like the opportunity of a lifetime. If he could scatter these Americans at North Point as decisively as Robert Ross had at Bladensburg, the city of Baltimore would surely be at his mercy.

* The author contacted the Brooke and Belmore families and it appears to be widely accepted that Belmore was the father of Marianne Brooke's daughter, Juliana, born in 1814.

19

The Battle of North Point

12 September

BRITAIN'S NEW COMMANDER knew he was facing an enemy that was, as he put it, 'strongly posted'. The Americans were drawn up on the edge of a wood protected by a palisade with a wide expanse of open ground in front of them. Brooke could spot around half a dozen guns in the American front line. 'I now saw', he recalled, 'there was no time to be lost, the enemy having about twelve thousand men.' Even by the usual standards of exaggerating the size of an enemy, this was ludicrous. The Americans had just 3,000 men, Brooke had a thousand more. But, even if he hoped the Americans would run away as fast as they had at Bladensburg, he recognised that he risked losing men in the initial assault, and that he needed to find a way of avoiding an all-out frontal attack on a powerful position. It didn't take him long to concoct a plan: bombard the enemy's centre and look for a way of turning his flank.

John Stricker, Brooke's opposing commander, obviously knew his business. 'The ground was well chosen,' wrote Gleig; 'for, besides the covering of wood which he secured for his own people, he took care to leave open fields in his front; by which means we were of necessity exposed to a galling fire, as soon as we came within range.' Stricker had opted to straddle the narrowest point of the North Point peninsula, but he was exposed at one spot. Over to his left, on his north side, there was a gap between his left-hand battalion, the 27th, and the marshy bank of Bread and Cheese Creek beyond. He moved the 450 men of the 39th there to stop the British creeping round the end of his line. But he could see he needed another battalion – ideally at a right angle to the 39th – to thwart any attempt by Brooke (though

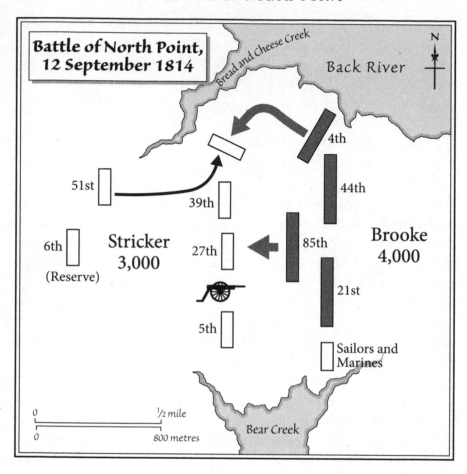

Battle of North Point,
12 September 1814

Bread and Cheese Creek

Back River

N

4th

51st

39th

44th

6th

(Reserve)

Stricker
3,000

27th

85th

Brooke
4,000

21st

5th

Sailors and
Marines

0 ½ mile

0 800 metres

Bear Creek

he still believed Ross was in command) to turn his left flank. And so Lieutenant Colonel Amey was told to move up his largely untried 51st Militia, which had been in the second line facing eastwards towards the enemy. It was now told to wheel around and face north, so that it would make a neat right angle with the 39th. This manoeuvre would have been hard enough for a well-drilled unit of regulars to achieve, but, with the British now opening fire with their artillery and rockets, it was a massive ordeal for the men of the 51st. There were 700 of them and there was soon utter confusion as Amey lost his sense of direction and control. 'The order being badly executed', Stricker reported later, 'created for a moment some confusion

in that quarter.' Stricker quickly sent in some of his best aides to ori-
entate the 51st and it struggled into line, but its morale was in shreds.

Brooke's guns – he only had three – were now exchanging fire
with Stricker's 4-pounders. And a handful of British rockets were
loosed off over the disoriented American left. The 4th Regiment was
despatched to circle round that flank.* It was now early afternoon,
the warmest part of a day which one American officer wrote was
already 'intensely hot'. But Brooke was determined not to lose
momentum. He lined up the 85th Light Infantry to his front with the
44th and 21st close behind. And while the artillery exchange went
on, in order to give the 4th Regiment time to work its way around
to the far right, he told his men to grab the chance of a quick lunch
from their packs. Gleig noticed how effective the handful of British
guns were in firing shrapnel shells at the Americans. Shrapnel had
been introduced in the Peninsula to great effect. The round shells
were fused to explode in the air and propel a lethal spray of musket
balls into enemy ranks. Here at North Point Gleig saw them making
'fearful gaps in the line'.

Brooke was not the only commander riding along his line waiting
for the moment to order an advance. George Cockburn, proud of the
fact there were seamen and marines near the front line, was, in typical
style, making himself visible too. Far too visible for comfort. He had
just had a narrow escape. Soon after Ross was shot, Cockburn saw an
American soldier taking aim at him from behind a tree. According to
Gleig, who recounts the story, instead of turning away or firing his
pistol at the man, as others would have done, 'the brave Admiral,
doubling his fist, shook it at his enemy, and cried aloud, "O you
damned Yankee, I'll give it to you!" Upon which the man dropped
his musket in the greatest alarm, and took to his heels.' By the time
Cockburn reached the battlefield a little later, he was, says his aide de
camp James Scott, 'well known to the enemy from his white horse

---

* The regiment was commanded by Major Faunce; its commanding officer, Arthur
Brooke's elder brother, Lieutenant Colonel Francis Brooke, missed the North
American campaign due to illness.

and gold-laced hat . . . The instant he was perceived, the fire of the enemy's guns seemed to follow him . . . the shot might be seen grazing before, behind, under, and passing over his horse. I several times heard the troops, as he approached in front of them, jokingly exclaim, "Look out, my lads, here is the Admiral coming, you'll have it directly."'

It wasn't long before Brooke felt ready to order the advance right along the line. The bugle sounded. Bayonets fixed, the men moved forward across the open ground. They quickly started taking casualties, first from the American artillery – now firing grapeshot – and then, as they approached closer, from rifle and musket. Gleig observed that the Americans were stuffing the barrels of their cannon with anything that could cause damage: 'old locks, pieces of broken muskets and everything which they could cram in . . .'.

On the American side John Stricker felt deeply bound to defend the honour of the United States and not to allow North Point to be another Bladensburg. It might be enough at least to be able to claim that he had delayed and weakened the British advance on Baltimore. His brigade consisted of the best troops the city could deploy. But already he had witnessed their fragility when the 51st under Colonel Amey had bungled its effort to shore up his extreme left. All he could do now was hope his left would hold as the main British advance smashed into his centre and right. He had stationed Colonel Sterett's 5th Regiment on his right. It had fought better than most at Bladensburg. Stricker now depended on it to stay steady under fire if he was to hold his position.

The British had about 500 yards of open ground to cover. They moved forward, reported Gleig, 'with their accustomed fearlessness, and the Americans with apparent coolness stood to receive them'. When the British were within 100 yards, the Americans fired their first small-arms volley. Smoke briefly obscured one line from the other. When a gust of wind blew it away, 'a hearty British cheer gave notice of our willingness to meet them; and firing and running, we gradually closed upon them, with the design of bringing the bayonet into play'. The British held their fire, as they'd been trained to do, until only a few yards away. It was futile to fire a musket at much more than seventy yards' range: at twenty to thirty yards, you were likely to hit. Still the smoke of the guns obscured the opposing lines from each other, and the British had to make do with firing at the flashes of the guns. Gleig received a blow in the groin from a grape-shot 'which would certainly have killed me had not my haversack which the motion of walking had turned round intervened to save me'.

It is at this stage of the battle – with the British within twenty yards of the Americans – that the accounts of both sides diverge sharply. British eyewitnesses all assert that, the moment the two lines met, the Americans ran for their lives. Cockburn says they 'gave way in all directions'. Scott says 'our gallant troops rushing on, scaled the pal-ings. The Americans could not stand cold steel and they fled in every direction.' Gleig says that when the British rushed forward with the bayonet, the Americans did not attempt to resist 'a shock which the flower of European armies had never been able to withstand . . . They lost in a moment all order, and fled, as every man best could . . .' Brooke makes the most ambitious claim: 'in less than 15 minutes the enemy's forces, being utterly broken and dispersed, fled in every direction . . .'

Most American accounts are rather different. What there is no dispute about on either side is that, at a critical moment in the battle, Stricker's left collapsed under pressure from the enveloping move-ment by Major Faunce's 4th Regiment. The 51st, which had made such a fiasco of its move forward, now folded in the face of this onslaught. Stricker himself admits: 'The 51st, unmindful of my object to use its fire in protection of my left flank . . . totally forgetful of the honour of the brigade, and regardless of its own reputation, delivered one random fire and retreated precipitately, and in such confusion as to render every effort of mine to rally them, ineffective.' But Stricker insists that on the rest of his line, where the 27th held the centre, and in particular on the right where Colonel Sterett's 5th was, fire was 'well returned by the artillery, the whole 27th and the 5th . . .'. Much of the line, in other words, appears to have held under pressure and at least some units stood their ground 'in spite of the disgraceful example set by the intended support on the left'. Captain James Piper reported (writing with hindsight a whole forty years later), 'The American troops stood firmly to their posts, pouring into them as they came up a most destructive fire . . .' But Piper goes on to say that this stand continued only until 'a gap in the line was opened by the 51st regiment, whose colonel misapprehended the general's order'. Piper suggests that the resistance continued *until* the left collapsed; Stricker suggests that it went on in spite of it. Either way, both American accounts go on to talk of an orderly withdrawal rather than the chaotic flight that the British claim. Stricker described his retreat with the words: 'I was constrained to order a movement back . . .' On this view it is possible to argue that North Point was an American success, certainly far short of a humiliating rout. As Piper put it: 'The great object of the expedition had been accomplished – by giving the enemy a specimen of Baltimore bravery and sharp shooting in earnest . . .' General Sam Smith, Stricker's Commander in Chief, was full of praise for him: 'General Stricker gallantly maintained his ground against a great superiority in numbers' (the Americans did their share of exaggerating too – Smith said the British had near twice the number they actually had) and only when the 51st gave way was he 'under the necessity of retiring to the ground in his rear'. But Robert Henry Goldsborough, the thirty-five-year-old US Senator and a major in the militia, is perhaps a more candid American eyewitness. He wrote a week later: 'The affair at Baltimore was . . . as little glorious to our arms as that at Bladensburg. Our militia were completely defeated and routed.' Once again, the attacking British suffered more casualties than the Americans, who were on the defensive behind their paling. British casualties were nearly 300 (thirty-nine killed, 251 wounded); the Americans lost under 200.

What is beyond dispute is that the British did not pursue the Americans far beyond the battlefield. Brooke says 'the day being far advanced' [it was actually only mid- to late afternoon] 'and the troops much fatigued we halted for the night on the ground of which the enemy had been dispossessed'. Scott and some seamen pursued the Americans into the woods they'd been defending. They caught up with one rifleman who, Scott reckoned, clearly believed the 'erroneous idea' which their officers had impressed upon them that they'd receive no mercy from the British. The man levelled his rifle from only six yards away, and when Scott told him to surrender, 'instead of complying with my command, he fired. The ball grazed my left side, cutting my flannel waistcoat, and unfortunately entered the breast of a fine young man close behind me, named Edmondson.' The American was shot dead by two of Scott's men as he ran away. But Scott then watched in horror as a young British lieutenant – before Scott could stop him – mistook Edmondson, still writhing on the ground, for a 'skulker' and despatched him with his sabre.

Brooke ordered the men to find a spot to bivouac just beyond the battlefield. 'A field of battle is a sickening sight when the fever of the blood has cooled, and the enthusiasm of desperate strife subsided into calm reflection,' wrote James Scott. He was sent by Cockburn to do what he could for the wounded. He found his sergeant, who'd been hit, 'near a small bush, under which he had taken shelter, stiff with the clotted gore that had issued from his wounds, but in tolerable spirits'. Scott had the man moved to a large house near by which was serving as a field hospital. Its owners had removed all their furniture, so the wounded lay about on the floor awaiting medical attention. There were too few doctors to give the men the immediate treatment many of them needed, but two American doctors stayed behind to help when their army withdrew. Gleig remarked that there was not 'the smallest distinction made between the Americans and the English . . .'. But few complained. 'A groan or shriek would, indeed, occasionally strike upon the ear of the bystander; and even a querulous exclamation, as the moving of another's leg or arm happened to bring it into contact with some unfortunate man's broken limb.' Gleig came across one wounded American in the woods and the man screamed in terror, assuming Gleig would finish him off. But Gleig managed to reassure him, and moved him to the hospital where he had his leg amputated. Amputation was often the only remedy doctors could safely offer a man with a musket ball lodged in a limb. There was reckoned to be a high risk of death from lead poisoning and gangrene if the ball could not be very quickly and cleanly removed.

George Chesterton, the Royal Artilleryman, saw several cartloads of wounded being wheeled off to the ships over very rough ground. 'Their piteous groans, as the ever-increasing inequities of surface caused painful jolts, and consequent irritation to their fresh and inflamed wounds, awakened the deepest commiseration.' He was sent back to the rear to stock up with ammunition for the guns, and passed a dead American officer. He noticed the man was wearing 'a good pair of Hessian boots'. No point in wasting them on a dead man, he thought, and he stooped down to pull them off. But then 'I suddenly relented, and inwardly denouncing the spoliation of the dead, hastily forbore and cursed my first intentions.' But ten minutes later he was back. His scruples, he said, had 'somewhat abated, and I returned to the spot unsentimentally disposed'. But he found that someone else, 'a less fastidious wanderer', had pre-empted him. The boots had gone. He wasn't too sorry that he'd been 'spared the perpetration of an ignoble deed'.

The night after his victory at North Point, Arthur Brooke could take his rest well satisfied with his first day as commander of the army. His first fight with the enemy had not been without cost, but he had won it. He had defeated the best men Baltimore could field in a bid to stop him. The road to a city far richer than Washington was now open. And the next day his final assault on it would be backed by the immense firepower of the Royal Navy. That night, 12–13 September 1814, the defenders of Baltimore prepared to face bombardment by the guns, rockets and bombs of the most powerful navy in the world.

20

The rockets' red glare

13 September

AT THE FIRST faint glimpse of dawn on 13 September most American eyes behind the walls of the forts on Baltimore's river front were focused on the forest of British masts just three miles away on the Patapsco River. The safety of their city depended on foiling any British attempt to silence their guns and attack Baltimore from the water to match Colonel Arthur Brooke's assault by land.

General Sam Smith had no doubt that the fate of his city would be decided that day. He had 12,000 men and several batteries of guns deployed along Hampstead Hill protecting the city from Brooke's approaching army. He argued that Stricker's force had done what it could to stem the British advance at the Battle of North Point. Smith had hardly expected him to turn them around. What mattered, Smith insisted, was that Stricker's action had boosted the city's morale. Stricker had been 'brave and skilful', his men had 'shown the coolness and valour of veterans'. But Brooke had not been stopped: Smith expected him to be at the very edge of the city within hours. And now that threat was reinforced by the Royal Navy: if its guns could shatter Baltimore's harbour defences, the city would be wide open to attack from the beaches as well. Smith looked to George Armistead and his men and guns in Fort McHenry and the string of smaller forts along the bank of the Patapsco.

Fort McHenry was critical to the shoreline's defence. The persistent efforts of Sam Smith and George Armistead had made it a formidable stronghold. Its sixty guns, solidly placed within the fort and in emplacements on the foreshore, could shatter any attempt by warships to enter the harbour. There were twenty 24-pounders

within the fort itself. Outside, in what were called the 'water batteries', were twenty-eight 36-pounders and twelve 18-pounders. They could smash any vessel that approached within a mile and a half of the muzzles of their barrels. They could spray lethal canister or grapeshot at any troops that managed to land and attack the fort's walls. This key stretch of coast was protected by several other batteries too, but principally by three close neighbours of Fort McHenry. On the far side of the harbour mouth – to the east – was the Lazaretto, three guns manned by forty-five of the flotillamen who'd fought so obstinately under Joshua Barney at Bladensburg. In the harbour mouth itself, between the Lazaretto and Fort McHenry, the Americans sank a number of ships to make it impassable.

Beyond Fort McHenry, a mile and a quarter north-west, was Fort

Babcock. It was commanded by flotilla Captain John Webster, who had had his hat and his horse shot through as he fought beside Joshua Barney at Bladensburg. He'd been a seaman since he was fourteen and had been third lieutenant on Barney's privateer *Rossie* in dozens of scrapes with the British. He'd fired many a broadside at the Royal Navy at sea. Now aged twenty-six and in command of fifty men, Webster had his chance to bombard the enemy from a battery firmly based on land. Sam Smith had picked Webster personally to man a vital link in Baltimore's defences. Webster later recalled that his position was 'open and exposed'. His six 18-pounder guns were not tucked snugly behind castle walls but protected only by a 'breastwork of about four feet high'. His powder magazine was dug into a hill a little way off, and so his men would have to sprint backwards and forwards to fetch the powder from it.

A quarter of a mile further on Lieutenant Henry Newcomb was in charge of eighty seamen and up to ten guns at Fort Covington. He had been singled out for command after his persistent and plucky efforts to disrupt the British navy's foray up the Potomac to Alexandria. His small gunboats had harried Captain Alexander Gordon's squadron and he'd steered a fireship at the British warships – only just managing to leap off it before it was enveloped in flames. Newcomb had failed to destroy the British in the Potomac: he was now determined to foil their attack on Baltimore. In his hour-by-hour account of the day he recorded that it began 'hazy' with 'moderate breezes'. At 6 a.m. he watched a line of British warships fanning out two and three-quarter miles from Fort McHenry and three miles from where he was.

It was a powerful array of up to eighteen warships. There were none of the huge line-of-battle ships with seventy-four or more guns: their hulls were too deep to clear the shallows of the Patapsco River. There were seven frigates and other smaller warships. But it wasn't the conventionally armed ships with their rows of gun ports on either side that seized the attention of the defenders of Baltimore. The vessels on which they concentrated their gaze were the five bomb ships clearly taking pride of place in the British line. They were fearful instruments of war. Each of them carried a handful of medium-sized naval cannon, but the centrepiece of each ship was a pair of giant mortar guns that took up a wide expanse of deck amidships. The mortars were placed on massive base plates on the deck between the ship's two masts. They packed an immense punch. They fired shells of 190 pounds – eight to ten times the weight of a typical naval round shot. And they could propel them for over two miles. That meant they could outrange anything the Americans could bring to bear on them. They were not very accurate but their destructive power could outreach the guns of Fort McHenry and its satellite forts by at least half a mile. The balance of power in this long-range gun battle would be heavily in favour of the British.

And so it proved. Britain's Commander in Chief, Vice Admiral Sir Alexander Cochrane, appears to have been so confident of suppressing Fort McHenry that he had transferred his flag to the frigate *Surprize* and sailed up the Patapsco with Captain Alexander Gordon's attacking squadron. And at six o'clock on that Tuesday morning, 13 September, Cochrane gave the signal to the bomb ships to begin their ranging shots. HMS *Volcano* fired the first shot, a hefty 13-inch mortar shell that exploded short of the coast. A second shot fell short too. All five bomb ships moved a little closer and by 7 a.m. all five were loosing off their giant mortar shells. Each time one of them fired, the downward force of the blast would make the whole deck tremble and momentarily thrust the ship's hull two feet deeper into the water. The huge shells would lift off and climb to the peak of a great arc before plunging to a point usually wide of the intended target. The rockets for their part were like flying bombs, each with a fiery red afterglow, with widely varied trajectories – some describing long, lazy, almost vertical paths, others screaming horizontally across the water. The rockets and mortar shells were hopelessly inaccurate, but it was the very randomness of their scatter that made them such terrifying weapons. They could fall directly overhead or they could miss by hundreds of yards. And while the direct fire of the ships' cannon, even if they'd been within range, would have done little damage to Fort McHenry's low profile, its walls and emplacements

Margaret Bayard Smith, whose letters describe her family's close friendship with the Madisons and the horror and shame of the British invasion. "Oh that I, a feeble woman, could do something," she wrote to her sister.

William Thornton, erudite Washington doctor and architect, whose British background inclined him to be civil to the invaders.

James Ewell, another well-to-do doctor, who, like Thornton, risked being seen as a traitor due to his conciliatory attitude to the British.

A British cartoon scorns James Madison and his war secretary fleeing their burning city with handfuls of hastily grabbed state papers. An American bystander observes: "I suppose this is what Maddie calls benefitting his country!"

Captain Charles Napier, "Black Charlie," skipper of the frigate *Euryalus,* whose gritty tenacity helped ensure the success of Gordon's Potomac expedition. He was wounded in the neck.

Captain James Alexander Gordon led the daring British naval expedition up the Potomac that secured the surrender of Alexandria. He and Napier came away with twenty-one captured ships and a pile of prize money.

Major General Ross is shot by a rifleman in the approach to Baltimore. His aides rush to help. Lowered from his horse, he died on a cart taking him back to the fleet—to the profound distress of his men.

Major General Sam Smith, saviour of Baltimore. A widely respected fifty-nine-year-old veteran of the War of Independence and tough-speaking U.S. senator, he readily accepted the task of ensuring his city didn't suffer the fate of Washington.

Major George Armistead, commander of Fort McHenry at Baltimore. His leadership and foresight inspired the fort's garrison to survive the British bombardment which lasted twenty-five hours.

Brigadier General John Stricker, commander of Baltimore's advance force dispatched to North Point to try to impede the British approach to the city. The British said he was sent packing: Stricker called it a fighting withdrawal.

Colonel Arthur Brooke, Ross's successor and Stricker's opponent at North Point. Competent but without Ross's charisma, he went on to face an agonising choice when hugely outnumbered at Baltimore.

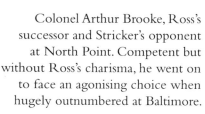

The Battle of North Point, September 12 1814, painted from memory by an American soldier. Stricker and his staff (right) have drawn up their men in a huge right angle at the edge of the wood, the 51st protecting their flank (left). The British can be seen in the far distance approaching over open ground.

Fort McHenry from the air. The star-shaped fortress with its low-profile ramparts looks today much as it did in September 1814. This view looks north with the entrance to Baltimore's inner harbour on the right.

The bombardment of Fort McHenry looking south across the inner harbour with the fort and its banner in the centre, and the British warships beyond. The British launched mortar shells and rockets at the fort from 6 a.m. on September 13 to 7 a.m. the next day.

Mary Pickersgill, the seamstress, who together with her daughter and two nieces made a massive flag to fly over Fort McHenry. She was commissioned by George Armistead to make it so large the British would see it from afar.

Pickersgill's star-spangled banner photographed with a soldier standing beneath it in 1872. At its full extent it measured 30 x 42 feet. It's now displayed in the Smithsonian Museum in Washington.

Francis Scott Key spots the flag still flying above Fort McHenry at dawn on September 14, 1814. It is not the Union Jack, as he had feared, but the star-spangled banner. He never knew the poem he wrote would become America's national anthem.

The score of "The Star-Spangled Banner," printed by a Baltimore publisher in the nineteenth century. Scott Key's poem "O say can you see . . ." was set to the music of an old English song club favorite and was adopted as the U.S. anthem in 1931.

An American cartoon celebrates the British departure from Baltimore. The United States was quick to claim it as a resounding victory. The American soldier who is prodding John Bull's bottom shouts: "We'll teach you to know what a flogging is!!!"

Twelve of the surviving "Old Defenders" of Baltimore sit for a photograph in 1870. George Lightner (second from the right in the back row) was a drummer boy in 1814. The last survivor of the battle—a nine-year-old powder monkey—died in 1898, aged ninety-four.

James Madison, aged eighty-two, in 1833. He and Dolley spent a happy retirement—he deep in study, she entertaining old friends — until his death in 1836.

A daguerreotype of Dolley Madison in the late 1840s, aged around eighty. She spent her last years in poverty when her son by her first marriage frittered away what money the family had left. She died in 1849, aged eighty-one.

Montpelier, the Madisons' mansion in rural Virginia, eighty miles south of Washington. After James's death, Dolley had to sell the house to pay her bills. Earlier, when the Madisons flourished, the Montpelier estate housed 120 slaves.

were a poor defence against the lobbing of mortars and rockets. Armistead's guess was that between 1,500 and 1,800 mortar shells alone – up to 150 tons of ordnance – landed around him in the next twenty-five hours. All the bomb ships had lurid names to awe their opponents: *Volcano*'s grim workmates were named *Aetna*, *Devastation*, *Meteor* and *Terror* and they were accompanied by a rocket ship, HMS *Erebus*, that fired even more erratically than they did.

Robert Barrett watched from the deck of the frigate *Hebrus* as the British guns pounded the forts. Just beyond them he and his mates could clearly see the masts of the merchant vessels and a 'beautiful new frigate, the Java', lying temptingly in the harbour, promising the British sailors a vast hoard of prize money if they could break in past the forts. Barrett was 'confident that all on board the advanced ships had little doubt that the British ensign would soon proudly wave in triumph over the embattled fortress, whose embrasures presented a formidable line of artillery'.

For the next twenty-four hours this thunderous bombardment continued – the howl of the mortar bombs and the shriek of the incoming rockets mixed with the roar of the replying American guns. From the start all the American guns responded, many of them using the shot specially heated in the furnaces that made the balls into lethal incendiary bombs if they hit the wooden ships. But it soon became horrifyingly clear that none of the American shots were reaching the British ships, which were anchored well out of range. No American shore battery had the range of the bomb and rocket ships.

'The enemy commenced the bombardment of Fort McHenry,' wrote the American Lieutenant Henry Newcomb, 'which was returned with shells and shot, but as they fell short, the fort discontinued firing, while the enemy continued to throw their shells with great precision and effect ...' George Armistead was soon near despair: 'This was to me a most distressing circumstance as it left us exposed to a constant and tremendous shower of shells without the most remote possibility of our doing him the slightest injury.' Armistead had earnestly requested a couple of heavy mortars. One had been delivered to him but without fuses or base. Another major worry for Armistead, as the bombs rained down around him, was the fact that the fort's powder magazine was not bombproof. At one heart-stopping moment a bomb landed on it but failed to go off. Another direct hit and Fort McHenry could be blown sky-high. Armistead had his men carry barrels of powder out of the magazine and spread them out behind a high wall in the fort where enemy fire was most unlikely to reach them.

John Webster had one desperate moment in Fort Babcock. Like Fort McHenry, Babcock had a powder magazine some way from the guns. Webster suddenly noticed that 'one of my seamen, an obstinate Englishman, attempted to lay a train of powder to the magazine; without thought I laid him out for dead with a handspike [a crow-bar]'. The man came to a little later and escaped before the firing stopped. By early afternoon the battered defenders of the forts had the further discomfort of heavy rain showers to cope with. Most of them standing around their guns had only their woollen blankets for protection.

In Baltimore itself, despite all the efforts of General Sam Smith, alarm among the citizens was now at fever pitch. Many had evacu-ated their homes and removed their furniture. Few stores were open. James Stevens, a Methodist preacher, wrote (in rather shaky spelling) to his sister in Pennsylvania that he could see on the one hand 'the wagons, carts and drays, all in hast mooving the people and the poorer sort with what they could cary and there children on there backs flying for their lives' and on the other hand he watched the British 'bumbs lite and burst on the shore at which explosions the hole town and several miles out would shake . . .'.

Around 2 p.m. the Royal Navy had a lucky strike. Through the driv-ing rain a British mortar shell dropped out of the sky on to a 24-pounder on Fort McHenry's south-west bastion. It was one of Judge Nicholson's guns. His lieutenant, Levi Clagett, was killed outright by the blast, which dismounted the gun and broke its car-riage wheel. Isaac Munroe was only twenty-five paces away. Moments earlier he'd been standing beside Sergeant John Clemm, 'a most amiable character', when a bomb had burst over their heads. Clemm was killed when 'a piece the size of a silver dollar, two inches thick, passed through his body in a diagonal direction from his navel, and went into the ground upwards of two feet'. Several more of Nicholson's men were wounded. In spite of this loss, it is astonishing how few casualties the Americans suffered as they endured hour after hour of pounding by British shells. In all they lost four men dead and twenty-four wounded. George Armistead was tireless in encouraging his men. 'No man ever behaved with more gallantry, firmness and constancy,' recalled Nicholson. 'We were like pigeons tied by the legs to be shot at, and you would have been delighted to have seen the conduct of Armistead.'

It was about this time, according to Armistead, that Cochrane, sensing that the Americans were in serious trouble, took the risk of ordering at least three of his bomb ships to move closer to the fort. They moved to within a mile and a half. It was the chance George Armistead had been waiting for. They were within range of his guns. He immediately ordered them all to open fire. Isaac Munroe watched Armistead mount the parapet and order the 24-pounders and then shortly afterwards the other guns to open up on the British ships that were now within range. 'We could see the shot strike the frigates in several instances, when every heart was gladdened and we gave three cheers.' Four musicians among the fort's artillerymen struck up 'Yankee Doodle' on their fifes and drums. Armistead reported that his command was 'obeyed with alacrity through the whole garrison, and in half an hour those intruders again sheltered themselves by withdrawing beyond our reach. We gave three cheers and again ceased firing.' The British bomb ship *Devastation* was hit in the port bow and *Volcano* was hit twice. It wasn't long before Cochrane pulled them back to where they could still inflict damage on the fort without being within range of its guns. 'We were again foiled,' recalled Isaac Munroe, 'and were reduced to the dreadful alternative of facing by far the most tremendous bombardment ever known in this country without any means of resisting it . . .' Robert Barrett was one of the crew of a launch sent from the *Hebrus* to reconnoitre the harbour mouth. But the American guns opened up so fiercely that Barrett saw the British bomb vessels wisely pulling back behind him. Another smallish British vessel was near by and Barrett watched as a 'black man, who was standing up in the centre, was cut clean in half by one of the enemy's shots. This was sufficient warning for us to shift . . .'

For most of the day and throughout the night of 13–14 September the American artillery remained powerless to respond to the British bombardment. Hour after hour Barrett could not conceal his excitement at the sheer immensity of the Royal Navy's firepower and he never appeared to doubt that it would lead to Baltimore's collapse. 'All this night the bombardment continued with unabated vigour, the hissing rockets and the fiery shells glittered in the air, threatening destruction as they fell, whilst to add solemnity to this scene of devastation, the rain fell in torrents.' Late that night, after more than twelve hours of the Royal Navy's attack on the forts, Cochrane ordered a further escalation. Captain Charles Napier, who had won great praise for his skill and bravery in the thrust up the Potomac against Alexandria, was ordered to mastermind a 'diversionary attack' up the Patapsco River. Napier was still suffering from the wound in his neck, which was to make him walk with a stoop for the rest of his life. But this mission was of the highest importance and it demanded a commander of his calibre. He was to take a fleet of small boats up the river – 'their oars', insisted Cochrane, 'must be muffled' – and go 'close to the shore', and then to anchor and 'remain perfectly quiet until one o'clock'. At 1 a.m. the British guns would open up again, and Napier's men would make as if to assault the forts from the beaches firing their muskets 'occasionally using blank cartridges'. The operation was designed to distract the Americans from the attack that Colonel Brooke's army would be making on the city's defences at 2 a.m. Once Napier had heard that the army's attack was 'seriously engaged, you will return to this ship for further orders'.

Napier transferred more than a thousand men to the launches and plenty of blank as well as regular ball ammunition for their muskets. Then, with the rain pelting down and making it very hard for any of the boat skippers to see more than a short distance ahead,

Napier's force moved off. The rain and the pitch dark soon fragmented this force, and half of the men found themselves heading direct for the harbour mouth. They were spotted by the American gunners in the Lazaretto battery and they soon turned around and scuttled back to the British fleet. Napier and the rest of the force managed to penetrate up the river as far as Fort Covington, but they were soon detected. John Webster in Fort Babcock, alerted by the increased British shelling that night, had already double-shotted his cannon with a mix of large 18-pound balls and grapeshot. And then, 'about midnight I could hear a splashing in the water. The attention of others was aroused and we were convinced it was the noise of muffled oars of the British barges.' He could even discern 'small gleaming lights in different places'. Some of the lights appeared to be showing as far up the river as Fort Covington. Webster then personally supervised the priming of the guns in the pouring rain and helped aim them carefully at where he reckoned the British were. 'I trained the guns and then opened on them, which caused the boats to cease rowing and a rapid firing followed from the barges, as well as from ourselves.' He was sure he could hear the balls strike the barges, and his men told him they could hear the British screaming. Henry Newcomb's guns in Fort Covington opened up too. The flashes of the British guns and the flare of the rockets now gave the Americans clear targets to aim at. It wasn't long before Napier ordered his flotilla to abort and make all haste back to the ships. The Americans claimed that they had destroyed one barge and that they found a number of bodies floating on the water the following morning.

Napier's foray had certainly commanded American attention and he must have hoped that it would help divert attention from Brooke's planned offensive that night. Even if he'd been unable to keep up the pressure until 2 a.m. as planned, Brooke would presumably still proceed with his scheduled attack. But, listen though they did, the British on their ships could hear no sound of firing from Brooke's army. Either his attack had been postponed or something had gone wrong.

21

You go on at your peril

13 September

Twenty-four hours earlier Arthur Brooke had gone to bed knowing that the following day, Tuesday 13 September, he would face the greatest challenge of his career. Ross's death had given him the chance to lead a British army to a historic victory. The Royal Navy would commence its bombardment of Baltimore's coastal forts the following morning. If they could be suppressed, the city would be exposed to assault from the sea on one side and from his army from the other. And if his forces could break through as they had at Bladensburg and North Point, the city would be at his mercy.

An encouraging message reached Brooke on the evening of the 12th from the British Commander in Chief, Vice Admiral Sir Alexander Cochrane. He was all ready to give his bomb ships the order to open fire as soon as the light came up the next day. Cochrane told Brooke that he had looked at the fortifications the Americans had thrown up in front of Baltimore, and 'It struck me that this entrenched camp may be turned.' Brooke wrote back to say that 'in the morning we hope to proceed at about twelve or one to work our destruction . . .' and he added: 'your fire I should think on the town would be of infinite service to us'. He ended by expressing 'my hope for our mutual success'.

It was another wet night. The rain was so heavy that soldiers struggled to keep their weapons dry. The lucky ones had leather cases which gave their muskets some protection; others did their best to shelter their guns under their arms. In the morning the troops were ordered to lighten their loads by dumping their blankets, most of which were sodden with the rain. Gleig got up, 'absolutely heavy with the load of moisture which hung about me . . . My very skin was perforated – I was wet to the bones and marrow.' The army moved off and soon there was the welcome sound of the supporting British naval bombardment over to their left. Gleig led a patrol to keep an eye on the army's flank, and it wasn't long before he came across two Americans as he struggled through some undergrowth. 'Holding a cocked pistol in my hand, I ran towards them and commanded them on pain of death to surrender.' Gleig had to knock a rifle out of the hand of one of them, who promptly burst into tears. He said he didn't mind what Gleig did to him as long as he would spare the life of his father, who was lying badly wounded on the ground. Gleig took one look at the father and saw that he was actually dead. 'God forbid that I should do injury either to a father or a son under such circumstances,' he said and moved on, leaving the young man to cope with his father's corpse.

After trudging through woods and clambering over a number of trees the Americans had cut down in their path, Brooke and his army suddenly broke out into much more open country which fell away before them and then rose to a ridge that concealed the city of Baltimore directly behind it. The ridge was heavily fortified. Brooke was immediately struck by the scale of the defences Baltimore's General Sam Smith had constructed: 'Found the enemy strongly posted on high hill, a regular ditch and strong redoubts . . .' He and his staff estimated that the line of ramparts and entrenchments was manned by as many as 15,000, perhaps even 20,000 men, five times the size of their own army. For once their estimate was about right. They also counted about 120 guns in well-dug emplacements. Some of them were heavy naval 32-pounders. Loaded with grape or canister they would pack a lethal punch against advancing infantry. As Gleig put it: 'A moment's survey of these hills served . . . to convince us that something more than a mere continuance of our march would be required to make the prize our own.' Brooke and Cockburn rode at a safe distance along the whole American line to make their own assessment. They were in no doubt that a head-on attack would be near suicide. But Brooke observed that the American left wing appeared poorly defended and that, 'by making a night attack, I might gain his flank and get into his rear'. This was, he reckoned, 'perfectly feasible', and he would attack at night when the American guns would be least effective. The assault would be launched at two o'clock the following morning – on 14 September. Two columns would wheel around the American left where the line of guns appeared to end and another column would stage a diversionary attack on the American right. It would only be a feint. Brooke's main punch would hit the Americans on their extreme left where their line was weak. But the navy's support would be critical through this operation, and so James Scott, Cockburn's right-hand man, was sent off to communicate the plan to Alexander Cochrane's ships bombarding Fort McHenry. Scott says that when he reached the beach the man who 'gave me a passage off to the Admiral' was none other than Captain Sir Thomas Hardy, former captain of the *Victory* who had famously kissed Nelson as he died of his wound at Trafalgar nine years earlier.

With the decision made to wait until the early hours for the night attack, Brooke's army remained stationary in front of the American lines all evening. From Cockburn and Brooke downwards hopes were high that the American position could be carried and that they'd be in Baltimore by breakfast. 'The odds were unquestionably tremendous ...' wrote George Gleig, 'yet there was not a man amongst us who entertained a doubt as to the issue of the battle, let it begin when it might. We despised the Yankees from our hearts, and only longed for an opportunity to show them how easily they could be beaten.'

Gleig and his comrades were again placed as sentries forward of the main force, and they were soon drenched in the rain which began again that evening. After a struggle with the sodden wood lying about, they finally got a fire alight to give them some warmth. Their spirits rose even more when they found an empty house a couple of hundred yards ahead of them. They looked everywhere – without success – for food, but then one of the soldiers noticed that 'the wily Yankee to whom this house belonged, unable or unwilling to remove his wine, had adopted the common precaution of blocking up the entrance to his vaults with brick work'. A soldier smashed through it with the butt of his musket, and they found a well-stocked wine cellar. 'In five minutes the cellar was crowded with men, filling, in the first place their own haversacks and bosoms, and then handing out bottles, with the utmost liberality, to their comrades.' Gleig and one of his friends laid hands on 'a flask of exquisite cognac with two magnums of superior Bordeaux'. They took them back to their post, tucked into a salt-beef supper, then lit their pipes and – in spite of the rain – sat by their fire 'in a state . . . of maximum enjoyment'.

George Chesterton was less lucky. He had to struggle to keep his artillery ammunition as dry as he could. He smothered it in blankets then, soaked to the skin, went off to report to his commanding officer. He searched for some time in the pouring rain and finally tracked him down snugly sheltering in a pigsty. 'He recommend me to take care of myself, so I joyfully made for a large and blazing camp-fire contiguous, where I hoped to dry my saturated garments.' No sooner had Chesterton managed to dry himself and his clothes than the heavens opened again, and 'I was again drenched.' He finally eased his way into a barn full of 21st Fusiliers fast asleep: one of them rather grumpily moved over to give him a piece of floor to sleep on.

Brooke had spread the word earlier in the evening that the army should be ready to mount his planned night attack once the navy resumed its bombardment of the coastal forts. And while it was still light he and Cockburn were just returning from a final inspection of the enemy's position when James Scott hurried back from his visit to the Commander in Chief. Cockburn, obviously in high spirits, greeted him cheerily and asked, 'Well Scott, have you delivered my message to the Commander in Chief? We have had an excellent view of their defences; before two o'clock tomorrow morning all that you now see . . . will be ours. What force is to assist us on the waterside?' Scott gave Cockburn an unsealed letter – which he had already scanned – with the words: 'I trust, Sir, the contents of this despatch will not frustrate your's [sic] and the General's plans' (Scott mistak-enly promotes Brooke to the rank of general). Scott watched

Cockburn's face fall as he studied the letter. Its 'perusal . . . dispelled the animated smile of confidence from his brow, and he handed it to General Brooke'.

The letter was from Cochrane, and it came as a crushing blow to both Cockburn and Brooke. It was addressed to Cockburn. 'My Dear Admiral. It is impossible for the ships to render you any assistance – the town is so far retired from the forts. It is for Colonel Brooke to consider under such circumstances whether he has force sufficient to defeat so large a number as it [is] said the enemy has collected, say 20,000 strong or even a less number . . .' The letter goes on to suggest that to go ahead 'will be only throwing the men's lives away and prevent us from going upon other services' (this clearly refers to Cochrane's ultimate aim of switching his campaign to the south and attacking New Orleans). 'At any rate a very considerable loss must ensue and as the enemy is daily gaining strength his loss let it be ever so great cannot be equally felt.'

Cochrane's letter is in striking contrast to his message to Brooke of the night before in which he states that the American position 'may be turned'. The letter is not an order. Cochrane was a lot senior to Brooke, but Brooke – like Ross before him – was free, as the army commander, to make up his own mind. Cochrane appears to accept this when he says 'It is for Colonel Brooke to consider . . .' But he then goes on to state bluntly that to go on with the fight would risk heavy losses and jeopardise the next stage of the campaign. He's saying to Brooke, 'You'll go on at your peril and you'll get no support from me.'

The other remarkable thing about the letter is that, at the foot of it, Cochrane indicates that it was written at 9.30 that morning, only two and a half hours after his bombardment of the forts had begun – hardly time enough to be sure whether his bomb ships would succeed or fail in suppressing Fort McHenry and the other gun positions protecting Baltimore harbour. Cochrane had of course watched the Americans sinking ships to close the harbour mouth. He must have realised that, even if he suppressed Fort McHenry, this barrier would preclude his ships penetrating the inner harbour to bring their guns within range of the city itself. Unless he could land guns on the shore and roll them forward, he would be powerless to give artillery support to Brooke. But he was to continue the blasting of the coastal forts for the best part of the next twenty-four hours. And he gave no intimation to anyone on the ships that he regarded any further fighting as futile. Quite the contrary: he continued it and even intensified it by moving his bomb ships forward in the early afternoon. And in the evening he gave the order for Captain Napier's midnight attack on the forts to coincide with Brooke's planned night attack. In spite of his disenchantment with the whole project from as early as breakfast time on 13 September, he continued with the bombardment in case Brooke rejected his advice and went ahead with his night attack.

Brooke faced an agonising decision. Cockburn was, predictably, forthright in urging him to press on – just as he had done when Cochrane had advised Ross to abandon his advance on Washington. 'The Rear Admiral', recalled Scott, 'was still for proceeding . . .' But Arthur Brooke felt he couldn't defy Cochrane. 'All my hopes were in a moment blasted,' he wrote in his diary. 'It would have been presumptuous in me to say I could take such a force without great loss, more especially having only about four thousand men. If I took the place I should have been the greatest man in England. If I lost, my military character was gone forever.' He did promise Cockburn that he would put the issue to a Council of War of his top military commanders, and invited Cockburn to attend it. Scott says Cockburn 'instantly declined', suggesting that the admiral was exasperated and deeply disappointed by what he saw as Cochrane's faintheartedness. The Council met till midnight. According to George Evans, who was there, Brooke summoned the meeting because he felt he was 'in an embarrassed situation'. The Council agreed unanimously on just one point, 'the conviction of success in the event of an assault – but three senior members considered the attempt improper in opposition to the judgement of the Vice Admiral. Being unable to obtain unanimous sanction, Col. Brooke decided on retreat.' So instead of attacking in the early hours, the army would retire to the ships. The Baltimore operation was off. The ambitious dream of securing an even richer prize than Washington was abandoned.

To young soldiers like George Gleig, who'd never experienced defeat in battle – either in the Peninsula and southern France or in America – the order to retire came as a bitter shock. 'It is impossible for me to convey any idea of the disappointment, or rather humiliation, experienced and expressed by persons of all ranks,' he wrote. 'In all night operations a compact body of veterans, well disciplined and orderly, are at all times an overmatch for whole crowds of raw levies.' To Scott it was 'a mortifying result after the brilliant success of the 12th'. But even Gleig, writing in a rather different tone in another book, recognised that without the coastal forts being suppressed and the navy assaulting Baltimore from the other flank, a land attack would have 'cost us dear'. The counsel that prevailed in the end was that of Harry Smith, Edward Codrington and now Cochrane, who felt that Baltimore was a battle too far. Admiral Codrington was in no doubt that left to himself Robert Ross would not have advanced on Baltimore but was talked into it by Evans and Cockburn. 'I was surprised that so sensible a man as General Ross should be led away by the opposite opinions,' he wrote to his wife when he sent her the news of Ross's death. He told her he believed that 'the operation was based on poor intelligence and that there was little chance of capturing Baltimore . . . it was well defended'. But George Cockburn was not going to give way to what he saw as the fainthearts. In a conversation with the American Skinner the next day he said: 'Ah, if it had not been for the sinking of those ships across the channel, with the wind and tide we had in our favour we would have taken the town.'

George de Lacy Evans, who had been as eager as Cockburn to persist with the attempt on Baltimore, was beside himself with frustration and fury at the aborting of the operation. He came close to accusing the navy of cowardice: he remarked in the memorandum he wrote at the time that 'our vessels were not permitted within cannon range' and that no one was killed on board. 'This was not the description of co-operation that General Ross had been led to expect. The enemy's batteries were not very formidable. Some distinguished naval officers volunteered to attack them or force the chain of small vessels which had been nearly sunk at the entrance of the harbour.'

And if Brooke had attacked Hampstead Hill, 'the extreme darkness of the night favoured us, we had observed the ground carefully . . . and at the very hour determined for the assault . . . a storm and torrent of rain commenced which must have rendered firearms nearly useless, and we should have probably penetrated the enemy's lines without having received a shot'. And Evans concluded his diatribe with the words, 'one of the most glorious opportunities which ever presented itself has irretrievably been lost'.

The men in Brooke's army would never tire of debating what would have happened if they'd pressed on with their night attack on Baltimore. Some argued that the loss of their general on 12 September was the death blow to the enterprise. If Ross had survived, and had led his men against the Hampstead Heights, the argument ran, the Americans would have been routed. With Ross rather than the competent but uninspiring Arthur Brooke at their head, even 20,000 militia wouldn't have stopped them. Baltimore would have suffered the fate of Washington. But Ross would have received the same disheartening news from Cochrane – that the navy couldn't suppress the forts and smash its way through the sunken ships and into the harbour. On past form Ross was as unlikely as Brooke to have been persuaded by Cockburn to defy their Commander in Chief and push on with the offensive.

And what prospects would there have been for that night attack, whether led by Brooke or by Ross? What chance was there that they would have overcome the Americans 'without a shot' as Evans believed? The assault would have been launched at the extreme left-hand edge of General Sam Smith's line on the north-east side of the city. By an irony Smith had shifted a large slice of his militia there under the command of William Winder, the loser at Bladensburg. To his credit Winder carried out the manoeuvre, according to Smith, 'with great skill and judgment'. The British would then have clashed immediately with the man they had humiliated three weeks earlier, now determined to redeem himself. And even if Winder had been beaten back, the thousands of Americans in entrenchments beyond would have had to be dislodged if the British were to secure their flank and rear as they pressed ahead. And the defenders of Baltimore were far better drilled and motivated by Sam Smith's weeks of meticulous preparation than the army Winder had commanded in the approaches to Washington. Besides they would have outnumbered the British attacking force by some ten to fifteen thousand men. The odds at Bladensburg had been two to one. Here they would have been up to five to one.

But if, despite all these doubts, the British had succeeded in smashing their way into Baltimore, they would have denied the Americans the single most satisfying outcome of the War of 1812. It was an event that was to become embedded in American history as one of the country's foundation myths. It took place at dawn the following morning as Cochrane decided to call an end to his bombardment of the forts twenty-five hours after it had begun.

The man who was to create this myth was the young American lawyer Francis Scott Key, who had successfully secured the release of Dr Beanes a few days earlier.* The pair had not yet been allowed to leave for home, and Key had spent the night anxiously watching the relentless British shelling of Baltimore's Fort McHenry. He was standing on the deck of the small ship on which the British had insisted on confining him to avoid him revealing their plans. He had a clear view of the smoke and debris thrown up by the explosions of the rockets and bombs, and his fertile imagination conjured up pictures of the suffering the British must be inflicting on the garrison of this and the other forts. It seemed to him less and less likely that the fort could survive the bombardment. As the first light on Wednesday 14 September began to distinguish the fort's embattled walls in the gloom, he strained his eyes to see any sign of life. Were there still Americans alive in it? Had the British silenced its guns? And – worst fear of all – was the fort in British hands? William Beanes was beside Key. His eyesight was poor: he could make out little in the morning haze. 'Can you see the flag?' he kept asking. 'Before it was light enough to see objects at a distance,' reported Key's brother-in-law,

* See above p. 168.

'their glasses were turned to the fort, uncertain whether they would see the stars and stripes or the flag of the enemy.' And then through the gloom Key could just spot the flagstaff inside the fort and a giant flag flying from it. It was unmistakable. It was not the Union Jack. It was the great banner with its fifteen stars and fifteen stripes which George Armistead had commissioned Mary Pickersgill and her daughter to make the previous summer. Key's spirit leapt. The Americans still held the fort. Baltimore had survived the British attack. And there and then 'in that hour of deliverance and joyful triumph, my heart spoke: and "Does not such a country and such defenders of their country deserve a song?" was its question'. The young lawyer jotted down the lines of a poem that was to become more celebrated than any other in American history.

> Oh say can you see, by the dawn's early light,
> What so proudly we hail'd at the twilight's last gleaming,
> Whose broad stripes and bright stars through the perilous fight,
> O'er the ramparts we watch'd, were so gallantly streaming?
> And the rockets' red glare, the bombs bursting in air,
> Gave proof through the night that our flag was still there –
> Oh say, does that star-spangled banner yet wave
> O'er the land of the free, and the home of the brave?

Francis Scott Key wrote these words in note form on the back of a letter which he happened to have in his pocket. He finished the poem, four verses in all, in the boat that took him ashore when the British released him. Once their mission had been abandoned, they had no reason to detain him any longer. He went to a Baltimore hotel and wrote the poem out in full and showed it to Judge Joseph Nicholson, his brother-in-law, who'd just returned from his post in Fort McHenry. Nicholson, who'd endured the entire bombardment inside the fort, told Key 'he was so much pleased with it that he immediately sent it to a printer'. And less than a week later it was published in a local paper and was widely welcomed by the public. Key set the words to the tune of an old English song club favourite 'Anacreon in heaven', and it became an immediate hit in America.

Over a century later, in 1931, it finally became the US national anthem.

The British seaman Robert Barrett saw the star-spangled banner too – from the deck of his frigate *Hebrus* as she and the other ships weighed anchor and turned away down the river. 'It was a galling sight for British seamen to behold. And, as the last vessel spread her canvas to the wind, the Americans hoisted a most superb and splendid ensign on their battery and fired at the same time a gun of defiance.' Barrett was another who believed that if Brooke and Cochrane had displayed 'ordinary judgement, perseverance and decision' they would have won the day. 'When the squadron retreated from Baltimore, sullen discontent was displayed and malevolent aspersions cast upon our veteran chief . . .'

Sam Smith's foresight and tenacity had paid off. He didn't realise that the British were leaving until daylight. He decided his troops were 'so worn out with a continued watching and with being under arms during three days and nights' that he made no effort to pursue Brooke back to the ships. But that was a mere trifle compared to what he and his fellow citizens felt they'd achieved. The events of that night and the following morning, 14 September, may have seemed little more than a frustrating setback for Britain, but the United States would interpret them as a glorious triumph. The British decision to end an inconclusive naval stand-off and to abort a major operation on land was transformed by American myth-makers into a resounding victory that would become an emblematic moment in US history. Without any clash on the battlefield the young American republic had humbled the might of the British empire. The rebuff to Britain at Baltimore decisively demonstrated America's independence of its former master. And this explosion of national pride was only to be magnified by the events of the remaining months of the war.

22

Unparalleled in history
Aftermath

WITH THE DEPARTURE of the British army from Baltimore the
so-called War of 1812 between Britain and America had only
four more months to run.

An exultant James Madison had even more to celebrate when he
addressed the new session of Congress on 20 September. A powerful
British thrust south from Canada had been thrown back at Plattsburg
in New York State and General Andrew Jackson had crushed
Britain's allies, the Creek Indians, in the south. The news only further depressed spirits on Alexander Cochrane's ships as they sailed off
to their West Indies base in Jamaica to prepare for the winter campaign against New Orleans. Cochrane put the best gloss he could on
the reverse at Baltimore, even claiming in a private letter to the head
of the Admiralty that he had always been against the Baltimore
operation. He wrote that he had been 'extremely urged by the
General to which I reluctantly consented'.

When the accounts of the setback reached London in late
October, newspapers put a brave face on it. The *Morning Post* called
it 'a most brilliant victory over the American army before Baltimore'.
The Prime Minister Lord Liverpool was more plain-spoken. He
wrote to his Foreign Secretary Lord Castlereagh that the news from
America was 'chequered'. One of his key negotiators at the peace
talks at Ghent in the Netherlands was more downbeat. The news was
'very far from satisfactory', and Baltimore 'will be considered by the
Americans as a victory . . .'. If the success at Washington had boosted
Britain's chances of winning the peace terms it wanted, Baltimore
and Plattsburg had changed all that. Liverpool's government was

now, like Madison's, deeply concerned by the cost of the war. It was involving Britain in 'prodigious expense'. In desperation he turned to the Duke of Wellington and asked him to take command in America, 'to place the military operations on a proper footing and give us the best prospects of peace'. Wellington, who thought the war a waste of money and lives, was quick to decline the invitation and to point out that the government could not hope to gain much at the peace talks. The Duke, then Ambassador in Paris after his successful campaign against the French in Spain and southern France, wielded immense influence. And his judgement as well as the severe economic pressures helped propel Liverpool's government towards a peace settlement at Ghent which effectively left each side where it had been before the war began. Both sides abandoned territorial ambitions. Britain renounced any claim to places like Maine, America scrapped any claim to Canada. No one mentioned the Royal Navy's outdated impressment policy that had been one of the war's main causes. The Treaty of Ghent was signed on 24 December 1814. Nothing was gained, nothing lost by either side: only the American Indians lost out. The British had been anxious to guarantee the rights of the tribes who had fought so loyally on their side. But they had little support from their Canadian subjects, and their own enthusiasm for the rights of Indians waned as the war went on and peace beckoned. The Indians were effectively ignored. The British government could heave a huge sigh of relief. Castlereagh wrote to Liverpool, 'I wish you joy at being relieved of the millstone of the American war.'

But the last tragic phase of the War of 1812 was about to be acted out – with neither of the combatants in America aware that peace had been signed. It took a month for news to cross the Atlantic, and only two weeks after the signing in Europe the armies of Britain and America faced each other just outside New Orleans. On 8 January 1815 Cochrane's much larger British force, with old comrades like Harry Smith, George Chesterton, George Gleig and James Scott now fighting under Wellington's brother-in-law, Major General Sir Edward Pakenham, threw itself against the army of

General Andrew Jackson. They were up against the ablest general in the United States. Jackson was as well entrenched as Sam Smith had been at Baltimore and his men equally motivated. Pakenham led a poorly co-ordinated attack on the American defences and what followed was a near massacre. Britain lost 700 dead including Pakenham himself, America just seven. Another 1,400 British were wounded and 500 captured. Harry Smith, who had been posted back to America after only a few weeks with his beloved Juana, described it as an 'awful disaster'. The American fire was the 'most murderous I ever beheld before or since'. New Orleans was an utterly futile waste of life: even if the British had triumphed, captured the city and plunged deep into Louisiana, they'd have had to hand every inch of it back under the peace treaty signed a fortnight earlier 5,000 miles away.

To James Madison's administration the news of Andrew Jackson's victory came like a gift from God. Dolley Madison had had a wretched autumn, much of it in tears, cursing the British and fretting for her husband's fractured reputation as a war leader mocked by most Americans. He had, after all, launched a country equipped with one of the tiniest navies into a struggle with the greatest naval power in the world. But after New Orleans the President could boast of a defeat of the British empire as conclusive as any in the whole war. It allowed Americans to banish the humiliation of Bladensburg and Washington to an obscure page of history – just as in Britain victory at Waterloo, only five months later, would eclipse the memory of New Orleans. James Madison had declared war on Britain over issues that had become irrelevant, a war that would win America no material gain and cost many lives. It was no second war of independence as some have dubbed it: Britain never intended to repossess the country it had lost thirty years earlier. But it did mark the coming of age of the United States, the birth of a new American pride and self-confidence. The raising of the star-spangled banner on 14 September 1814 became a symbol of this new determination. James Madison and his successors unashamedly abandoned their reservations about defence. They signalled their support for strong regular armed forces, and set the country on a path of expansion on land and at sea. During the next forty years the United States thrust out west from its small enclave on the Atlantic seaboard to the Pacific 3,000 miles away. This great new enterprise soon made the drive to compete with British seapower in the Atlantic seem far less important.

Madison and his wife Dolley took up residence in one of the very few fashionable properties in Washington left intact – the Octagon House, which still stands on the corner of 18th Street and New York Avenue. It was built for the wealthy Tayloe family by William Thornton, designer of the Capitol, and the Madisons did their best to revive the colourful lifestyle that had made them so popular in the White House. Both James and Dolley were in the Octagon House on 14 February 1815 when the news finally reached them from Ghent that they were officially at peace with Britain.

At eight o'clock that night Dolley Madison threw open the doors and in poured congressmen, senators and other leading citizens right across the political spectrum. An eyewitness watched Dolley Madison 'in the meridian of life and queenly beauty' presiding over the joy and splendour of the scene. 'No one could doubt, who beheld the radiance of joy which lighted up her countenance and diffused its beams around, that all uncertainty was at an end, and that the government of the country had, in very truth . . . "passed from gloom to glory".' Even the servants weren't forgotten. Dolley Madison's cousin Sally Coles rushed to the top of the basement stairs shouting 'Peace, Peace!' and the butler was ordered to serve out wine freely in the servants' hall. Paul Jennings, the Madisons' black servant, played the President's March on his violin. He recalls the major-domo, Sioussat, being 'drunk for two days', and 'such another joyful time was never seen in Washington'.

The city gradually recovered from the war. The Capitol was rebuilt after a proposal to shift the capital from Washington was narrowly defeated in Congress. James and Dolley Madison were never again to occupy the White House. It took its original designer, James Hoban, and his team three years to restore and re-whiten the walls and completely refurbish the interior.* The next President to move in was James Monroe, Madison's natural successor as President, who'd played such a leading role throughout the crisis of 1814. He took up residence in the reconstructed White House more than three years after the British had set it on fire. His wife, Elizabeth, was nowhere near as amiable and accessible as Dolley Madison had been. Under President Monroe, however, the United States, by expanding its borders and its influence in the Americas with its imperious 'Monroe Doctrine', became an increasingly important world power.

Of those Americans who had fought at Bladensburg, only Joshua Barney emerged with any credit. He had little time to enjoy being a national hero: he never really recovered from his wounds and died in 1825. William Winder, like John Armstrong, had suffered too much obloquy to have any career prospects. Remarkably he was cleared by a court of inquiry and 'commended' for having heroically 'done his duty under circumstances beyond his control'. He died ten years later. James Madison generously wrote to Winder's son in 1834, assuring him that his father had behaved 'with gallantry, activity and zeal . . . during the action'. John Pendleton Kennedy, the man who had turned up on the battlefield in dancing pumps, switched from soldiery to literature and became a popular American novelist, striking up a friendship with the British writer William Thackeray. He also flourished as a politician. He entered Congress and became Navy Secretary in 1852. Francis Scott Key returned to his law practice and became the capital's Attorney General in 1833. He never knew that one day the words he'd written at Fort McHenry would become the most famous song in the United States, its national anthem.

George Armistead continued as the commandant of Fort McHenry, but his health was not good and he died in Baltimore, a national hero, in 1818 at the age of thirty-eight. By an irony both his grandson and the grandson of Francis Scott Key were imprisoned in Fort McHenry

---

* Hoban made it all happen relatively quickly because he agreed to use wood rather than brick for many internal partitions. These were not built to last and the building had to be totally reconstructed in 1948–52.

for their southern confederate leanings in the American Civil War – when the fort became a federal prison with a fearsome reputation. Sam Smith, who more than anyone deserves the credit for saving Baltimore, remained a formidable figure in the US Congress for another nineteen years and died at the age of eighty-six in 1839.

At the end of the Madison Presidency James and Dolley retired to their beloved country estate at Montpelier. James Madison loved country pursuits; Dolley hankered after the buzz of Washington, but she made up for it by entertaining generously and she saw much of her old friend Margaret Bayard Smith. The Madisons remained devoted to each other. 'Mr Madison dearly loved and was proud of his wife,' wrote Mary Cutts, Dolley's niece. 'She was his solace and comfort, he could not bear her to leave his presence . . .' Dolley Madison was desolate after James's death in 1836 and spent her last few years in some poverty, aggravated by the selfish extravagance of her son Payne Todd. She sold Montpelier, returned to Washington and was partly supported by Paul Jennings, the old White House servant who gave her some of his savings. He remained devoted to the family, saying that James Madison was 'one of the best men who ever lived'. His devotion to Dolley in her last years is all the more remarkable for the fact that she was so broke that she had to sell him as a slave to her neighbour. When Dolley Madison finally died, aged eighty-nine, in 1849, the US President Zachary Taylor said: 'She was truly our First Lady for a half century.' James Madison is remembered as one of the greatest United States political leaders. He is admired more for his early contributions to America's constitutional development than for his Presidency, and certainly not for his role as Commander in Chief in the War of 1812. America may have emerged from the war a wiser, more self-assured nation than when it went in, but the war was ill conceived and mismanaged. And for that Madison must take much of the blame.

For Britain the bitter memories of the war with the United States soon faded. America's threat to British interests gradually gave way to much deeper concerns about Russia and then Germany. Over the rest of the century worries about American expansion and trade that had been the basis of the War of 1812 turned into a mutual interest in global security and commercial enterprise to the benefit of both sides of the Atlantic. Any pride there may have been in the heady days of 1814 at having given the Americans 'a good drubbing' by burning Washington was soon replaced by many with the thought that the action had been unworthy of a country that called itself civilised. A British traveller who witnessed the rebirth of Washington a few years later remarked that the British invaders had 'acted, perhaps, agreeably to their orders, but certainly in opposition to the feelings, judgment, and character of the British people'.

Of the admirals who'd destroyed Washington, Edward Codrington went on to command the allied navies which defeated the Ottoman Turks at Navarino in 1827 in the struggle for the liberation of Greece. Alexander Cochrane became Commander in Chief of the important west country dockyard of Plymouth. George Cockburn, to no one's surprise, had a colourful and hyperactive career on his return. After the Battle of Waterloo in June 1815 he was deputed to accompany Napoleon to exile on the island of St Helena. He pronounced Napoleon 'uncouth and disagreeable', and insisted that he should never be referred to as 'Emperor' but only as 'General Buonaparte'. Cockburn carried out his task with a relish and ruthlessness that made Napoleon describe him as 'rough, overbearing, vain, choleric and capricious . . . never consulting anybody; jealous of his authority; caring little of the manner in which he exercises it and sometimes violent without dignity . . .'. Cockburn went on to become a Tory MP and First Naval Lord at the Admiralty in 1841 at the age of sixty-nine. A right-winger by instinct, he was nevertheless an innovator, and an enthusiastic advocate of the development of the steamship. He died at eighty-two, an admiral of the fleet. One of the pallbearers at his funeral was James Scott, his former devoted ADC in the American campaign, who later became an admiral himself.

Arthur Brooke went with Pakenham to New Orleans but left for home in a fit of pique when he wasn't given command of a brigade. He thought the British government owed him more after Baltimore, and told them so: he ended up a lieutenant general but never saw any more active service. George de Lacy Evans was a lot luckier. When the government refused him the double promotion that Robert Ross had requested for him, he made a great fuss. The rank of captain, he complained to Whitehall, was 'a totally inadequate reward'. It worked: at the Battle of Waterloo just a month later he was an acting lieutenant colonel, and went on to command a division in the Crimean War with the rank of general. He also won a seat in the House of Commons and was a passionate promoter of army reform. But his forthright and intolerant personality lost him friends and weakened his influence. George Gleig, the prolific diarist, went on to write a biography of the Duke of Wellington and became chaplain general to the forces. He called for better education for the military and wrote another fifty-seven books. He died at ninety-two in 1888. Harry Smith was a great survivor too. He was to become a baronet and a lieutenant general. In 1847 Sir Harry and the wife he adored, Juana, were posted to South Africa. He was a very popular governor of the Cape, and when he and Juana left, the South Africans named a number of towns after them – including Harrismith and Ladysmith.

When Harry Smith and Juana had visited Robert Ross's wife Elizabeth back in September 1814 before the news of Baltimore had reached London, none of them knew that the husband she missed so desperately was dead. 'Poor thing!' wrote Smith later, 'at that very moment of her excessive happiness he was in a soldier's grave.' Elizabeth Ross – 'My Ly' as Robert Ross had called her – was shattered by the news of his death, which reached her in late October. Ross's body, preserved in 129 gallons of rum, wasn't taken home to Ireland: it was transported to the British colony of Nova Scotia and buried in St Paul's churchyard in Halifax, the capital. But the government honoured Ross's dying wish and provided generously for Elizabeth and her family. The Prince Regent also granted them a special privilege: they and their direct descendants would from then on be able to call themselves 'Ross of Bladensburg'. The last to bear the title, Kathleen Ross of Bladensburg, died a spinster on Christmas Day 1974.

As for the achievement of Ross's army, it was left to that great nineteenth-century chronicler of military campaigns Baron de Jomini to characterise it as an 'extraordinary' undertaking: 'The world was astonished to see a handful of seven or eight thousand Englishmen making their appearance in the midst of a state embracing ten millions of people, taking possession of the capital, and destroying all the public buildings – results unparalleled in history.' It was actually under five thousand in the midst of more than seven million, but few people would deny that what took place in those few weeks in August and September 1814 was, indeed, 'extraordinary'.

Author's Note

I was inspired to examine this remarkable story when I discovered how few people knew it had ever happened. What made me write it went way beyond that. The events themselves are astonishing enough: just as striking is the richness and abundance of eyewitness accounts on both sides. The clarity, humanity and wit of British and American men and women who were there bring the story alive as if it had happened today. I have listed in the Bibliography all those who provide the most vivid material. The Notes refer to these books and other accounts by their authors' names. Many of the sources I found readily available in the United States National Archives and the Library of Congress in Washington and in the British Library in London and the Public Record Office in Kew. Many of the older volumes are also available online, but I have always referred to the original titles for those who prefer to handle the old books themselves. I have received valuable help from a whole range of other libraries and research institutions in North America and Britain. I am grateful too to the many individuals who have pointed me towards key source material and shown me the buildings and the countryside in which the action took place.

The most notable memory I have of two detailed research visits to the United States is of the burn marks still visible on the masonry of the White House. My thanks to Bill Allman, the White House curator, for allowing me to see them. Bill also provided me with a copy of the report on the current state of the George Washington portrait which Dolley Madison had removed from the White House Dining Room. Ed Furgol guided me round the Washington Navy Yard and its treasure house of exhibits and memories of the 1812 war. Ralph Eshelman, an encyclopaedic expert on the 1814 campaign, took me on an exhaustive tour of Bladensburg battlefield and the Maryland tidewater. We explored the Patuxent River by boat and saw where Joshua Barney had tucked away his barges in St Leonard's Creek. Scott Sheads, writer and commentator on the Baltimore campaign and resident historian at Fort McHenry, gave me a thorough tour of the North Point peninsula and access to eyewitness evidence in the fort's library.

I had prompt personal help from researchers and librarians in a number of places in the US – in particular from Jeffrey Flannery, Head of Research in the Manuscripts Division in the Library of Congress, Ted O'Reilly at the New York Historical Society, John Buchtel and Scott Taylor at the Georgetown University Library, Janet Bloom at the Clements Library at the University of Michigan, David Haugaard at the Historical Society of Pennsylvania, Ann Southwell at the University of Virginia Library, Barbara Wolanin at the Capitol, Yvonne Carignan at the Washington Historical Society, Maria Downs at the White House Historical Association, Scott Scholz at the Dumbarton House Museum, David Sullivan at the Company of Military Historians, Dan Hinchen of the Massachusetts Historical Society, and Nathan Ochsner and Iris Bierlein of the Maryland Historical Society in Baltimore. I was also warmly received by Nora Hoffmann-White of the Sewell-Belmont Museum, Pauline Nathan at the Smithsonian Museum of American History, and Tom Chapman and Tiffany Cole at James and Dolley Madison's mansion at Montpelier. I am also hugely indebted to Susan Strange, my Washington researcher, who left no file unturned to dig out some more telling quotations. In Canada Peter Gubbins took me on an exhaustive tour of Fort York in Toronto.

In the UK I must thank Martin Salmon, who helped me find manuscripts at the National Maritime Museum in Greenwich, Arnold Hunt of the British Library, who helped me decipher manuscripts, Peter Duckers at the KSLI Museum in Shropshire, Matthew Sheldon, Heather Johnson and Margaret Newman at the Portsmouth

Naval Museum Library, Lucas Elkin at Cambridge University Library, Mike Dowell, archivist at the Devon Record Office, Lee Duncan of Richmond Library, Sandy Leishman of the Royal Scots Fusiliers Museum, Daniel Sherman of the Royal United Services Institute, and the staff at the Public Record Office in Northern Ireland who found me all the letters of Robert Ross. Lord Brookeborough, his wife Janet and Juliana Grose (née Brooke) were very kind in pointing me to family memories of Colonel Arthur Brooke. I am immensely grateful to Kevin Chambers of the National Archives at Kew who has lent me his massive dossier of correspondence and despatches on the British campaign including the letters of British government ministers and the Duke of Wellington. A great friend and colleague at the BBC, Andrew Green, kindly rummaged through the Newspaper Archives at Colindale for the articles in British newspapers. I owe a lot to the inspiration, valuable advice and hospitality I received from John McCavitt, the leading Irish expert on Major General Robert Ross and his family. He was most generous with his time and through him I met Steven and Jackie Campbell, descendants of Robert Ross, who have a very fine portrait of him in their hall. I am grateful too to Phil Mowat of the Ulster American Folk Park who let me handle Colonel Brooke's leather-bound diary of the American campaign. Another member of the Ross family, Lieutenant General Sir Robin Ross, has been full of ideas and advice, as has Francis Hamilton, who has a fine collection of Ross memorabilia at his lovely home at Melrose in the Scottish borders.

There is a wealth of reading available about this remarkable episode in the War of 1812, much of it still in print. Two essential primary sources are old stalwarts from the Peninsular War campaign under Wellington, Harry Smith, whose *Autobiography* is a classic of wit and acerbic commentary, and George Gleig, who wrote no fewer than three detailed accounts, his diary, his memoir *A Subaltern in America* and *The Campaigns of the British Army at Washington and New Orleans*. The last was recently republished by Leonaur under the title *Fire and Blood*. James Scott, Rear Admiral George Cockburn's ADC, provides a boisterous and sometimes exaggerated account of his boss's adventures. Cockburn himself and the other commanders, Vice Admiral Sir Alexander Cochrane, Major General Robert Ross and Colonel Arthur Brooke, left letters, diaries and despatches that give us their accounts of what happened. On the American side three women, Dolley Madison, the President's wife, and two other Washington socialites, Margaret Bayard Smith and Anna Maria Thornton, revealed their feelings throughout the crisis in their personal letters and diaries. John Pendleton Kennedy's biography has the best first-hand account of the ordinary American militiaman's story, and the US commanders at all levels in Washington and Baltimore have given us their accounts in great detail in their reports and correspondence. Much of it is usefully preserved in the Congress report on the invasion of Washington which is published online – see the Bibliography. Another valuable resource, a short-cut to much of the manuscript material on both sides, is volume 3 of *The Naval War of 1812: A Documentary History*. The words of James Madison and James Monroe are published in books of their writings and may also be found in their abundant MSS in the Library of Congress. I have corrected the spelling and punctuation in primary source material where it would simply be a distraction to leave it. Wherever the misspelling seems to me to add character or colour, I have left it.

Of the many secondary sources who have written about these events, I have listed the ones I have made use of in the Bibliography, but I would mention in particular the remarkably vivid and well-researched account by Anthony S. Pitch in *The Burning of Washington* published in 1998 and Ralph Ketcham's excellent recent biography of James Madison. The best American account of the whole War of 1812 is by Professor Donald R. Hickey of Nebraska's Wayne State College, *The War of 1812: A Forgotten Conflict*. As this book went to the printers I got a glimpse of *Through the Perilous Fight*, a lively and detailed account of the events of August–September 1814 by the *Washington Post*'s Steve Vogel.

This book would not exist but for the support and perceptive advice of both my agent, Julian Alexander, and Roland Philipps, who found time to edit the book as well as to manage John Murray, the publishers. I am again grateful to the production team who made such a success of *To War with Wellington* which was published in 2010 – Becky Walsh and Lyndsey Ng at John Murray, my painstaking cartographer Rodney Paull, my tireless picture researcher Juliet Brightmore and the best copy editor in the business, Peter James. I have had the usual backing of my talented family, my historian son Dan, author of the finest book on Wolfe's victory in Canada in 1759 and a fount of knowledge and good judgement, my mother-in-law Eluned MacMillan, my sister-in-law Margaret MacMillan, who has been busy with her own book on the causes of the First World War whose centenary coincides with the bicentenary of Britain's burning of Washington – and of course my wife Ann, journalist and managing editor of the Canadian Broadcasting Corporation in London, who has been as tireless as ever with her editorial skill and personal encouragement.

Notes and References

The authors' names refer to their alphabetical listing in the Bibliography.

I have used the following abbreviations for references used frequently:

AMT   Anna Maria Thornton, 'Diary', in Bryan, ed.

ASP   American State Papers, Military Affairs, *Capture of the City of Washington*, Report to the House of Representatives, 29 November 1814

DPM   Dolley Payne Madison

F and B   *Fire and Blood*, a book by George Gleig

LC   Library of Congress, Washington, DC

MB   Mary Barney, author of *Biographical Memoir of Joshua Barney*

MBS   Margaret Bayard Smith, letters in *Forty Years of Washington Society*

MHM   *Maryland Historical Magazine* published by the Maryland Historical Society

NA   Natioinal Archives, Kew, London

NARA   National Archives and Records Administration, Washington, DC

NMM   National Maritime Museum, Greenwich

NW   *The Naval War of 1812: A Documentary History*, vol. 3, ed. Crawford

PRONI   Public Record Office Northern Ireland

Sub   *A Subaltern in America*, a book by George Gleig

WSD   *Wellington, Supplementary Despatches*

1: Introduction

1 tasted like 'nectar': Scott, p. 304

1 'ancestors had got up to': White House transcript, 14/3/2012

1 'kind of late – but sorry!': Tony Blair, speech to Congress, 17/7/2003

Chapter 1: 17 August – Eager souls panting for fame

5 very heart of the United States: Swann to Armstrong, 17/8/1814, quoted in the *American and Commercial Daily Advertiser*, Baltimore, 20/8/1814

6 'homeless and defenceless': letter to editor of the *Virginia Patriot*, 17/8/1814

6 'Spain and Portugal': Barrett, 'Naval Recollections', p. 457

7 was George Gleig: Gleig, *Diary*, 15/8/1814

7 'good drubbing': Torrens to Murray, 14/4/1814, NA Wo3/607

8 'mere matter of marching': Jefferson to William Duane, 4/8/1812, Thomas Jefferson Papers, LC, online http://hdl.loc.gov/loc.mss/mtj. mtjbib021175. This boast soon became a classic, because the United States ended the war with not an inch of Canadian territory. As one Canadian historian remarked, 'Canadian and British historians have been dining out on that quote ever since'

8 'against the Americans': *The Times*, 15/4/1814

8 'laurels even in America': Gleig, *F and B*, p. 14

9 'heart was ready to burst': Smith, *Autobiography*, p. 182

9 'insensible and in a faint': ibid., p.188

9 'falling into his hands': Arnold, pp. 150–1

10 'temporary inconvenience': Ross to Ned Glascock, 12/3/1814, in Ross, 'Memoir', p. 413

10 'all those gloomy ideas': Ross to wife, 10/7/1814, PRONI D20041a/3/3

10 handsomely to his earnings: Ross to wife, 30/7/14, PRONI D2004/1a/3/7

10 'an Irishman': Ross to wife, 22/6/1814, PRONI D2004/1A/3/2

11 'and to human nature': Marine, p. 23

11 'each of his ears on delivery': in *Niles' Weekly Register*, 21/8/1813

11 'placed to his account': Scott, p. 114

12 'without disparagement to either': ibid., p. 165

12 'owners offered resistance': Babcock, p. 119. See also *Baltimore Patriot*, 26/8/1814, under the title 'From our own correspondent'. It

says: 'we have talked with a Mr Bayley a US mail contractor' who was in Washington and who reported, 'All private property was respected and two soldiers caught plundering received 100 lashes each'

12 'killing our own people': William Napier, *Life and Opinions*, vol. 1, pp. 224–5

12 'danced round the wreck': Chamier, vol. 2, pp. 125 and 135

13 'man under his command': Barrett, 'Naval Recollections', p. 456

13 'without one man missing': Scott, pp. 261–2

13 'you may find assailable': Cochrane to commanding officers of the North American station, 18/7/1814, *NW*, p. 140

14 Cochrane wrote to Cockburn: Cochrane to Cockburn, 1/7/1814, *NW*, p. 129

14 'completely at our mercy': Cockburn to Cochrane, 25/6/1814, *NW*, p. 116

14 'spot within the United States . . .': Cockburn to Cochrane, 17/7/1814, *NW*, p. 137

15 'don't tell the Yankees!': Codrington to wife, 3/8/1814, in Codrington, *Memoir*, abridged edn, p. 228

15 'which might be doubtful': Codrington to wife, 29/7/1814, in Codrington, *Memoir*, 1875 edn, vol. 1, p. 312

Chapter 2: 17 August – The great little Madison

17 'weak and barren country': Richard Rush to John Adams, 5/9/1814, Richard Rush Papers, LC

17 the President's House: the first newspaper to name the President's House as the White House appears to be the *Baltimore Whig* of 22/11/1810. See Freidel and Pencak, p. 23, which cites numerous examples of the use of the term 'White House' before August 1814. See also Seale, p. 157. There is also a chirpy quote in the *Federal Republican* newspaper of 10/2/1813 – sixteen months before the invasion of 1814 – which reads: 'If the despatches from France and the news from the Chesapeake and Virginia don't drive the poor little Viceroy in the White House crazy, he must be as tough as a pine knot.' It was President Theodore Roosevelt who made the name, the White House, official in 1901

18 'withered little apple-john': Irving to Brevoort, 13/1/1811, in Washington Irving, *Letters*, vol. 1, p. 23

18 'up for a funeral': Winslow Marston Watson, *In memoriam: Benjamin Ogle Tayloe*, LC Washington 1872, p. 118 http://archive.org/details/inmemoriambenjam00wats

18 'hearts of the Quaker lads': Cote, p. 259

18 'staring at thee': Cutts, p. 14

19 'the great little Madison': ibid., p. 15

19 'curl would escape': ibid.

19 'he dreams of you': Cote, p. 118

19 'a queen of hearts': ibid., p. 128

19 'partner I've ever had': Boller, p. 37

19 'support to her husband': Cutts, p. 26

19 'Mr Madison alone': Boller, p. 38

20 a crippling $4 a yard: Gerry, p. 181

20 never forgot a name: Cote, p. 321

20 'like a queen': ibid., p. 258, and MBS, p. 62

20 'pleasant word for everybody': Irving to Brevoort, 13/1/1811, in Washington Irving, *Letters*, vol. 1, p. 23

20 'mouth for him to kiss': Mrs Frances Few, Diary, 3/3/1809, Georgia Dept of Archives and History, virtual vault, ad hoc collection, p. 10

21 'an overseer to do it': Jennings, p. 15

21 'knows better than yourself': Albert Gallatin to Henry Clay, 22/4/1814, written from London, in Adams, ed., *Gallatin*, vol. 1, pp. 606–7

21 'modeling the government': *Cobbett's Weekly Register*, 7/5/1814

22 to parade her in the streets: Kent, p. 77

22 any threat Cockburn might make: DPM to Edward Coles, 13/5/1813, in Allgor, pp. 306–7

22 'determined to stay with him': DPM to Hannah Gallatin, 28/7/1814, in ibid., pp. 310–11

22 she offered her cheek: MB, p. 137

23 'all eyes will be upon you': Jones to Barney, 18/2/1814, in *NW*, p. 33

23 Barney replied: Footner, pp. 264–5

24 'with whom one cannot treat': Napoleon to Cadore, in Adams, *History*, vol. 5, p. 229

25 'not be a spot on it': Goodwin, p. 136

25 'republican party and cause': Monroe to Madison, 27/12/1813, James Madison papers, Series 2, Additional correspondence, LC

26 'magnitude of the achievement': Rush letter to Congress, 15/11/1814, in ASP, p. 541

26 'a favourite one': Madison to Armstrong, 20/5/1814, Madison Papers, LC

27 'a more prompt compliance': Boileau to Winder, 27/8/1814, in ASP, p. 551

27 on the nation's cities: Stagg, p. 412

27 'already have given his blow': Winder to Armstrong, in ASP, p. 543

27 'on the spur of the moment': Winder to Congress, in ASP, p. 552

28 'an attack by the enemy': Van Ness to Congress, in ASP, p. 580,

28 'ought to be protected . . . ?': Burr to Nourse, 5/7/1814, Nourse Family Papers, 3490-a, University of Virginia

Chapter 3: 18–19 August – Into the Patuxent

29 he found it a bearable 83: Codrington to wife, 12/8/1814, in Codrington, *Memoir*, abridged edn, p. 228

29 'tipped with foam': Gleig, *F and B*, p. 65

30 'upon opposite tacks': Chesterton, vol. 1, p. 114

30 'stalking through a wood': Smith, *Autobiography*, p. 197

30 'the cultivation so rich': Gleig, *Diary*, 18/8/1814

30 'which formed a background . . .': Gleig, *Sub*, p. 66

30 'this favoured country': Barrett, 'Naval Recollections', p. 457

31 'their blooming country': Chesterton, vol. 1, p. 115

31 'to the drum boy': Brooke, Diary, PRONI D3004

32 a half pounds of biscuit: Gleig, *Sub*, pp. 9–10

33 'and threw us a line': ibid., p. 7

33 Gleig described in 1814: ibid.

33 'occupied one of the shelves': ibid., p. 8

33 'capture of some sheep': Chesterton, vol. 1, p. 116. George Laval Chesterton – Laval was his mother's maiden name; his uncle was the French General Laval – had obtained his commission through a lucky family connection: his mother knew Spencer Percival, who'd been Prime Minister in 1812

35 'distance from the coast': Bathurst to Barnes (the government's original choice of army commander before Ross), 20/5/1814, in *NW*, p. 73

36 this to Madison himself: Skinner to Madison, 13/8/1814, in Brant, vol. 6, p. 289

36 'possible join the British': MBS, p. 90, quoting MBS to Mrs Kirkpatrick, 20/7/1813

36 'to keep them in awe': Gerry, p. 199

36 should immediately be freed: Bathurst to Barnes, 20/5/1814, in *NW*, p. 73

36 'whole of their race': Cockburn to Cochrane, 10/5/1814, in *NW*, p. 65

37 'wives and children': Scott, p. 188

37 'hurled from his throne': Cochrane to Cockburn, 1/7/1814, in *NW*, p. 129

37 'use when they had it': Lovell, *Personal Narrative*, p. 152

37 barges in Barney's flotilla: Ball, p. 467

37 destroying Barney's flotilla: Barney to Jones, 19/8/1814, NARA, RG 233, Select Committee Papers and Reports (HR13A-D15-3)

38 'your power, his progress . . .': Jones to Barney, 19/8/1814, in *NW*, pp. 186–7

38 'myself and assistants . . .' : ASP, p. 554

38 'obligations as militia men?': Winder to Armstrong, 19/8/1814, in ASP, p. 547

38 'He concurred in the opinion': Monroe, 13/11/1814, in ASP, p. 536.

38 'degree than any other': Monroe to Armstrong, 18/8/1814, in Monroe, *Writings*, p. 289

39 'preparation to repel it': Monroe to Madison, 20/8/1814, in ASP, p. 537

39 'would they do here?': Van Ness, in ASP, p. 581

39 'much more consequence': ibid.

39 'a Corporal's Guard': Armstrong to Spencer, 22/12/1814, in Skeen, p. 205

40 'captivating glitter': Tuckerman, p. 64

40 'belonging to the army': ibid., pp. 65–6

40 'glitter of a dress parade . . .': ibid., p. 71

41 'urgent business': ibid., pp. 71–3

41 'and a steady resolve': ibid., p. 75; Marine, p. 108.

41 'as a matter of laughter': Tuckerman, p. 72; Marine, p. 106

41 'semi liquid state . . .': Tuckerman, p. 74

Chapter 4: 20–22 August – A black floating mass of smoke

42 'perhaps the flotilla': Barney to Jones, 20/8/1814, in *NW*, p. 187

42 'with the utmost confidence': Jones to Barney, 20/8/1814, in *NW*, p. 188

43 'and gain intelligence': Winder, in ASP, p. 554

43 'as soon as she beheld us': Gleig, *Sub*, p. 20

43 'another hearty cheer': ibid., p. 22

44 'those engaged in it': ibid., p. 26

44 'they reached Nottingham . . .': Adams, *History*, vol. 8, p. 129

45 'as ever wore a sword': Smith, *Autobiography*, p. 193

45 'a *coup de main*': ibid., p. 197

45 army on the alert: Gleig, *Sub*, p. 32

45 'hospitable barn chatting . . .': ibid., p. 36

46 'aiming at the city . . .': Monroe to Madison, 21/8/1814, in ASP, p. 537

46 'of precautions on ours': Madison to Monroe, 21/8/1814, in Madison, *Writings*, p. 291

46 'officers and persons': Winder, in ASP, p. 555

47 'a thousand atoms': Scott, p. 277

47 'from our view': ibid., p. 278

47 'honour of his flag . . .': Barrett, 'Naval Recollections', p. 459

47 'piece of cold steel': Scott, p. 279

47 the expedition was over: Davies to mother, 31/8/1814, in Burnett, p. 224

48 'nothing of importance': Roosevelt, vol. 2, p. 47

48 'enemy a serious check . . .': ASP, p. 555

49 'attacking them in ambush': Ball, pp. 467–8

49 march on Washington: MB, pp. 263–4

49 commander in chief: ibid., p. 264. Barney's biographer refers to Winder, clearly echoing Joshua Barney's own view, as 'the commanding general – if indeed he could properly be so called'

49 'remove the records': Monroe to Madison, 22/8/1814, in ASP, p. 538

50 locked up for weeks: Pleasonton to Winder, 7/8/1848, in Hildt, ed., pp. 65–6

51 'have prevented it': Booth to Tingey, 22/8/1814, in *NW*, p. 204

51 Booth remarked: ibid.

51 'public and private': DPM to her sister, 23/8/1814, in Mattern and Shulman, eds, p. 193, and Seale, pp. 228–9

52 Ross's British veterans: Gen. Williamson, quoted in John S. Williams, *History*, pp. 175–6

52 'with my shoes on': ibid., p. 175

52 'fortune to gaze': Gleig, *Sub*, p. 41

52 'bottle of peach whisky': ibid., p. 45

52 'promise of neutrality . . .': Evans, 'Memorandum of operations on the shores of the Chesapeake in 1814', National Library of Scotland, Edinburgh, p. 6

53 remarked Gleig: Gleig, *Sub*, p. 46

Chapter 5: 23 August – Not till I see Mr Madison safe

55 'we captured': Cockburn to Cochrane, 22/8/1814, in *NW*, p. 196

56 'characteristic zeal': Evans, *Facts*, p. 12

56 'Upper Marlborough': Cockburn to Cochrane, 22/8/1814, in *NW*, p. 196.

56 'get back the better . . .': Cochrane to Cockburn, 22/8/1814, in *NW*, p. 197

56 read it till 24 August: Evans, *Facts*, p. 3

56 'we gave three cheers': Davies to mother, 31/8/1814, in Burnett, p. 224

57 'favourable bias': Evans, *Facts*, p. 12

57 'on the city of Washington': Cockburn to Cochrane, 27/8/1814, in *NW*, p. 220. Cockburn wrote this letter four days after the successful raid on Washington – by which time he knew that Cochrane, far from expressing disapproval, would be keen to claim his share in running it

57 'marines and seamen': Evans, 'Memorandum', 23/8/1814, p. 7

57 'upon the capital': Scott, p. 280

57 'confidence and discipline . . .': Evans, 'Memorandum', p. 7

58 'return to the shipping . . .': Gleig, *F and B*, p. 77

58 'serious consequences . . .': ibid., p. 79

58 'was to effect it': Gleig, *Sub*, pp. 46–7

58 'consultations and calls . . .': Winder, in ASP, p. 555
59 'life and reputation': McLane, pp. 234–5
60 'devoted husband M.': Madison, *Writings*, pp. 293–4
60 'faithful in their duty': MB, p. 264
61 'assail us by daylight': Smith, in ASP, p. 564
61 'a serious check': Winder, in ASP, p. 555
61 'of comfortable living': Smith, in ASP, p. 564
62 'Bladensburg and the city': Stansbury, in ASP, p. 561
62 'my [dancing] pumps': Marine, pp. 110–11
62 'saved Washington': ibid., p. 108
63 'stalks around us': DPM to sister, 23/8/1814, in Cutts, p. 193
64 'security and peace': MBS to her sister Mrs Kirkpatrick, 25/8/1814, in MBS, pp. 98–100
64 'coachmen absent . . .': Mrs Jones to DPM, 23/8/1814, in Clark, pp. 162–3
65 'salute, melted away': Gleig, *Sub*, pp. 52–8, and Gleig, *Diary*, 23/8/1814
65 'his sanguine advice': Malcolm to wife, 2/9/1814, Poultney Malcolm Papers, Clements Library, University of Michigan
65 'was too rash': Scott, p. 280
66 'to return immediately': ibid., pp. 281–2

Chapter 6: 24 August, morning – Be it so, we will proceed

67 runs his account: Scott, p. 282
68 'We must go on': ibid., p. 283
68 'we will proceed': Scott, pp. 283–4
68 'not hesitate to disregard': Evans, 'Memorandum', 24/8/1814
68 'gallant band': Scott, p. 284
69 'the consequences of failure': Ross to wife, 1/9/1814, PRONI, Ross Papers, MS 1a/3/8
70 'to be 13,000 strong': King, pp. 438–9
71 stay alert all night: Burch to Congress, in ASP, p. 574
71 'way to the Navy Yard': Winder to Congress, in ASP, p. 557
71 'his march into the city': ibid.

72 'General Winder's force . . .': ibid., p. 561

72 'marched off their legs': AMT diary, 23/8/1814, p. 174

73 'before they could be obtained . . .': Minor to Congress, in ASP, p. 569

73 finally turned up: Madison memorandum, in Madison, *Writings*, p. 295

74 advise his commanders?: Campbell to Congress, in ASP, p. 598

74 'from the Executive': Madison memorandum, 24/8/1814, in Madison, *Writings*, p. 296

74 'or from the government': Armstrong to Congress, in ASP, p. 539

74 'latter would be beaten': Rush to Congress, in ASP, p. 542

75 'his advice or opinions . . .': Madison memorandum, in Madison, *Writings*, p. 296

75 by Madison and Richard Rush: ibid.

75 'beaming upon my face': Tuckerman, p. 79; and in Marine, p. 112

76 'be properly so called': MB, p. 264

76 enemy crossing the bridge: ibid.

76 'corporal and six men': Armstrong to Congress, in ASP, p. 540

77 'into the brushwood . . .': Scott, pp. 284–5

77 'gaily and rapidly': Gleig, *Sub*, p. 63

77 'inability to keep up': Gleig, *F and B*, p. 82

77 'head hit the ground . . .': Gleig, *Sub*, p. 65

77 'unable to go on': Gleig, *F and B*, p. 84

77 'and commanding attitude': ibid., pp. 84–5

78 'to occupy Washington': Gleig, *Sub*, p. 67

78 'agricultural occupations': ibid.

79 'now in Bladensburg': Simmons to Congress, in ASP, pp. 596–7

80 to come back for it: Simmons to Congress, in ASP, p. 596

80 'as circumstances admitted': Madison memorandum, in Madison, *Writings*, p. 297

80 'encourage the resistance': Rush to Williams, 10/7/1855, in John S. Williams, *History*, p. 279

80 'spectator of the combat': Armstrong to Congress, in ASP, p. 539

81 'of fear and trembling': letter from 'a citizen of Washington', *Federal Republican*, 17/9/1814

81 'strangers were expected': Jennings, p. 8

Chapter 7: 24 August, afternoon – Bladensburg: a fine scamper

82 'this glittering army': Kennedy, in Marine, p. 106

82 'I never could learn': Stansbury to Congress, in ASP, p. 562

84 'this is not my plan': Sterett to Congress, in ASP, p. 568

84 'blundering tactician': Armstrong, *Notices*, vol. 2, p. 148

85 'did not interfere': Stansbury to Congress, in ASP, p. 561

85 'must be repulsed': Smith, *Autobiography*, pp. 198–9

86 'people at a funeral': Gleig, *Sub*, p. 68

86 'was swept down': Gleig, *F and B*, p. 87

86 'across his countenance': Gleig, *Sub*, p. 70

86 'gall us with their fire': ibid., p. 71

87 'in an instant': ibid., p. 73

87 'major or a dead captain': Captain Knox letter, 23/11/1814, in Barrett, *85th KLI*, p. 153

87 'woodpeckers and bullfrogs . . .': Skinner letter to *Baltimore Patriot*, 23/5/1849

87 'fire ill-directed': Smith, *Autobiography*, p. 199

87 'with their appearance': Furlong diary in Buchan, p. 170

87 and unnecessary risk: Ross is roundly criticised by Fortescue, vol. 10, pp. 144–5

88 'in full to the enemy!': Smith, *Autobiography*, p. 199

88 'of the stream': Gleig, *F and B*, p. 87

88 'confusion whatever . . .': Fulford's account in Marine, p. 114

88 'wait a wee, wie your skirling': Scott, p. 286

88 'Rear Admiral . . .': ibid.

89 'his round shot': ibid., p. 288

89 'exclaimed, "excellent!"': ibid., p. 289

89 'to the other world': ibid.

90 'which it was supported': Pinkney to Congress, in ASP, p. 573

90 'as I myself did': ibid.

90 'in the enemy's ranks': ibid.

90 'prisoners or cut to pieces': ibid., p. 573

91 'possible use of their legs': Bluett Diary, p. 32, Royal Naval Museum, Portsmouth

91 'handkerchief round it': Captain Bowlby account, National Army Museum
91 'were fruitless': Stansbury to Congress, in ASP, p. 562
91 'and personal bravery': ibid.
91 'precipitation and disorder': Winder to Congress, in ASP, p. 558
92 'absolute and total disorder': ibid.
92 'broken by a bullet': Kennedy, in Marine, p. 112
92 'which it was to be effected': Lavall to Congress, in ASP, p. 570
92 'open and scattered order': Johnson, in ASP, p. 529
92 'madness and bravery': Lavall to Congress, in ASP, pp. 570–1
93 'journeymen mechanics': John S. Williams, *History*, pp. 102–3

Chapter 8: 24 August, afternoon – Barney's last stand

95 'apparently in much disorder': Barney to Jones, 29/8/1814, in *NW*, p. 207
96 'by their guns first': Jennings, pp. 7–8
96 'worn-out soldiers': Ball, p. 468
96 'completely cleared the road': Barney to Jones, 29/8/1814, in *NW*, p. 207
97 'cutting the sinues [sic]': Burnett, pp. 224–5
97 'a mower's scythe': *Niles' Weekly Register*, 27/8/1814
97 'totally cut up': Barney to Jones, 29/8/1814, in *NW*, p. 207
97 'saw on horseback': Ball, p. 468
97 'loading and firing . . .': Gleig, *Sub*, p. 75
97 'rallying the men': ibid.
97 'command issued': ibid., p. 95
98 'fuses still in their hands . . .': Gleig, *F and B*, p. 89
98 'like sheep chased by dogs': Ball, p. 468. Charles Ball's life provides a revealing commentary on the attitudes of American slaves at this time. In the 1812 war he was one of many blacks who preferred to remain loyal to the American republic in spite of his extraordinary experiences in attempting to escape from slavery. He'd run away from a southern plantation before the war and after his service with Barney during the war he worked on as a free man in Maryland with his wife and family. In 1830 his past caught up with him: a slave-owner from Georgia

reclaimed him and forced him back to work in the south. Ball again escaped, but when he finally made his way back to Maryland he found his wife and family had been sold as slaves. He never saw them again. It wasn't till the 1860s that America's slaves were emancipated by Abraham Lincoln (Ball, passim)

98 'enemy pressed them': McKenney, p. 363
99 'loss of blood': MB, p. 266
99 'pick up my hat': Webster, in Marine, p. 178
99 'attendance of a surgeon': MB, p. 267
100 'want to be conveyed?': ibid.
100 'wouldn't have done that!': ibid., p. 268
100 'like a child': ibid.
100 they wouldn't accept it: Weller, p. 146
101 'desperate as necessary . . .': Winder to Congress, in ASP, p. 559
101 'was insupportable': Smith to Congress, in ASP, p. 565
101 'superior authority': ibid.
101 'denied the opportunity': Williams, *History*, p. 238
102 '50 or 60 wounded': Winder to Congress, in ASP, p. 548
102 'to make prisoners': Codrington, *Memoir*, abridged edn, p. 231
102 'they are not soldiers . . .': Gleig, *F and B*, p. 110
102 British crossing the bridge: Winder to Congress, in ASP, p. 559
103 'the art of war': McKenney, p. 368
103 And so on: privately printed pamphlet in 1816, special collections, University of Virginia, quoted in full in Seale, pp. 240–5

Chapter 9: 24 August, evening – Save that painting!

104 'heat and fatigue': MBS, p. 113
104 'cities of the ancient world': Ewell, p. 56
104 'Washington? No never!': ibid., p. 58
105 'that all was lost': ibid., p. 61
106 'ruffians are at hand!': ibid.
106 'shrieking by her side': ibid.
106 used a single one: ibid., pp. 64–5
106 'mourned for my country': DPM to sister, probably Lucy, 24/8/1814, in Mattern and Shulman, eds, p. 193. This letter, though dated 24

August 1814, appears to have been compiled by DPM from memory later: she may have embellished it with hindsight

106 '[you are] going to do . . .': Anna Cutts to DPM, 23/8/1814, in ibid., p. 194

107 'husband and his friends': DPM to sister, probably Lucy, 24/8/1814, in ibid., p. 193

107 'but I wait for him': ibid.

108 'Washington is secured . . .': ibid.

108 canvas had been cut: The White House curator Betty C. Monkman typed a note dated 25 September 1978 and attached it to a report on the thorough examination of the painting that was made in the 1970s. It said: 'According to Marion Mecklenburg, the conservator, there is no evidence that the canvas of the Washington portrait was ever cut to remove it from its frame nor is there any evidence that the painting was removed from its stretcher and rolled . . . The only damage to the painting which had occurred over the years was due to environmental reasons or the glues used by various restorers. There is no evidence of mechanical damage to the portrait' (email to author from White House curator William Allman, 9/4/2012)

109 by Dolley Madison: AMT, pp. 174–5

110 'and retire in your gig': Jones memorandum, 24/8/1814, in NW, p. 215

110 Tingey recalled: Tingey to Jones, 27/8/1814, in NW, p. 215

110 'apparently panic-struck': Booth to Tingey, NA, RG 45 PC 30 entry 350; also carried in full in Irwin, pp. 9–27

111 'followed me': ibid.

111 'of destroying it': Smith, *Autobiography*, p. 200.

111 'it under contribution': Gleig, *F and B*, p. 91

112 killed and three wounded: King, p. 447, quoting Chester Bailey in the Philadelphian newspaper *Poulson's Advertiser*

112 'towards the President's palace': Scott, p. 298

112 'connected with government': Gleig, *F and B*, p. 92

112 the Americans paid compensation: Cochrane to Monroe, NA ADM 1/506 18/8/1814, disc 596

113 Americans escaped: Gleig, *F and B*, p. 92; Scott, p. 299

113 'by order of Cockburn': Davies to mother, 31/8/1814, in Burnett, pp. 223–5. Davies also claimed that the US shots from the house killed a corporal and wounded a private soldier

Chapter 10: 24 August, evening –
The barbarous purpose

114 'destruction of the property': Tingey to Congress, in ASP, p. 578
114 'irretrievable conflagration': ibid.
115 'inextinguishable fire': ibid.
115 'palsied my faculties . . .': Booth, in NW, p. 213
116 'ignorant of architecture': Latrobe letter to Mazzei, 29/5/1806, quoted in Pitch, p. 105
116 'spread for flight': Latrobe letter to the Editor of the National Intelligencer, 30/11/1807
116 'peculiar to our country': ibid.
116 'monarchical splendor': Scott, p. 300
116 'the young nation': ibid., p. 301
117 'carried unanimously': Ingersoll, vol. 2, p. 185; Cutts, p. 104
117 'Governor of Bermuda': Pack, pp. 17–18
118 'or more sublime': Gleig, F and B, pp. 93–4
118 'have been spared': ibid., p. 93
118 'destroying the city . . .': Smith, Autobiography, p. 200
118 'with a dismal gloom': Ewell, p. 65
119 'perfect gentlemen': ibid., p. 66
119 'sentinel to guard it': ibid.
120 'house immediately': ibid., p. 67
120 'domestic relations': ibid.
120 'flame of former friendship': ibid., p. 68
121 'property we knew not': Hunter, 'Diary', p. 81
121 'such a horrid scene': ibid., p. 81
121 be burned down: ibid.
121 'the city and ourselves': ibid., p. 82
122 'ever committed': ibid.
122 'was that night': ibid
122 'I'll put him to death': William Gardner letter to Federal Republican, 16/9/1814
122 'ought to manifest': Seale, pp. 326–7
123 'faithfully and successfully': Seaton, p. 118
123 lashed or shot: William Gardner letter to Federal Republican, 16/9/1814
123 'property will be respected': ibid.

123 'taken good care of': ibid.
123 'spent in fright': Ingersoll, vol. 2, p. 186
124 who'd come back later: ibid.

Chapter 11: 24 August, night – The dreadful majesty of the flames

125 'of the United States': Brooke, Diary
125 'pleased to select . . .': McLane, p. 21
125 'mortifying to dwell on': ibid.
127 wrote James Scott: Scott, p. 303
127 'immediate use . . .': Gleig, *F and B*, p. 95
127 'some very good wine also': Smith, *Autobiography*, p. 200
127 'down with Madison': Martha Peter to Timothy Pickering, 28/8/1814, Pickering Papers, microfilm edition, reel 15, Massachusetts Historical Society
127 'having taken to his heels . . .': Ross letter home quoted in Smyth, vol. 1, p. 325
128 'I must give to the flames': MBS, p. 111, letter of 30/8/1814
128 remind him of 'her seat': ibid., pp. 112–3, refers to Cockburn 'adding pleasantries too vulgar for me to repeat'. She was describing the scene at third hand. She says she heard the news from Anna Maria Thornton, who presumably had been briefed by the unfortunate Mr Weightman afterwards
128 'draught in the banqueting room': Scott, p. 304
128 'exhibit her in London': P. Morris to A. Morris, 14/9/1814, Dumbarton House collection, Washington DC, and Gerry, p. 180
128 among the family treasures: *Morning Post*, 5/10/1814; *Aberdeen Journal*, 9/10/1861, p. 8
128 'inexhaustible source': Chesterton, vol. 1, p. 132
129 wrap up in the tablecloth: *Morning Post*, 5/10/1814
129 'was there in person': the French Ambassador Louis Serrurier to French Foreign Minister Talleyrand, 27/8/1814, in Tucker, p. 565. The French Bourbon monarchy in the person of Louis XVIII had been restored to the throne after Napoleon's abdication in the spring of 1814
130 wrote Harry Smith: Smith, *Autobiography*, p. 200

130 'wrapt in flames and smoke': Margaret Bayard Smith, letter of 30/8/1814, p. 111

130 to his government: ibid.

130 'wrapt in one entire flame': William Gardner letter to *Federal Republican*, 16/9/1814

130 'President's house': Smith, *Autobiography*, p. 200

131 'buildings demolished': Furlong diary, in Buchan, p. 171

131 'indiscriminate plunder': Barrett, 'Naval Recollections', p. 459

131 'with a barbarian character': Chesterton, vol. 1, p. 129

131 has remained ever since: Seale, p. 207

132 before fleeing the city: McElroy, Papers and recollections, Georgetown University Library, Special Collections Research Center

132 'possible suffocation': Scott, p. 305

132 'an Irish renegade': ibid., p. 306

133 he said gleefully: Ingersoll, vol. 2, p. 189

133 'a traitorous proprietor': Scott, p. 308

133 'same compliment': ibid., p. 212

133 'England for a curiosity': J. W. Taylor to Mrs Taylor, 8/10/1814, in Dangerfield, p. 5

133 'publicly offered': Scott, p. 308

133 'better than expected': *Niles' Weekly Register*, 27/8/1814

133 'profited of the general distress': *National Intelligencer*, 13/9/1814

134 'sailors and marines': MBS, p. 112

134 'were paid for': ibid.

134 'than Jemmy did!': ibid.

134 'the prejudices that existed': ibid., p. 113

Chapter 12: 25 August – Damn you! You shan't stay in my house

135 'in the dark horizon': Rush to Williams, 10/7/1855, in Williams, *History*, p. 274

136 'smouldering city': Ingersoll, vol. 2, p. 207

136 as them, they said: ibid., p. 208

136 'so get out!': Jennings, p. 11

136 'their misfortune': Madison, *Writings*, p. 298n

137 'gave him immediate relief': Ewell, p. 68. There is some disagreement among diarists and historians about the exact sequence of events overnight on 24 August and on the following day. There is no doubt about what happened. The precise timetable is disputed: I have given my best estimate of it

137 'shall not pass unnoticed': Ewell, p. 69

138 'certainly have been saved': ibid., p. 70

138 'consanguinity and interest': Ingersoll, vol. 2, p. 190

138 'got to your city': Ewell, p. 70

138 'time he was in Washington': ibid., p. 71

138 'Cockburn! Impossible!': ibid., p. 72

138 'altogether private property': ibid., p. 74

139 'smouldering rubble': Scott, pp. 311–12

140 lay there for hours: Ingersoll, vol. 2, p. 188

140 him a doctor: Scott, pp. 320–1

141 'all the models': Dr Thornton letter to *National Intelligencer*, 7/9/1814

141 'invaders of the country': ibid.

141 'enlightened nations': Dr Thornton letter to *National Intelligencer*, 30/8/1814

141 'injure private property': AMT, pp. 175–6

142 'of very intelligent mind': William Gardner letter to *Federal Republican*, 16/9/1814

142 'same day and shot': ibid.

142 identify her attacker: Ewell, p. 75

143 with the enemy: APS, p. 590

143 'of their city . . .': Ewell, pp. 72–3

143 'allowed a fair price': ibid., p. 73

144 'horribly mangled': ibid., p. 78; Scott, p. 312; Ingersoll, vol. 2, p. 189. Scott says that twelve died and more than thirty were wounded

144 'thrown up by the explosion': Williams, *History*, p. 269

144 'which I shall never forget': Ewell, p. 78

144 'the ground beneath': Moore, pp. 102–3

144 'sun had long set': Gleig, *F and B*, p. 99

145 'their beam ends': Smith, *Autobiography*, p. 203

145 'vast sheet of foam': Barrett, 'Naval Recollections', p. 460

146 'to justify the attempt': Evans, 'Memorandum', pp. 13–14

146 'great loss or difficulty': Cockburn journal, COC 11 MS pp. 136–7, NMM

147 'they do we are gone': David Winchester to Gen. James Winchester, 25/8/1814, box 2, folder 7, James Winchester Papers, Tennessee Historical Society, Nashville

147 'ventured to propose': Evans, 'Memorandum', p. 14

147 'suffered to pass unheeded': Scott, p. 327

147 under another commander: Smith, *Autobiography*, p. 201

Chapter 13: 26–27 August – Into the Potomac

148 'take the same resolution': Madison to wife, 27/8/1814, in Madison, *Writings*, p. 300

148 'taken place, not dispirited': MBS, p. 107

148 'you ever beheld': Rush to Charles Ingersoll, 8/9/1815, in Howard, p. 211

149 'smouldering ruins . . .': MBS, p. 209

149 'blackened wall remained': ibid.

149 'nothing but ashes': ibid., pp. 209–10

149 'had most dread of': ibid., pp. 11–19

152 'no pilots could be procured': Elers Napier, *Life and Correspondence*, vol. 1, p. 76

153 'evacuating the town': ibid., p. 78

153 'banks of the river': ibid.

153 'only apprehension': ibid.

154 'by main strength': Gordon to Cochrane, 9/9/1814, in *NW*, p. 238

154 'defence of the place': Dyson to Armstrong, 29/8/1814, in ASP, p. 591

Chapter 14: 28–29 August – A tempest of dissatisfaction

156 'of all the shipping': terms delivered 29/8/1814, in ASP, p. 591

157 'cruel and unfounded': R. I. Taylor to Congress, 20/11/1814, in ASP, p. 593

157 'been our misfortune': letter to Congress, in ASP, pp. 593–4

157 'their person or houses': Charles to Nancy Simms, 3/9/1814, in *NW*, p. 246

157 'and he went off': ibid., p. 247

157 'the town in a blaze': Elers Napier, *Life and Correspondence*, vol. 1, p. 83

158 'plunder and destroy': AMT, p. 177

158 'spirit animate our people . . .': MBS, p. 115

158 'torn to pieces': ibid.

158 'as we expected . . .': ibid., pp. 114–15

158 'your present quarters': Clark, p. 172

159 'disgraced administration': MHM special edition, vol. 1, spring 2012, p. 120

159 'completely panic struck': *Federal Republican*, 2/9/1814

159 'an imbecile administration': *Portsmouth Oracle*, 3/9/1814

159 'our bleeding country': *Virginia Gazette*, in Lord, p. 215

159 'its best parts in ashes': Richard Rush to John Adams, 5/9/1814, in Powell, p. 52

159 'with great fever': Monroe to Winder, 21/9/1814, in Howard, p. 226

159 Anna Maria Thornton: AMT, p. 177

160 'friend or foe': *New York Evening Post*, 29/8/1814. See http://www.newsinhistory.com/content/document/v2:10945d65c96b4140@newsinhistory-1098f8943260b698-1098f894a54a66e8-1098f89568589918/

160 'a coward and a fool': Fearon, p. 286

160 'of all classes of people': Jones to Rodgers, 29/8/1814, in *NW*, p. 243

160 height of the crisis: Monroe memorandum, in Monroe, *Writings*, p. 374: 'He [meaning Monroe] forbade the measure.' But note that in the original text of this memo the words are 'The President forbade the measure.' See Howard, p. 333 n. 13

160 'that air of unyielding determination . . .': Margaret Bayard Smith, *What is Gentility?*, Washington, DC, Pishey Thompson, 1828, p. 154 (a novel about Madison)

161 'speak without tears': MBS, p. 110

161 'bottomless pit': AMT, p. 178

161 to such terms: ibid.

161 the President's call to arms: ibid., p. 177

161 'wishes of the government': Dr Thornton letter to *National Intelligencer*, 7/9/1814

162 'were disposed to hang him': Stagg, p. 420, quoting William Williams to James Barbour, 28/8/1814

162 'member of the cabinet': McKenney, p. 46

162 'anything to do with them': Madison, *Writings*, p. 301

162 giving no more orders: McKenney, p. 47. Madison's words, according to McKenney, were: 'Say to General Smith, the contingency – namely, that of any future orders being given by General Armstrong – shall not happen'

162 'the enemy at Alexandria': Madison memorandum, 29/8/1814, in Madison, *Writings*, pp. 300ff

163 'and in proper time': ibid., p. 302

163 'forward by myself': ibid., p. 303

163 'on a visit to his family . . .': ibid., p. 304

163 'destructive of order . . .': *Baltimore Patriot*, 3/9/1814, reprinted in *Niles' Weekly Register*, vol. 7, p. 6

163 the defeat at Bladensburg: Armstrong, *Exposition*, p. 11

163 'longer connect myself': Armstrong to Spencer, 3/9/1814, MSS Dept, New York Historical Society

Chapter 15: End of August – Do not attack Baltimore!

165 'height of military glory . . .': Gleig, *F and B*, pp. 106–7

165 'air was horrible': ibid., p. 103

166 'attentively to their prisoners': ibid., p. 104

166 'in forgetfulness': Scott, p. 325

167 demanded a drink: Delaplaine, p. 148

167 his two house guests: Evans, 'Memorandum', p. 14

167 'gleamed a meteor of war . . .': Delaplaine, p. 41

168 the south of France: Skinner letter to *Baltimore Patriot*, 23/5/1840

168 'wounded have been treated': Ross to Mason, 7/9/1814, in Delaplaine, p. 157

169 proper military conduct: Chesterton, vol. 1, pp. 135ff

169 'war-girt coast': ibid., p. 135

169 'Americans were abroad': ibid., p. 136

169 'free with his stock': ibid.

169 the terrified wife: ibid., pp. 137–8

169 'national enmities': ibid., p. 139

170 allowed ashore: Codrington orders of 25/8 and 3/9/1814, in *NW*, pp. 230–1

170 'the parties could bear': Codrington order of 25/8/1814, in *NW*, p. 230

171 'words to express': Gordon to Cochrane, 9/9/1814, in *NW*, p. 238

171 'capture of Washington': Codrington diary of 10/9/1814, in Codrington, *Memoir*, abridged edn, p. 233

171 'the Captains and crews . . .': Roosevelt, vol. 2, p. 47

171 'and good fortune': Armstrong, *Notices*, vol. 2, p. 133

171 'city of Washington': Ross to Bathurst, 30/8/1814, in *NW*, p. 323

171 'numerous population . . .': Cochrane to Croker, 2/9/1814, in *NW*, p. 226

172 'the capital unprotected': Ross to Maria Suter, 2/9/1814, PRONI 1A/3/9, and to wife, 1/9/1814, PRONI 1A/3/8

172 'never again to separate': Ross to wife, 1/9/1814, PRONI 1A/3/8

172 'soldier,' wrote Smith: Smith, *Autobiography*, pp. 104 and 107

173 'simple statement of facts': ibid., p. 206

173 achieved at Washington: ibid.

173 'previous discomfiture': ibid., pp. 206–7

173 'what I have stated': ibid., p. 207

Chapter 16: End of August – Is my wife alive and well?

175 'Is she well?': Smith, *Autobiography*, p. 211

175 'scenes of our lives': ibid., p. 212

175 when she was grieving: ibid., p. 213

176 'nor will I now': ibid.

176 news he had brought: ibid., p. 215

176 'officer's promotion': ibid.

176 'He is my brother': ibid., p. 216

177 'put to flight': *The Times*, 28/9/1814

177 'transatlantic imitator': *Morning Post*, 28/9/1814

177 'capital of America': Williams, *History*, p. 255

178 'glorious on the victors': *Liverpool Mercury*, 28/10/1814

178 'the continent of Europe': *The Annual Register 1814*, vol. 56, pp. 184–5

178 against the burning of Washington: *The Times*, 14/10/1814, and Longford, p. 379

178 what had we gained?: Whitbread, 8/11/1814, Hansard, House of Commons, vol. 29, cols 46–7

178 'them on this unnatural war . . .': Liverpool to Cochrane, 28/9/1814, Cochrane Papers 2574

178 'experienced at Washington . . .': Bathurst to Ross, 29/9/1814, NA WO6/2 Downing Street

179 'from the United States': Bathurst to Ross, 28/9/1814, NA WO6/2, read in conjunction with Bathurst to Ross, 6/9/1814 WO6/2

180 'peculiar to Spain': Smith, *Autobiography*, pp. 217–19

180 'under her husband': ibid., p. 217

180 'was awfully overcome': ibid., p. 223

180 by the end of 1814: Arthur, p. 241, table 16

180 of its pre-war level: ibid., p. 242, table 17

181 'the American people': Greville, Hansard, House of Lords, 8/11/1814, col. 15

Chapter 17: 1–11 September – The star-shaped fort and its banner

182 'my near relatives': Cochrane to Lord Melville, 3/9/1814, in *NW*, p. 269

182 without reinforcement: Cochrane's first letter after the sack of Washington, written to Lord Bathurst on 28/8/1814 (NA WO1/141), ruled out any immediate attack on Baltimore. 'Our present force is not adequate to the attempt without inviting more risk than it would be prudent to do'

183 'attended all our efforts': Cochrane to Melville, in *NW*, p. 270

184 'the attack of that place': Evans, 'Memorandum', p. 19

184 'insured by postponement': Codrington letter, 10/9/1814, in Codrington, *Memoir*, abridged edn, p. 234

184 'surrounding country': Scott, pp. 331–2

184 'bull by the horns': ibid., p. 332

185 'bread out of my mouth': ibid., p. 326

185 'likelihood die soon . . .': Wallace, pp. 145–6

185 wrote one Baltimorean: Capt. James Piper, in 'The Defense of Baltimore', p. 104

185 'we are gone': David Winchester to his brother James Winchester, 25/8/1814, Winchester Papers, box 2, folder 2

187 'killed in one day!': see the website of the American Revolution Round Table, http://samson.kean.edu/~leew/arrt/heroes/samsmith.html

187 'a few strokes of the axe': Smith to Armstrong, 18/3/1813, in Sheads, 'Two Sidelights', p. 253

187 'the defence of such a post?': Smith to Armstrong, 21/3/1814, in ibid.

188 'the man that skulks . . .': Robert Henderson in the *American and Commercial Daily Advertiser*, 20/7/1814, in Sheads, *Guardian*, p. 25

189 'call,' replied Smith: Samuel Smith Papers, MSS 18974, reel 5, cont. 7–8, LC, quoted on the Baltimore militia website http://maryland1812.wordpress.com/category/maryland-militia/

189 'been selected': Winder to Smith, 26/8/1814, in Robinson, 'Controversy over the Command at Baltimore in the War of 1812', p. 179

189 was assuming command: Smith to Winder, 26/8/1814, in ibid., p. 179

189 to be Sam Smith: Monroe to Winder, 11/9/1814, in ibid., p. 193

190 'produce disunion': minutes of the Committee of Vigilance and Safety, in Hoyt, pp. 199–224

190 'tents or camp kettles': Smith to Monroe, 3/9/1814, Smith Papers

190 'number to this post': Smith to governing general in Philadelphia, 5/9/1814, Smith Papers

191 'different from what you are . . .': Minerva Rodgers to John Rodgers, 25/8/1814, Rodgers-Macomb Papers, LC

191 'in the common cause': George Douglas to Henry Wheaton, in Sheads, *Guardian*, pp. 60–1

192 'little confidence of our success': Nicholson to Mrs Albert Gallatin, 4/9/1814, New York Historical Society, Albert Gallatin Manuscript 238

192 'for a gallant defence': Isaac Munroe, *Yankee Newspaper*, 30/9/1814, in Sheads, 'Yankee Doodle Played', p. 381

Chapter 18: 12 September – Many heads will be broken tonight

193 noted in his ship's log: Cockburn ship's log, COC 11, pp. 136–7, NMM

193 'assistance within my power': Cockburn to Cochrane, 15/9/1814, in *NW*, p. 279

193 'without intermission': Gleig, *Sub*, p. 107

194 'was before us': ibid., p. 108

194 'moment might bring forth': ibid., p. 114

194 'and 12 by water': Codrington, *Memoir*, abridged edn, p. 234

195 'to the exhaustion': Lovell, *Personal Narrative*, p. 162

195 'across the channel': Gleig, *Sub*, p. 108

195 'ship off if necessary . . .': Barrett, 'Naval Recollections', p. 462

195 'the process': ibid., p. 463

196 'all the Yankees': Codrington, *Memoir*, abridged edn, p. 234

196 'expel the invader': Madison, *Writings*, p. 305

196 'invincibles shall be beaten': *Niles' Weekly Register*, 10/9/1814, p. 8

196 'proper use of it': George Douglass to Henry Wheaton, in Sheads, *Guardian*, p. 69

197 'tonight – or hell': Hawkins, p. 9

197 'to be desirable': Gleig, *Sub*, p. 117. There are a number of inconsistencies in Gleig's different accounts of this and other episodes. His claims to have been present at some of these actions should be taken with some scepticism.

198 'if it rains militia': Marine, p. 150

199 'in taking aim . . .': ibid., p. 122

199 'pierced his side': ibid.

199 reload their weapons: see Jenkins, p. 362

199 'fallen to the ground': Gleig, *Sub*, p. 123

199 'loudly for a surgeon': Gleig, *F and B*, p. 123

200 'dearer to him than life . . .': Cockburn to Cochrane, 15/9/1814, in *NW*, p. 280

200 'avail to no good purpose': Skinner letter in *Baltimore Patriot*, 23/5/1849

200 in the Union Jack: Lovell, *Personal Narrative*, p. 163

200 'wife and family . . .': Crofton to Glascock, 7/8/1815, Ross Papers, PRONI

200 'all her earthly bliss!': Codrington to wife, 13/9/1814, in Codrington, *Memoir*, abridged edn, p. 234

200 'concealed from the troops': Evans, 'Memorandum', p. 21

200 'by the army': Scott, p. 336

201 'Ross had obtained it': Gleig, *Sub*, p. 123

201 'man in the army': Cpl Brown, 21st Fusiliers Diary, Museum of Royal Scots Fusiliers, Edinburgh
201 'give vent to their tears': Chesterton, vol. 1, p. 145
202 'guide an army': Gleig, *F and B*, p. 124
202 'strongly posted': Brooke, Diary

Chapter 19: 12 September – The Battle of North Point

203 'about twelve thousand men': Brooke, Diary
203 'came within range': Gleig, *F and B*, p. 125
205 'in that quarter': Stricker to Smith, in Marine, p. 163
205 'intensely hot': Piper, in 'The Defense of Baltimore', p. 106
205 'gaps in the line': Gleig, *F and B*, p. 127
205 'took to his heels': ibid., p. 129
206 'you'll have it directly': Scott, p. 337
206 'they could cram in . . .': Gleig, *F and B*, p. 127
206 'to receive them': Gleig, *Sub*, p. 132
206 'bayonet into play': ibid., p. 133
207 'intervened to save me': Gleig, *Diary*, p. 169
207 'way in all directions': Cockburn to Cochrane, 15/9/1814, in *NW*, p. 280
207 'fled in every direction': Scott, p. 338
207 'man best could . . .': Gleig, *Sub*, p. 134
207 'fled in every direction . . .': Brooke to Bathurst, 17/9/1814, in *NW*, p. 283
207 'to rally them, ineffective': Stricker to Smith, in Marine, p. 163
207 'and the 5th . . .': ibid., p. 164
208 'support on the left': ibid.
208 'the general's order': Piper, in 'The Defense of Baltimore', p. 106
208 'movement back . . .': Stricker, in Marine, p. 164
208 'shooting in earnest . . .': Piper, in 'The Defense of Baltimore', p. 106
208 'to the ground in his rear': Smith to Monroe, 10/9/1814, in *NW*, p. 296
208 'defeated and routed': MHM special edition, vol. 107, spring 2012, p. 106
208 'had been dispossessed': Brooke to Bathurst, 17/9/1814, in *NW*, p. 283

209 'named Edmondson': Scott, p. 339

209 wrote James Scott: ibid., p. 341

209 'tolerable spirits': ibid.

209 'broken limb': Gleig, *Sub*, p. 136

210 'the deepest commiseration': Chesterton, vol. 1, p. 148

210 'of an ignoble deed': ibid., pp. 149–50

Chapter 20: 13 September – The rockets' red glare

211 'valour of veterans': Smith to Monroe, 19/9/1814, in *NW*, p. 294

213 powder from it: Webster, in Marine, p. 179

213 from where he was: Newcomb despatch to Commodore Rodgers, 18/9/1814, in *NW*, p. 292

215 'formidable line of artillery': Barrett, 'Naval Recollections', p. 463

215 'precision and effect . . .': Newcomb despatch to Commodore Rodgers, 18/9/1814, in *NW*, p. 292

215 'the slightest injury': Armistead to Monroe, 24/9/1814, in Marine, p. 168

216 'a handspike [a crowbar]': Webster, in ibid., p. 180

216 'miles out would shake . . .': Stevens to Pennell, 29/9/1814, *MHM*, vol. 51 (1956) p. 356

217 men were wounded: Isaac Munroe letter to *Boston Yankee*, 30/9/1814

217 'conduct of Armistead': Nicholson to Monroe, 17/9/1814, in Sheads, 'Joseph Hopper Nicholson', p. 148

217 'struck up 'Yankee Doodle'': Munroe letter to *Boston Yankee*, 30/9/1814

217 'again ceased firing': Armistead to Monroe, 24/9/1814, in *NW*, p. 303

217 'means of resisting it . . .': Munroe letter to *Boston Yankee*, 30/9/1814

218 'warning for us to shift . . .': Barrett, 'Naval Recollections', p. 463

218 'rain fell in torrents': ibid.

218 'quiet until one o'clock': Cochrane to Napier, 13/9/1814, *NW*, p. 279

218 'for further orders': ibid., p. 278

219 British screaming: Webster, in Marine, p. 179

Chapter 21: 13 September – You go on at your peril

220 'may be turned': Cochrane to Brooke, 12/9/1814, *NW*, p. 376

220 'mutual success': Brooke to Cochrane, 12.30 a.m., 13/9/1814, in *NW*, p. 277

221 'bones and marrow': Gleig, *Sub*, p. 142

221 'death to surrender': ibid., p. 145

221 father's corpse: ibid., p. 146

221 'strong redoubts . . .': Brooke, Diary

221 'prize our own': Gleig, *Sub*, p. 147

222 be least effective: Brooke to Bathurst, 17/9/1814, in *NW*, p. 282

222 nine years earlier: Scott, p. 344

222 'easily they could be beaten': Gleig, *Sub*, pp. 149, 156

223 'vaults with brick work': ibid., p. 153

223 'superior Bordeaux': ibid., p. 154

223 'of maximum enjoyment': ibid

223 'my saturated garments': Chesterton, vol. 1, pp. 151–2

223 floor to sleep on: ibid., p. 152

223 'on the waterside?': Scott, p. 345

224 'to General Brooke': ibid.

224 'cannot be equally felt': Cochrane to Cockburn, 13/9/1814, in *NW*, p. 278

225 'still for proceeding . . .': Scott, p. 345

225 wrote in his diary: Brooke, Diary

225 'was gone forever': ibid

225 faintheartedness: Scott, p. 345

225 'decided on retreat': Evans, 'Memorandum', 13/9/1814

226 'crowds of raw levies': Gleig, *Sub*, pp. 158–9

226 'success of the 12th': Scott, p. 347

226 'cost us dear': Gleig, *F and B*, p. 136

226 'was well defended': Codrington to wife, 13/9/1814, in Codrington, *Memoir*, 1875 edn, vol. 1, p. 320

226 'have taken the town': J. S. Skinner letter to editor of the *Baltimore Patriot*, 23/5/1849

226 'entrance of the harbour': Evans, 'Memorandum', p. 25

227 'irretrievably been lost': ibid., p. 26

227 'great skill and judgment': Smith to Monroe, 19/9/1814, in *NW*, p. 296

229 'flag of the enemy': Chief Justice Taney, in Marine, p. 187

229 'was its question': Scott Key speech in Frederick County in Rukert, p. 41, and in Sheads, *Guardian*, p. 105

229 American history: Taney, in Marine, p. 188

229 'home of the brave?': Key's original MS is in the Maryland Historical Society in Baltimore

230 the US national anthem: Taney, in Marine, p. 188

230 'gun of defiance': Barrett, 'Naval Recollections', p. 464

230 'upon our veteran chief . . .': ibid., p. 465

230 back to the ships: Smith to Monroe, 10/9/1814, in *NW*, p. 297

Chapter 22: Aftermath – Unparalleled in history

231 'which I reluctantly consented': Cochrane to Melville, 17/9/1814, in *NW*, p. 289

231 'before Baltimore': *Morning Post*, 18/10/1814

231 America was 'chequered': Liverpool to Castlereagh, 21/10/1814, in WSD, vol. 9, p. 367

231 had changed all that: Goulburn to Bathurst, 21/10/1814, in ibid., p. 366

232 'prodigious expense': Liverpool to Castlereagh, 2/11/14, in ibid., pp. 401–2

232 'prospects of peace': Liverpool to Castlereagh, 4/11/14, in ibid., pp. 404–5

232 at the peace talks: Wellington to Liverpool, 9/11/14, in ibid., pp. 424–6

232 peace beckoned: see Taylor, pp. 435–6

232 'millstone of the American war': Castlereagh to Liverpool, 2/1/1814, in WSD, vol. 9, p. 523

233 'beheld before or since': Smith, *Autobiography*, pp. 246–7

234 'from gloom to glory': Ingersoll, vol. 2, p. 65

234 'seen in Washington': Jennings, pp. 13–14

235 'during the action': Madison letter to William Winder Jr, 15/9/1834, James Madison Papers, microfilm reel 24, series 1, LC

236 'to leave his presence': Mary Cutts memoir, Cutts Collection, LC, quoted in *Memories of Montpelier* online at http://www.nps.gov/nr/twhp/wwwlps/lessons/46montpelier/46facts3.htm

236 'who ever lived': Jennings, p. 15

236 'for a half century': Boller, p. 36

237 'of the British people': Fearon, p. 283

237 'uncouth and disagreeable': Morriss, p. 140

237 'violent without dignity . . .': O'Meara, vol. 1, p. 34

238 'a totally inadequate reward': Evans to Torrens, NA WO31/418 15/5/1815

238 'in a soldier's grave': Smith, *Autobiography*, p. 217

239 'unparalleled in history': Jomini, pp. 385–6

Bibliography

1) Books

Adams, Henry, *History of the USA during the Administrations of Thomas Jefferson and James Madison*, 9 vols, NY, Charles Scribner's Sons, 1890–1

Adams, Henry, ed., *The Writings of Albert Gallatin*, 3 vols, Philadelphia, J. B. Lippincott, 1879

Allgor, Catharine, *A Perfect Union: Dolley Madison and the Creation of the American Nation*, New York, Henry Holt, 2006

Anthony, Katherine S., *Dolley Madison: Her Life and Times*, Garden City, NY, Doubleday, 1949

Armstrong, John, *Exposition of Motives for Opposing the Nomination of Mr Monroe for the Office of President of the United States*, Washington, DC, 1816; online at http://www.archive.org/stream/expositionofmotioo wash/expositionofmotioowash_djvu.txt

Armstrong, John, Jr, *Notices of the War of 1812*, New York, Wiley & Putnam, 1840

Arnett, Ethel Stephens, *Mrs James Madison: The Incomparable Dolley*, Greensboro, NC, Piedmont Press, 1972

Arthur, B., *How Britain Won the War of 1812*, Woodbridge, Boydell & Brewer, 2011

Auchinleck, G., *History of War between Britain and the US*, Toronto, Pendragon House, 1972

Babcock, K. C., *The Rise of American Nationality 1811–19*, New York, Haskell Publishers, 1906

Ball, Charles, *Slavery in the United States: A Narrative of the Life and Adventures of Charles Ball, a Black Man*, Detroit, Mich., Negro History Press; reprint of 1837 edn

Barker, Jacob, *Incidents in the Life of Jacob Barker of New Orleans*, Washington, DC, n.p., 1855

Barney, Mary, *A Biographical Memoir of the Late Commodore Joshua Barney*, Boston, Gray & Bowen, 1832

Barrett, C. R. B., ed., *The 85th King's Light Infantry by One of Them* (Lt Col. F. R. Gubbins), London, Spottiswoode, 1913

Boller, Paul, *Presidential Wives*, New York, Oxford University Press, 1988

Bowling, Kenneth, *Recreating the Federal City: Potomac Fever*, Washington, DC, American Institute of Architects Press, 1985

Brant, Irving, *James Madison*, 6 vols, New York, Bobbs-Merrill, 1961

Buchan, John, *History of the Royal Scots Fusiliers*, London, Thomas Newton, 1925

Burnett, T. A. J., *The Rise and Fall of a Regency Dandy: The Life of Scrope Berdmore Davies*, London, John Murray, 1981

Burrows, John W., *The Essex Regiment – 1st Battalion (44th), 1741–1919*, Southend-on-Sea, J. H. Burrows, 1923

Carter, Thomas, *Historical Record of the Forty Fourth, or The East Essex Regiment of Foot*, London, W. O. Mitchell, 1864

Chamier, Frederick, *The Life of a Sailor*, 3 vols, London, Richard Bentley, 1832

Chesterton, G. L., *Peace, War and Adventure: An Autobiographical Memoir*, 2 vols, Longman, Brown, Green, 1853

Clark, Allen C., *Life and Letters of Dolly Madison*, Washington, DC, W. F. Roberts, 1914

Cockburn, George, *Buonaparte's Voyage to St Helena, Comprising the Diary of Rear Admiral Sir George Cockburn*, Boston, Lilly, Watt, Colman & Holden, 1833

Codrington, Edward, *Memoir of the Life of Admiral Codrington*, ed. Lady Bourchier, 2 vols, London, Longman Green, 1875; vol. 1 online at http://archive.org/stream/cu31924087998500/cu31924087998500_djvu. txt. There is an abridged version in one volume, published 1876, online at http://archive.org/stream/memoirlifeadmir04codrgoog/memoirlife admir04codrgoog_djvu.txt

Cote, Richard N., *Strength and Honor: The Life of Dolley Madison*, Mount Pleasant, SC, Corinthian Books, 2005

Cowper, L. I., *The King's Own: The Story of a Royal Regiment*, vol. 2: *1814–1914*, Oxford, Oxford University Press, 1939

Crawford M. J., ed., *The Naval War of 1812: A Documentary History*, 3 vols, Washington, DC, Naval Historical Centre, 2002

Cutts, Lucia Beverley, *Memoirs and Letters of Dolly Madison, Wife of James Madison, President of the United States*, Boston, Houghton Mifflin, 1886

Dangerfield, George, *The Awakening of American Nationalism, 1815–28*, New York, Harper & Row, 1965

Delaplaine, Edward S., *Francis Scott Key*, New York, Biography Press, 1937

Eshelman, Ralph and Kummerow, Burton, *In Full Glory Reflected*, Maryland Historical Society Press, Baltimore, 2012

Eshelman, Ralph, Sheads, Scott and Hickey, Donald, *The War of 1812 in the Chesapeake*, Johns Hopkins University Press, Baltimore, 2010

Evans, George de Lacy, *Facts Relating to the Capture of Washington*, London, Henry Colburn, 1829

Ewell, James, *Concise History of the Capture of Washington*, Philadelphia, Jewell, 1817

Fearon, Henry Bradshaw, *Sketches of America*, London, Longman, Hurst, Rees, Orme & Brown 1819; online at http://www.archive.org/stream/ sketchesofameric00fear/sketchesofameric00fear_djvu.txt

Footner, H., *A Sailor of Fortune: The Life and Adventures of Commodore Barney*, New York and London, Harper & Brothers, 1940

Fortescue, Sir John, *A History of the British Army*, 20 vols, London, Macmillan, 1899–1930

Freidel, Frank and Pencak, William, eds, *The White House: The First Two Hundred Years*, Boston, Northeastern University Press, 1994

George, Christopher T., *Terror on the Chesapeake*, Shippensburg, Pa, White Mane Books, 2000

Gerry, Elbridge, *The Diary of Elbridge Gerry*, New York, Brentano's, 1927

Gleig, George, *Diary*, carried in full in C. R. B. Barrett, *The 85th King's Light Infantry by One of Them* (Lt Col. F. R. Gubbins), London, Spottiswoode, 1913

Gleig, George, *Fire and Blood*, Milton Keynes, Leonaur, 2007; reprint of *The Campaigns of the British Army at Washington and New Orleans*, 1827

Gleig, George, *A Subaltern in America*, Philadelphia, Carey & Hart, 1833

Goodwin, Maude Wilde, *Dolly Madison*, London, John Murray, 1896

Hackett, F. W., *Captain Thomas Tingey USN*, reprinted from *Proceedings of the US Naval Institute*, 33, no. 1 (1907) pp. 119–23

Hawkins, Rev. William, *Life of John H. W. Hawkins*, Boston, Dutton, 1863

Historical Record of the Fourth, or the King's Own, Regiment of Foot, London, Longman, Orme, 1839

Howard, Hugh, *Mr and Mrs Madison's War*, New York, Bloomsbury Press, 2012

Hunt-Jones, Conover, *Dolley and the 'Great Little Madison'*, Washington, DC, Institute of Architects Foundation, 1977

Ingersoll, Charles Jared, *Historical Sketch of the Second War between the USA and GB*, 2 vols, Philadelphia, Lea & Blanchard, 1849

Ingraham, Edward D., *A Sketch of the Events which Preceded the Capture of Washington: by the British, on the twenty-fourth of August, 1814*, Philadelphia, Carey & Hart, 1849; online at http://books.google.com/books?id=Jvgu AAAAYAAJ&pg=PP10&dq=Ingraham,+Edward+D.+A+sketch+of+t he+events+which+preceded+the+capture+of+Washington+:+by+the +British,+on+the+twenty-fourth+of+August&ie=ISO-8859- 1&output=html&cd=1

Irving, Pierre, *Life and Letters of Washington Irving*, 4 vols, New York, Putnam & Son, 1869

Irving, Washington, *The Letters of Washington Irving to Henry Brevoort*, ed. George S. Hellman, 2 vols, New York, Knickerbocker Press, 1915

James, William, *Naval Occurrences of the War of 1812*, London, Egerton, 1817

Jennings, Paul, *A Coloured Man's Reminiscences of James Madison*, Brooklyn, Beadle, 1865

Jomini, Baron de, *The Art of War*, Philadelphia, Lippincott, 1862; online at http://www.gutenberg.org/files/13549/13549-h/13549-h.htm

Kent, Zachary, *Dolley Madison*, Berkeley Heights, NJ, Enslow, 2010

Ketcham, Ralph, *James Madison*, Charlottesville, University of Virginia Press, 1971

Kroll, Steven, *By the Dawn's Early Light: The Story of the Star-Spangled Banner*, New York, Scholastic Press, 2000

Lewis, Ethel, *The White House*, New York, Dodd, Mead, 1937

Lloyd, Alan, *The Scorching of Washington*, New York, Luce, 1974

Longford, Elizabeth, *Wellington: The Years of the Sword*, London, Harper & Row, 1969

Lord, Walter, *The Dawn's Early Light*, New York, W. W. Norton, 1972

Lossing, Benson J., *The Pictorial Field Book of the War of 1812*, New York, Harper & Brothers, 1868

Lovell, W. S., *From Trafalgar to the Chesapeake*, ed. R. F. Mackay, Annapolis, Naval and Military Press, 2003

Lovell, William Stanhope, *Personal Narrative of Events 1799–1815*, London, William Allen, 2nd edn 1879; online at http://archive.org/stream/personalnarratioolovegoog/personalnarratioolovegoog_djvu.txt

McCullough, David, *John Adams*, New York, Simon & Schuster, 2001

McKenney, Thomas L., *Memoirs Official and Personal*, New York, Payne & Burgess, 1846

Madison, James, *The Writings of James Madison*, ed. Gaillard Hunt, 9 vols, New York, G. P. Putnam, 1900–10; all the Madison MSS are available on the Library of Congress website at http://memory.loc.gov/ammem/collections/madison_papers/mjmquery.html

Malcolmson, Robert, *Capital in Flames: The American Attack on York, 1813*, Annapolis, Naval Institute Press, 2008

Marine, William Matthew, *The British Invasion of Maryland 1812–15*, Baltimore, Society of the War of 1812 in Maryland, 1913

Mattern, David and Shulman, Holly, eds, *The Selected Letters of Dolley Payne Madison*, Charlottesville, University of Virginia Press, 2003

Monroe, James, *The Writings of James Monroe*, ed. Stanislaus Murray Hamilton, 9 vols, New York, G. P. Putnam, 1901

Morriss, Roger, *Cockburn and the British Navy in Transition*, Exeter, University of Exeter Press, 1997

Muller, Charles, *The Darkest Day: 1814: The Washington–Baltimore Campaign*, Philadelphia and New York, J. B. Lippincott, 1963

Napier, Elers, *The Life and Correspondence of Admiral Sir Charles Napier*, 2 vols, London, Hurst & Blackett, 1862

Napier, William, *The Life and Opinions of Charles James Napier*, 4 vols, London, John Murray, 1857

Norton, Louis A., *Joshua Barney, Hero of the Revolution and 1812*, Annapolis, Naval Institute Press, 2000

O'Meara, Barry E., *Napoleon in Exile*, 2 vols, London, Simpkin & Marshall, 1822

Pack, A. J., *Admiral Sir George Cockburn: The Man who Burned the White House*, Emsworth, Hampshire, Kenneth Mason Publications, 1987

Perrett, Bryan, *The Real Hornblower: The Life of Admiral Sir Alexander Gordon*, New York, Henry Holt, 2006

Pitch, Anthony S., *The Burning of Washington: The British Invasion of 1814*, Annapolis, Naval Institute Press, 1998

Ralfe, J., *A Naval Biography of Great Britain*, 4 vols, London, Whitmore & Fenn, 1828

Roosevelt, Theodore, *The Naval War of 1812*, 2 vols, New York, G. P. Putnam, 1902

Rukert, Norman, *Fort McHenry: Home of the Brave*, Baltimore, Bodine & Associates, 1983

Scott, James, *Recollections of a Naval Life*, London, Bentley, 1834

Seale, William, ed., *The President's House: A History*, 2 vols, Washington, DC, White House Historical Association, 2004

Seaton, William, *William Winston Seaton of the 'National Intelligencer'*, Boston, James R. Osgood, 1871

Sheads, Scott S., *Guardian of the Star Spangled Banner: Lt. Colonel George Armistead and the Fort McHenry Flag*, Baltimore, Toomey Press, 1999

Sheads, Scott S., *The Rocket's Red Glare: The Maritime Defence of Baltimore in 1814*, Centreville, Md, Tidewater Publishers, 1986

Shomette, Donald, *Flotilla: Battle for the Patuxent*, Baltimore, Johns Hopkins University Press, 2009

Skeen, Carl E., *John Armstrong Junior: A Biography*, Syracuse, NY, Syracuse University Press, 1981

Smith, Harry, *Autobiography of Lieutenant-General Sir Harry Smith*, London, John Murray, 1903

Smith, Margaret B., *Forty Years of Washington Society*, ed. Gaillard Hunt, London, T. Fisher Unwin, 1906

Smyth, Benjamin, *A History of the Lancashire Fusiliers (Formerly XX Regiment)*, 2 vols, Dublin, Sackville Press, 1903

Stagg, J. C. A., *Mr Madison's War*, Princeton, Princeton University Press, 1988

Standiford, Les, *Washington Burning*, New York, Crown Publishers, 2008

Taylor, Alan, *The Civil War of 1812*, New York, Alfred Knopf, 2010

Tucker, Glenn, *Poltroons and Patriots*, Indianapolis, Bobbs-Merrill, 1956

Tuckerman, Henry T., *Life of John Pendleton Kennedy*, New York, G. P. Putnam, 1871

Van der Voort, P. J., *The Pen and the Quarter-deck: A Study of the Life and Works of Captain Frederick Chamier RN*, Leiden, Leiden University Press, 1972

Wallace Adam, *The Parson of the Islands: A Biography of the Late Rev. Joshua Thomas*, Philadelphia, Perkinpine & Higgins, 1861

Wellington, Duke of, *The Dispatches of Field Marshal the Duke of Wellington*, 13 vols, ed. John Gurwood, London, John Murray, 1837–8

Wellington, Duke of, *Supplementary Despatches and Memoranda of Field Marshal Arthur, Duke of Wellington*, ed. his son the Duke of Wellington, 11 vols, London, John Murray, 1858–64

Whitehorne, Joseph A., *The Battle for Baltimore 1814*, Baltimore, Nautical and Aviation Publishing, 1943

Williams, H. Noel, *The Life and Letters of Admiral Sir Charles Napier*, London, Hutchinson, 1917

Williams, John S., *History of the Invasion and Capture of Washington, and of the Events which Preceded and Followed*, New York, Harper & Brothers, 1857

2) Articles

Arnold, James Riehl, 'The Battle of Bladensburg', *Records of the Columbia Historical Society*, vol. 37–8 (1937) pp. 145–68

Barrett, Robert, 'Naval Recollections of the Late American War', *United Service Journal and Naval and Military Magazine*, part 1 (1841); online at http://books.google.com/books?id=3czpYoN7zmoC&printsec=frontcover#v=onepage&q&f=false

Brown, David, 'Diary of a Soldier 1805–27', *Journal of the Royal Highland Fusiliers*, no. 8 (June 1973) pp. 23–36

Bryan, W. B., ed., 'Diary of Mrs William Thornton: Capture of Washington by the British', *Columbia Historical Society Proceedings*, vol. 19 (1916) pp. 172–83

Cassell, Frank, 'Response to Crisis: Baltimore in 1814', *MHM*, vol. 66 (1971) pp. 261–87

'The Defense of Baltimore', *MHM*, special edn, vol. 107, no. 1 (Spring 2012) pp. 102–9

Eaton, H. B., 'Bladensburg', *Journal of the Society for Army Historical Research*, vol. 55 (Spring 1977) pp. 8–14

George, Christopher T., 'The Family Papers of Major General Robert Ross, the Diary of Colonel Arthur Brooke and the British Attacks on Washington and Baltimore in 1814', *MHM*, vol. 88 (1993) pp. 300–16

Hildt, J. C., ed., 'Letters Relating to the Burning of Washington', *South Atlantic Quarterly*, vol. 6 (January 1907) pp. 58–66

Hoyt, William D., 'Civilian Defense in Baltimore, 1814–15', *MHM*, vol. 39 (1944) pp. 199–224, 293–309

Hunter, M., 'The Burning of Washington, Diary', *New York Historical Society Bulletin*, 8 (October 1925) pp. 80–3

Irwin, R. W., ed., 'The Capture of Washington in 1814 as Described by Mordecai Booth', *Americana*, no. 28 (January 1934) pp. 9–27

Jenkins, Wheeler R., 'The Shots that Saved Baltimore', *MHM*, vol. 77 (1982) pp. 362–4

King, Horatio, 'The Battle of Bladensburg: Burning of Washington in 1814', *Magazine of American History*, vol. 14 (November 1885) pp. 438–57

McCormick, John H., 'The First Master of Ceremonies at the White House', *Records of the Columbia Historical Society*, vol. 7 (1904) pp. 170–94

McKenney, Thomas L., 'A Narrative of the Battle of Bladensburg in a Letter to Henry Banning, Esq., by an Officer of General Smith's Staff', *Portico*, vol. 5 (January–February 1818)

McLane, Allen, 'Col. McLane's Visit to Washington in 1814', *Bulletin of the Historical Society of Pennsylvania*, vol. 1 (June 1845) pp. 16–22

Maguire, W. A., 'Major General Ross and the Burning of Washington', *Irish Sword: The Journal of the Military History Society of Ireland*, vol. 14 (Winter 1980) pp. 117–28

Moore, Virginia Campbell 'Reminiscences of Washington as Recalled by a Descendant of the Ingle Family', *Records of the Columbia Historical Society*, vol. 3 (1900) pp. 96–114

Mullaly, Franklin R., ed., 'A Forgotten Letter of Francis Scott Key', *MHM*, vol. 55 (1960) pp. 359–60

Napier, Charles, 'Narrative of the Naval Operations in the Potomac', *United Services Journal*, part 1 (March 1833) pp. 469–81

Pakenham, Valerie, 'Sir Edward Pakenham and the Battle of New Orleans', *Irish Sword: The Journal of the Military Society of Ireland*, vol. 9 (1969–70) pp. 32–7

Powell, J. H., 'Some Unpublished Correspondence of John Adams and Richard Rush, 1811–16', *Pennsylvania Magazine of History and Biography*, vol. 61 (1937) no. 1, pp. 26–53, and no. 2, pp. 137–64

Robinson, Ralph, 'Controversy over the Command at Baltimore in the War of 1812', *MHM*, vol. 39 (1944) pp. 176–98

Robinson, Ralph, 'New Light on Three Episodes of the British Invasion of Maryland in 1814', *MHM*, vol. 37 (1942) pp. 273–90

Ross, Sir John, 'Ross of Bladensburg', *National Review* (London) (May 1929) pp. 443–50

Ross, Robert, 'Memoir of Major General Robert Ross', *United Service Journal*, part 1 (1829) pp. 412–16

Sheads, Scott S., 'A Black Soldier Defends Fort McHenry, 1814', *Military Collector and Historian*, 41 (Spring 1989) pp. 20–1

Sheads, Scott S., 'Joseph Hopper Nicholson: Citizen-Soldier of Maryland', *MHM*, vol. 98 (2003) pp. 133–51

Sheads, Scott S., 'Two Sidelights', *MHM*, vol. 84 (1989) pp. 252–8

Sheads, Scott S., 'Yankee Doodle Played: A Letter from Baltimore 1814', *MHM*, vol. 76 (1981) pp. 380–2

Skeen, Carl E., 'Monroe and Armstrong: A Study in Political Rivalry', *New York Historical Society Quarterly*, vol. 57 (1973) pp. 121–47

Skeen, Carl E., 'Mr Madison's Secretary of War', *Pennsylvania Magazine of History and Biography*, vol. 100 (1970) pp. 336–55

Thornton, Anna Maria, 'Diary', see Bryan, ed.

Weller, M. I., 'The Life of Commodore Joshua Barney, Hero of the Battle of Bladensburg', *Records of the Columbia Historical Society*, vol. 14 (1911) pp. 67–183

3) Other archive material

American State Papers, US Congress, Military Affairs 16, *Capture of the City of Washington*, Report to the House of Representatives, 29 November 1814, ordered by the 2nd Session of the 13th Congress; online at http://memory.loc.gov/cgibin/ampage?collId=llsp&fileName=016/llsp016.db&recNum=529

Annual Register, or a view of the History, Politics and Literature for the year 1814, London, Baldwin, Cradock & Joy, 1815

Armstrong, John, Letter to Spencer, New York Historical Society MS

Barney, Joshua, Letters, National Archives, Washington, DC

Bluett, John Courtney, Diary, Royal Naval Museum, Portsmouth, MS ref. 1995/48

Booth, Mordecai, Letters to Tingey, National Archives, Washington, DC

Bowlby, Captain Peter, of the 4th King's Own, Diary, National Army Museum, London, typescript

Brooke, Sir Arthur, MS diary of campaign, PRONI D3004; the original is at the Ulster-American Folk Park, Omagh, Northern Ireland

Brown, Corporal, 21st Fusiliers diary, Museum of Royal Scots Fusiliers, Edinburgh

Cockburn, Rear Admiral George, Papers, Library of Congress, Washington, DC, MS Dept

Cockburn, Rear Admiral George, Memoir of Services, National Maritime Museum Library, Greenwich, MS Dept

Cochrane, Vice Admiral Sir Alexander, Papers, Library of Congress, Washington, DC, MS Dept; also available at the National Library of Scotland, Edinburgh

Evans, George de Lacy, 'Memorandum of operations on the shores of the Chesapeake in 1814', National Library of Scotland, Edinburgh

Few, Frances, Diary, Georgia Dept of Archives and History, Atlanta, Ga

Fulford, Henry, Correspondence: see Marine, *British Invasion of Maryland*

Gallatin, Mrs Albert, Letters, New York Historical Society

Jefferson, Thomas, Thomas Jefferson Papers, Library of Congress, Washington, DC

McElroy, Rev. John, Papers and recollections, Georgetown University Library, Special Collections

Malcolm, Admiral P., Letters, Clements Library, University of Michigan

National Archives, Kew, London, War Office documents 1814

Nourse, C. J., Correspondence, Nourse Family Papers, University of Virginia

Pickering, Timothy, Letters, Pickering Papers, Massachusetts Historical Society

Rodgers, Minerva, Letter to John Rodgers, Rodgers Macomb Papers, Library of Congress, Washington, DC

Ross, Major General Robert, Papers and letters, PRONI D2004, Belfast

Shiner, Michael, Diary/papers, all online at Naval Historical Society website http://www.history.navy.mil/library/online/shinerdiary.html and http://www.ibiblio.org/hyperwar/NHC/shiner/shiner_diary.htm#diary

Smith, General/Senator Samuel, Papers and letters, Library of Congress, Washington, DC, MS Dept

BIBLIOGRAPHY

US newspapers: *Virginia Patriot, National Intelligencer, Baltimore Patriot, Baltimore Whig, Niles' Register, Federal Republican, Boston Yankee,* etc. are available online on Newsinhistory.com

Webster, John, Account of 1814 campaign: see Marine, *British Invasion of Maryland*

Winchester, James, James Winchester Papers, Tennessee Historical Society, Nashville

Illustration Credits

Courtesy of Architect of the Capitol, Washington: 9 above right (painting by George B. Matthews after Gilbert Stuart). Benson J. Lossing *The Pictorial Field-Book of the War of 1812*, 1868: 6 below right, 7 above left. Benson J. Lossing *The Pictorial Field-Book of the Revolution* vol I, 1859: 7 above right. Brown University Library, Rhode Island/ Bridgeman Art Library: 2 below. Courtesy of Stephen Campbell: 2 above right. © Chicago History Museum/Bridgeman Art Library: 10 below (painting by Alonzo Chappel c.1859). © Corbis Images: 3 above (painting by John Vanderlyn c.1816), 7 below left (painting by James Herring after John Vanderlyn), 8 above (drawing by George Munger, 1814), 13 above (photo Paul A. Souders), 14 above right. De Agostini Picture Library/A. de Gregorio/Bridgeman Art Library: 16 below (painting by Anne Marguerite Hyde de Neuville, c.1818). Mary Evans Picture Library: 5 above right (engraving by J. Cochran, c.1835, after Thomas Lawrence). © The Huntington Library, Art Collections and Botanical Gardens, San Marino, California / Bridgeman Art Library: 7 below right (painting by Philip Tilyard, c1825). Library of Congress/Prints and Photographs Division, Washington DC: 3 below (drawing by Benjamin Henry Latrobe, between 1814–1820), 8 centre (drawing by George Munger, 1814), 9 below (cartoon published by S.W. Fores London, 1814), 14 above left, 15 above (cartoon by William Charles, c.1814). © Collections of Maine Historical Society: 16 above right (daguerreotype, c.1840). Courtesy of the Maryland Historical Society/Baltimore City Life Museum Collection/Museum Department: 4 above (Image ID CA682 painting by Rembrandt Peale c.1817), 11 above (Image ID CA681 painting by Rembrandt Peale, 1817), 11 below (Image ID CA684 painting by Rembrandt Peale, 1817), 12 above left (Image

ID CA 683 painting by Rembrandt Peale, c.1817–18). Courtesy of the Maryland Historical Society/Museum Department: 12 below (Image ID 1939.11.1 painting by Thomas Ruckle Sr, c.1814). Courtesy of the Maryland Historical Society/Special Collections: 15 below (Image ID GPVF photograph by W. Ashman, 1876). Courtesy of the Maryland Historical Society and the National Park Service, Maryland, NPS/© Richard Schlecht, 2011: 4 below (detail). © National Maritime Museum, Greenwich, London: 2 above left (painting by Jon James Halls c.1817), 10 above left (engraving by T. Blood, 1814), 10 above right (painting by Thomas Musgrave Joy, 19th century). Courtesy of the National Museum of Health and Medicine, Maryland: 9 centre left (frontispiece, James Ewell's *The Medical Companion* 1847, 10th edition). National Museums Northern Ireland: 12 above right (painting attributed to Martin Cregan, c.1838). © National Portrait Gallery, London: 6 below left (painting by William Charles Ross c. 1840). © Collection of the New-York Historical Society/Bridgeman Art Library: 3 above right (painting by Bass Otis, c. 1817), 13 below (engraving by John Bower, 1814), 16 above left (painting by Asher Brown Durand, 1833). Peter Newark American Pictures/Bridgeman Art Library: 1 above, 14 below left and below right. Private Collections: 5 above left (engraving by C. Turner, 1824, after William Beechey), 5 below (painting © James Brereton/photo Bridgeman Art Library), 6 above right. Redwood Library and Athenaeum, Newport, Rhode Island, Gift of the Artist: 9 above left (painting by Charles Bird King, c. 1829). The Royal Green Jackets (Rifles) Museum, Winchester: 6 above left. White House Historical Association 21 (White House Collection): 8 below. White House Historical Association 5720: 1 below (painting © Tom Freeman 2004).

Index

NOTE: Ranks and titles are generally the highest mentioned in the text

Adams, John Quincy 18, 126, 159
Adams, Henry 44
Aetna, HMS 152, 215; *see also* bomb ships
Albion, HMS 113
Alexandria, Virginia: delegation from sent to Winder 142–3; surrender of and 'contribution' paid by 154–60, 161, 162, 171, 184; attempt to disrupt attack on 213
American Constitution: role of James Madison 3, 18, 20, 236
American War of Independence: US victory in 5, 8, 82; death of Cochrane's brother during 13; Barney's privateering during 22; Monroe's fighting in 24, 39, 46; surrender of Saratoga during 32; devastating of the Hunter family's estate during 120; mementoes in Washington War Office 140; Sam Smith's fighting during 187; flags made by Mary Pickersgill's mother during 188; Stricker's fighting during 197
Amey, Lieutenant Colonel 204, 206

Amputation: importance of 209–10
'Anacreon in heaven' (tune) 229
Andrei, Giovanni 116, 117
Anna Maria, HMS 152
Annapolis: as possible target of attack 5, 14, 16, 27, 37, 38, 59, 70, 193–4; march of Maryland militia from 98
Annual Register 178
Argus (US sloop) 109, 115
Armistead, Major George 187–8, 211, 215–17, 229, 235
Armstrong, Brigadier General John (US Secretary of War): ineptitude of 3, 27–8, 38, 39–40, 49–50, 73–6, 80–1, 102, 103; warned of British invasion 5; appointment and early career 23–4; tension with James Monroe 24, 25–6, 84; councils of war with President Madison and military commanders 52, 80; urging of retreat to Washington 59, 100–101, 104, 105; message to Thomas Tingey 110; censure and dismissal 154, 158, 161–4, 235; commending of James Gordon's military skill 171; Sam Smith's complaints to

Armstrong, Brigadier General John
(US Secretary of War) (*cont.*)
187; Winder's complaint to
concerning Sam Smith 189
artillery: small size of British land
artillery 33, 53, 59, 168; Joshua
Barney's 46, 96, 98; US
superiority in land artillery 61;
US guns hurried from Eastern
Branch Bridge to Bladensburg
71; at Battle of Bladensburg 83,
85, 86, 87, 96, 98, 102; at Battle
of North Point 204–6, 207;
Navy bombardment of Fort
McHenry and Baltimore forts
210, 211–21, 220–1, 224–5, 228,
229; Fort McHenry's 215, 217;
see also bomb ships; Congreve
rockets

Back River 198
Badajoz, Spain 9, 12, 69, 173, 179
Ball, Charles 37, 49, 96, 97, 98
Baltimore: successful defence of 3,
4, 166, 196–7, 210, 211–21, 220–1,
224–5, 228, 229; as possible target
of attack 5, 14, 16, 27, 28, 37–9,
146–7; Winder appointed
commander of military district
embracing 25, 27; Maryland
(Baltimore) militia 27, 41, 60, 82,
83, 84, 91; reservations concerning
attacking 147, 171, 173–4, 182–4,
193, 226; British preparations for
attack on 178, 185, 193; run on
banks 180; preparations for
defence of 185–92, 196–7; Ross's
advance towards 194–6, 197–200;
Brooke appointed to replace Ross
201–2; Battle of North Point
203–10; abandoning of assault on
220–30; aftermath of defeat at
231–2; *see also* Fort McHenry

Baltimore militia 60, 83, 84, 91–2,
187, 191–2, 196, 206, 207, 208
Baltimore Patriot 163
Bank of Washington: spared 121,
138
Banks: run on in Baltimore and
Philadelphia 180
Barbary pirates 167
Barney, Commodore Joshua: early
privateering career 4, 22, 146,
197, 213; at Battle of Bladensburg
93, 94–8, 102, 103, 235; wounding
and capture at Battle of
Bladensburg 99–100, 123, 138;
and construction of flag at Fort
McHenry 188; death 235; *see also*
flotilla: Barney's; flotillamen,
Barney's
Barney, Mary 22, 76, 99, 100
Barrett, Robert (midshipman) 6,
131, 145, 195, 215, 217–18, 230
Bathurst, Lord (Secretary of War)
34–5, 36, 45, 171, 173, 174, 175,
176, 178–9
battalions, US: Major Pinkney's rifle
battalion 60; 5th Baltimore
volunteer regiment 91–2, 206,
207; General Stansbury's 91;
Ragan's and Schutz's 91; 27th
203, 204, 207; 39th 203, 204; *see
also* militia
Bayard Smith, Margaret: on
President Madison 3, 160; and
Dolley Madison 20, 161, 236; on
slaves 36, 149; on panic in
Washington 63–4; abandoning of
Washington 104, 118; on
Cockburn 133–4; return to
Washington 149, 158
bayonet charge: effectiveness 84, 92,
98, 207
Beal, Major 187
Beall, Colonel William 94, 98

Beanes, Dr William 53, 166–8, 228–9

Bear Creek 198

Belmore, Lord 201–2

Benedict, Maryland: as landing site for British troops 14, 16, 29, 32–4, 154, 188; scouted by Monroe 38, 39, 46; British fleet moored at 42, 53, 65, 66, 145, 165; Charles Ball on US failure to engage British in woods from 49; William Beanes taken to 167, 188

Bently, Mrs 64

Bermuda 14

Blackrock: British raid 137

Bladensburg, Maryland: preparations for defence of 59, 60, 61–2, 70–2, 74–6, 79–81; vulnerability of bridge at 64, 70, 74, 76, 79, 82–3; ford 70, 76, 82, 87, 88, 90, 91, 102; British advance to 77–9; Congreve rockets used at 80, 89, 91, 105, 152; first phase of Battle 82–93; British reckless crossing bridge 85–8, 90, 91, 93, 96, 101–2, 201; Joshua Barney's last stand at Battle of 94–103, 123, 138, 190, 212–13, 235; reaction to British victory 107, 110, 155, 158, 163, 185, 189, 196, 203, 208, 233; British advance from 111; dead-strewn battlefield 165–6; US treatment of British officers at 168; Brooke's role at 202; Sterett's 5th Regiment at 206; odds of victory at 228

'Bladensburg Races'(poem) 103

Bladensburg, Kathleen Ross of 238

Blair, Tony 1

blockade of US trade by Royal Navy 146, 180

Bluett, John 91

bomb ships 5, 151, 152, 195, 213–15, 217–18, 220, 224–5

bombardment of Fort McHenry and Baltimore forts 210, 211–21, 224–5, 228, 229

Bonnie Prince Charlie 32, 150

Booth, Mordecai 50–1, 110–11, 114, 115

Boston 34, 154

Boston Gazette 11

Bowlby, Captain Peter 91

Boyne, Battle of the 31

Bradley, Willie 63

Bread and Cheese Creek 198, 203

Brigades: Ross's division of men into 31–2

Britain: response to sacking of Washington 175–81

British Regiments: 4th King's Own Regiment 31, 91, 93, 98, 205, 207; 21st North British (later Scots) Fusiliers 32, 87, 111, 131, 139, 201, 205, 223; 44th East Essex Regiment 31, 93, 98, 201, 205; 85th Light Infantry (Buckinghamshire Volunteers) 31, 43, 86–9, 90, 91, 93, 96–8, 102, 128, 139, 197, 205

Brooke, Colonel Arthur: command of the 44th in France 31; at Battle of Bladensburg 93, 98; on US capitulation at Washington 125; placed in command after death of Ross 201–2; at Battle of North Point 203–10; planned offensive at Baltimore and aborting of 211, 218, 219, 220–8, 230; subsequent career 237–8

Brooke, Field Marshal Alan 201

Brooke, Juliana 202

Brooke, Lieutenant Colonel Francis 205

Brooke, Marianne 201–2

Brookeborough, Lord 201
Buffalo: British raid on 137
Burch, Captain Benjamin 71
Burrell (sentry) 65
Bush, George, Jr 135
Bussaco, Battle of 12, 151

Cameron, David 1
Campbell, George (Treasury
   Secretary) 73, 74, 75
Canada: US raids on 7, 8, 13, 14;
   burning of York (modern-day
   Toronto) 8, 58, 112, 129, 137;
   British reinforcing of 21, 24;
   Treaty of Ghent provisions on
   179, 232; final British thrust from
   231
canister: US use of 96, 212, 221
Cape St Vincent, Battle of 11
Capitol: design and building of 17,
   72, 109, 140, 234; rescuing of
   papers from 50; Armstrong's
   recommended retreat to 59;
   falling back to 100–1;
   abandoning of 110–11; British
   advance on 111–13, 114; torching
   of 115–22, 135, 138; flames doused
   by storm 145; burnt-out shell of
   148–9; rebuilding of 234
Capitol Hill 104, 112, 120
Carbery, Colonel 73
Carroll, Daniel 107–8
Castlereagh, Lord 231, 232
casualty figures: at Battle of
   Bladensburg 101, 102; during
   voyage back down Potomac
   170–1; at Battle of North Point
   208; of US troops' forts defending
   Baltimore 217; at New Orleans
   233
cavalry: despatched to track British
   landing party 43, 48, 59, 67;
   British lack of 44, 46, 53, 59, 69,

94; at Battle of Bladensburg 84,
   92–3; allowing British army to
   fall back after sack of Washington
   165; tracking British advance
   towards Baltimore 197
Chamier, Frederick 12
Chesapeake Bay: British fleet's
   arrival at 5–6, 8, 11, 15, 16, 21, 23;
   heat and storms of 29; and
   possible attack on Baltimore 146;
   Peter Parker's naval thrust in 150;
   Gordon's squadron rejoining fleet
   at 170, 171; fleet's movement in
   prior to advance on Baltimore
   182, 184, 186; see also Patuxent
   River; Potomac River
Chesterton, George 33, 128, 131,
   168–9, 201, 210, 223, 232
Christ's Church, Baltimore 192
Churchill, Winston 201
Ciudad Rodrigo, Spain 69
Clagett, Levi 216
Clemm, Sergeant John 216–17
Cochrane, Vice Admiral Sir
   Alexander: leading of British
   invasion into the Chesapeake
   13–16, 29, 30, 150; pros and cons
   concerning campaign 34–7, 65,
   171, 182–4; reservations
   concerning attack on Washington
   53, 56, 65–6, 183; reports back to
   55, 56, 57, 171; order to abandon
   attack on Washington 66–9, 147,
   182, 183, 225; letter to Monroe
   112; and Napier 151; and
   successful assault on Washington
   170, 171, 178, 182, 183; and
   possible attack on Baltimore 173,
   183–4, 193; and possible attack on
   New Orleans 179, 180, 182–3,
   184; impact of dithering following
   assault on Washington 191, 193;
   anchoring of fleet at North Point

192; and navigating the Potomac 193, 195; and death of Ross 200; and assault on Baltimore 214, 217, 218, 220, 222, 224–8; failure at Baltimore 230, 231; defeat at New Orleans 232; appointed Commander in Chief at Plymouth 237

Cockburn, Rear Admiral George: fearsome reputation and early Chesapeake campaign 2–3, 11–14, 21–2, 30, 36, 106, 151, 191; and rules of engagement 12, 33, 43, 134, 138–9; advocating of assault on Washington 14, 15, 16, 53–4, 55–8, 171; and Barney's flotilla 23, 35, 42, 44–5, 46–7, 55, 57, 94; advance up the Patuxent 29, 30, 49; on President Madison 35–6, 138; and recruiting of blacks 36–7; picking up of spies 53; advance towards Washington 64, 65–6; Malcolm's jealousy of 65; ignoring of Cochrane's orders 67–9, 147, 182; shots fired at 76; at Bladensburg 88, 89, 91, 99–100, 103; and assault on Washington 106, 111, 112–13, 116–20, 122, 123, 182; and burning of White House 125, 126, 127–30; and burning of Treasury Building 131–2; and destroying of *National Intelligencer* building 132–3; US praise of his restraint 133–4; first night in Washington 136–7; and torching of Navy Yard 139; conversation with William Gardner 141; and delegation from Alexandria 142–3; return of to ships 145, 165; advocating attack on Baltimore 146, 147, 173, 182, 184, 193, 201, 226, 227; accuses Beanes of betrayal 168; landing at Benedict

and advance towards Baltimore 188, 197–200; and Battle of North Point 205, 207, 209; and assault on Baltimore 221, 222, 223, 224, 225; and failure of assault on Baltimore 226, 227; subsequent career 237; *see also* discipline: British

Cockburn, Sir James 117

Codrington, Rear Admiral Edward: advance towards Washington 15, 29, 65, 102; discipline imposed by 169–70; on surrender of Alexandria 171; debate with Cochrane over plans after sacking of Washington 183–4; and assault on Baltimore 194, 195, 196, 226; on death of Ross 200; subsequent career 237

Codrington, Jane 184, 194

Colebrooke estate 201

Coles, Catherine 19

Coles, Sally 234

collaboration: accusations of 142, 144, 161

Collins, Elizabeth 18

Columbia (US frigate) 109, 114–15

Committee of Vigilance and Safety 188–9, 190

Congress *see* Library of Congress; House of Representatives; Senate

Congreve rockets: at Bladensburg 80, 89, 91, 152; in Washington 105, 117, 121; in assault on Baltimore 204, 205, 210, 214–15, 218, 219, 228, 229

cotton gin: patenting of 140–1

Creek Indians 231

Creighton, Captain John 110–11, 114

Crimean War 238

Crofton, Captain Edward 200
Culloden 32, 150
Cutts, Anna 106–7
Cutts, Lucy 19
Cutts, Mary 236

dancing pumps: worn into battle by
  John Pendleton Kennedy 4, 62,
  75, 235
Davies, Samuel (midshipman) 47,
  56, 96, 113, 129
de Jomini, Baron 239
de Staël, Madame 178
Delaware River 14, 187
Devastation, HMS 152, 215, 217; see
  also bomb ships
discipline, British 12, 43, 133–4,
  142, 153, 156, 168–70, 178, 196,
  198, 201; see also private property:
  British respect for
District of Columbia militia 39, 60,
  84, 95, 100–1
'diversionary attack' on Fort
  McHenry 218–19, 225
Douglas, George 191
Downing Street 175
dressing room: Madison's in White
  House 128
Dylan, Bob 1
dysentery 173
Dyson, Captain Samuel 154

Eastern Branch Bridge 61, 64, 70–1,
  72, 75–6, 84, 110
Edmondson (British soldier) 209
Egypt: military campaign in 13, 31,
  201
18th Street, Washington 234
Elba, island of 8, 177
engagement, rules of 12, 43, 168–9,
  196; see also discipline: British;
  private property: British respect
  for

Erebus, HMS 152, 215
Euryalus, HMS 151, 152
Evans, George de Lacy: early career
  10; advocating assault on
  Washington 45, 53–4, 55–7, 67,
  68; on Upper Marlborough 52–3;
  on Ross's tactics in advancing to
  Bladensburg 70; spotting of
  sharpshooters 76; in advance
  towards Washington 111; and
  attack on Washington 115;
  advocating assault on Baltimore
  146, 147, 182, 184, 226–7; Ross's
  appeal for double promotion of
  173, 238; on death of Ross 200;
  on Brooke's Council of War
  concerning Baltimore 225;
  subsequent career 238
Ewell, Dr James: fears of prior to
  British invasion 104–6;
  cooperation with British troops
  118–20, 132, 137–9, 142, 144,
  161; on panic in Alexandria
  143; on Greenleaf Point accident
  144; after British withdrawal
  149
Ewell, Mrs 118, 137
expansionism of US: following
  victory at New Orleans 234, 235,
  237

Fairy, HMS 170
Faunce, Major 205, 207
Federal Hill 192
Federal Republican 81, 159
Federalists 24, 25, 158–9
5th Baltimore volunteer regiment
  91–2, 206, 207
51st Militia 204, 205, 206, 207,
  208
fireships 161, 170, 213
flags: Mary Pickersgill's making of
  for Fort McHenry 188, 228–9

flotilla, Barney's: creation of and harrying of British fleet by 4, 22–3, 35, 37–8, 42, 44, 45, 96, 99, 146; destruction of 46–8, 49, 53, 55–6, 57, 65, 150

flotillamen, Barney's: at Long Old Fields 59, 60–1; at Eastern Branch Bridge 61, 71, 75–6, 84; at Battle of Bladensburg 78, 84, 93, 94–103, 123, 138, 190, 212–13, 235

ford, at Bladensburg 70, 76, 82, 87, 88, 90, 91, 102

Fort Babcock 187, 212–13, 216, 219

Fort Covington 187, 212, 213, 219

Fort George 187

Fort McHenry: design 40, 186–7; reinforcing defence of 188–91; preparations for attack on 195; bombardment of 210, 211–22, 224–5, 228, 229; as federal prison 235–6

Fort Mifflin 187

Fort Stevens 81

Fort Washington 150, 153–4, 158

Franzoni, Giuseppe 116

Frazier, Lieutenant Solomon 46

French embassy, Washington: sparing of 129

Fuentes d'Oñoro, Battle of 31, 86

Furlong, Charles 130–1

Galba, Emperor 23

Gales, Joseph 132, 133, 134

Ganges (US warship) 109

gangrene: danger of 210

Gardner, William 123, 130, 141–2, 144

George II, King 150

George III, King 175–6

Georgetown, Washington: government papers and documents taken to 50; US

retreat through 101; home of Thornton family 118, 140, 141; sparing of university in 131–2; fears of British invasion 142; home of the Scott Keys 167

Gerry, Vice President Elbridge, Jr 36

Ghent peace talks and treaty 179, 231–2, 234

Gleig, George: diary 3; early career 7, 31; enthusiasm for British invasion 8–9; on start of voyage up the Patuxent 29, 30; on landing at Benedict 32–3; foraging 43; on advance towards Washington 44, 45; on Upper Marlborough 52; on William Beanes 53; and delay in committing to assault on Washington 57–8; posting to 'chateau' near British camp 64–5; on US militia 77–8; on Bladensburg 82, 86–7, 97–8, 102; on assault on Washington 111–12, 113, 117–18, 127, 165; on storm after assault on Washington 144; on US treatment of injured 166; rejoining of fleet in the Patuxent 168; on advance towards Baltimore 193–4, 195, 197–8, 199; on death of Ross 200–1; on Brooke 202; on Battle of North Point 203, 205, 206–7, 209; on assault on Baltimore 220–1, 222–3; on defeat at Baltimore 226; in defeat at New Orleans 232; subsequent career 238

Goldsborough, Senator Robert Henry 159, 208

Goliath, HMS 150–1

Gordon, Captain James Alexander 143, 150–7, 161, 170, 171, 195, 213, 214

Gordon, Lydia 151
Gorsuch, Robert 197
grapeshot 96, 206, 207, 212, 219, 221
Grassi, Father 131–2
Greenleaf Point 143–4
Greville, Lord 181

Hampstead Hill, Baltimore 186, 191, 211, 227
harbour, Baltimore: sinking of ships to block entrance 212, 224, 226, 227
Hardy, Captain Sir Thomas 222
Harrismith, South Africa 238
heat: effect on troops 29, 32, 41, 43–4, 61, 77, 94, 104, 195, 199, 205
heated shot, US 170, 192, 215
Hebrus, HMS 6, 195, 217, 230
Hoban, James 126, 234–5
House of Commons 178, 238
House of Representatives 17, 50, 116–17, 148–9; *see also* Capitol
Howard, Colonel John 189
Huffington (flotillaman) 99
Hunter, Reverend Dr Andrew 120
Hunter, Mary 120–2

impressments: Royal Navy practice of 7, 109, 140, 179, 232
India: Evans' fighting in 53
Indians, American 7, 179, 231, 232
Intrépide (captured French ship) 15
Iphigenia, HMS 174
Irving, Washington 18, 20

Jackson, General Andrew 231, 233
Jacobite rebellions 32
Jamaica: British West Indies base in 231
Java (US frigate) 215
Jefferson, Thomas 8, 18, 19, 20, 23, 24, 25, 36, 125

Jennings, Paul 20, 81, 107, 108, 127, 136, 234, 236
'Jonathan' (British nickname for US enemy) 34
Jones, Colonel 141
Jones, William (US Navy Secretary) 23, 37–8, 52, 64, 109–10, 135, 160
Jones, Mrs (wife of William) 64

Kains, Archibald 131
Kennedy, John Pendleton 4, 40–1, 62, 75, 82, 92, 235
Kentucky: joining of the US 188
Kettle Bottom shoals 152, 170, 195
Key, Francis Scott 167–8, 228–30, 235
Key, Polly Scott 167
Kildrummy Castle 150
Knox, Captain John 87

Ladysmith, South Africa 238
Latrobe, Henry 109, 116
Lavall, Lieutenant Colonel Jacint 84, 92
Lazaretto battery 187, 212, 219
L'Enfant, Pierre 122
Lewis, John 140
Lewiston: British raid on 137
Library of Congress 17, 117, 118, 138
Lincoln, Abraham 81
Liverpool, Lord 8, 145, 178, 179, 181, 231, 232
Liverpool Mercury 177–8
London Statesman 177
Long Old Fields, Maryland 48, 52, 58, 59, 60, 61, 64, 70, 72
Longford, Lord 183
looters: American 122, 133, 139, 149; British 142, 167
looting: British ban on 12, 122–3, 153; *see also* discipline: British; engagement: rules of

Louisiana: British designs on 179, 233; *see also* New Orleans
Love, Matilda 135
Lower Marlborough, Maryland 44
Lowndes Hill, Bladensburg 79
Lynx (US schooner) 109, 115, 139

McComas, Private Henry 199
McElroy, Reverend John 131–2
McHenry, James 186
McKenney, Major Thomas 162, 164
McLane, Allen 125
Macleod's Tavern 123
Madeira wine: drinking of in White House 1, 127
Madison, Dolley: acclaimed for conduct during crisis 3, 138; first husband 18–19; furnishing of White House 19–20, 126, 129, 130; fears concerning British raids 21; on measures to defend America 22; on slaves 36; amid scenes of panic in White House 51; letter from James concerning troops in the field 59–60; urged by James to leave White House 63; letter from Mrs Jones to 64; preparations for meal in White House 81, 107; friendship with the Ewells 104; remains at White House as British advance 106–7; flight from White House 107–9, 118, 127, 135–6; cushion of taken from White House as trophy 128; delayed return to Washington 148, 158; return to Washington 160–1; and restoration of James's reputation 233; move to Octagon House 234; in contrast to Elizabeth Monroe 235; retirement to Montpelier estate 236
Madison, President James: role in formulating American

constitution 3, 18, 20, 236; and restoration of American self-belief 3–4, 160, 172, 181, 196, 231, 233–4; declaration of war on Britain (June 1812) 7, 129; censured in British press 8, 177; unprepossessing character 18; marriage to Dolley 19; treatment of White House slaves 20–1; enlisting help of Joshua Barney 22, 23, 96, 146; appointment of key defence staff 23–6, 103; and defence of Washington 28, 80–1; Cockburn's challenge concerning 35–6; fears concerning attack on Washington 38, 62–3, 75; disenchantment with 42, 53, 63, 81, 103, 136, 158–60, 181, 233; instructions to Monroe concerning British fleet 46; warned by Monroe to destroy bridges to Washington 49; decision to join troops in the field 51–2, 75, 81; Winder's report to concerning troops in the field 58–9; review of troops 59–60; impatience with Armstrong 73–4, 75, 162–4; approval of Barney and his flotillamen's redeployment at Bladensburg 76, 84; flight from Bladensburg 79–80; friendship with the Ewells 104; brief return to White House 108; flight from Washington 108, 118, 123, 135; meeting with military commanders 109; Cochrane's demand to for compensation 112; possessions taken as trophies from White House 117, 128; and White House ostentation 125; mocked by British officers 127, 133, 138; pleas to Winder by town council of Alexandria in presence

Madison, President James (*cont.*)
    of 142; return to Washington
    148–9; appointment of Monroe as
    War Secretary 164; sanctioning
    of Scott Key's mission to secure
    release of William Beanes 167–8;
    and peace negotiations 179, 180;
    appointment of Sam Smith to
    command of 10th Military
    District 189; move to Octagon
    House 234; letter to Winder's son
    235; retirement to Montpelier
    estate 236; *see also* Ghent peace
    talks and treaty
Maffitt, John 135
Magraw, Tom 108
Maine: dispute over 179, 232
Malcolm, Clementine 65
Malcolm, Rear Admiral Pulteney
    15, 65
Marie-Antoinette, Queen 4, 22
marines: US 32, 64, 84, 93, 94, 97,
    98, 103; British 57, 68, 130, 134,
    194, 205
Martinique, island of 13; *see also*
    flotillamen: Barney's
Maryland militia 27, 40, 94, 98
Maryland Point 153
medicine chest: survives torching of
    White House 131
Meldrum: estate 128
Melwood: Ross and Cockburn's
    dining at 'chateau' in 64–5
Meteor, HMS 152, 215
military stores: removal from
    Washington's Navy Yard
    50–1
militia: US dependence on 12,
    26–8, 41, 77–8; inexperience of
    15, 61, 67, 77–8, 95, 106, 191–2;
    Maryland militia 27, 40, 94, 98;
    Virginia militia 27, 60, 72–3, 101,
    190; Pennsylvania militia 27, 190;

Washington DC militia 28, 84,
    94, 100, 162; District of Columbia
    militia 39, 60, 84, 95, 100–1;
    Baltimore militia 60, 83, 84,
    91–2, 187, 191–2, 196, 206, 207,
    208; 51st Militia 204, 205, 206,
    207, 208
Miller, Colonel Samuel 94, 95, 97
Minor, Colonel George 60, 72–3,
    101
Mississippi river 179, 183
Monroe, Elizabeth 235
Monroe, James: role in restoring
    American self-belief 3–4, 160,
    161; tension with Armstrong
    24–5, 163–4; early unconcern over
    lack of defences 26, 28; scouting
    of the front line 38–9, 42, 46, 48,
    49; as an alternative battlefield
    commander 73, 79, 80, 82, 84, 85,
    90, 92; and retreat through
    Washington and Georgetown
    101; lampooned in 'Bladensburg
    Races' 103; Cochrane's letter to
    112; letter to James Madison
    concerning British withdrawal
    148; recognition of anger of the
    American people 159; as
    Secretary of War 164, 189, 190; as
    President 164, 235
Montpelier (Virginia): Madisons'
    mansion in 20, 21, 236
Morning Post 177, 231
Morris, Phoebe 128
mortars 5, 152, 214, 215–17; *see also*
    bomb ships
Munroe, Isaac 192, 216, 217
muskets: effectiveness of 83–4, 98,
    207

Napier, Captain Charles John
    ('Black Charlie') 12, 151–4, 157,
    170, 171, 218–19, 225

Napier, Colonel Charles James 151
Napoleon I (Bonaparte): abdication
7; campaign against 2, 7, 21, 31,
33, 69, 165, 177, 179, 201; exile 8,
177, 237; dislike of John
Armstrong 24; sale of Louisiana
to America 179
'Narrow Way, The' (Bob Dylan) 1
national anthem (US) 166, 229–30,
235
National Intelligencer: destruction of
offices 132–3; commending of
Cockburn's restraint 133
Navarino, Battle of 237
Navy Yard, Washington:
transporting of supplies from 50;
sending to for powder to destroy
bridges to Washington 70, 71;
Tingey ordered to prepare for
destruction of 109–11; torching
of 114–15, 117, 121–2; arrival of
Wainwright's naval demolition
party at 139
Ned (brother of Elizabeth Ross)
9–10
Nelson, Admiral Viscount Horatio
11, 195, 222
New England 34, 53, 154
New Orleans 179, 180, 182, 183,
224, 231, 232–3, 237
New York 107, 146, 154, 160
New York Avenue, Washington
234
New York Evening Post 160
Newark, New Jersey: British raid on
58
Newcomb, Lieutenant Henry 213,
215, 219
newspaper reports: on Madison and
his government 8, 81, 159, 160,
161, 163; on Cockburn 11, 132;
on Barney 97; on British conduct
133; in Britain concerning

burning of Washington 177–8;
on panic in Baltimore 184; on
rekindled patriotism of
Americans 196; on Baltimore
triumph 231
Niagara peninsula 177
Niagara River 187
Nicholson, Judge Joseph 191–2, 216,
217, 229
Nile, Battle of the 5, 13, 151
Niles' Weekly Register 133, 196
North Point: British fleet's arrival at
192, 193, 196; advance up
peninsular of 197–9; death of
Ross at 199–200; Battle of
203–11, 220
Nottingham, USA 44, 45, 46, 48,
57–8
Nova Scotia 238

Obama, Barack 1
Octagon House 234
Ohio 7, 146
Orion, HMS 15
Orr, Mrs 106, 118
Orthez, Battle of 9, 79

Pakenham, Major General Sir
Edward 180, 183, 232, 233, 237
Pakenham, Kitty 183
Parker, Captain Peter 150
Patapsco river: British advance
towards 184, 192; initial landing
194; advance up 195, 197;
Stricker's defensive position on
peninsular 198; British ships
anchored in 211, 213–14; Napier's
diversionary attack 218–19; *see
also* bombardment of Fort
McHenry and Baltimore forts
Patent Office: sparing of 140–1
Paterson, Lieutenant Colonel
William 32

Patuxent River: landing site at
    Benedict 14, 16, 32–3; clash of
    Barney's and Cockburn's ships in
    23, 48; British advance up 29–31,
    32, 37, 39, 46, 150, 178; Barney's
    flotilla trapped in 42, 46, 48, 55;
    British ships in upper reaches of
    54, 55; lashed by storm following
    sack of Washington 145; British
    return down 168–9, 178, 184
Peninsular campaign: Harry Smith's
    time in 2, 9, 10, 173; Gleig's time
    in 7, 9, 32, 44, 86, 226; Evan's
    time in 10, 53; Ross's time in 10,
    79, 112; Napier's time in 12, 151;
    Thornton's time in 31; discipline
    enforced in 156; introduction of
    use of shrapnel shells during
    205
Pennsylvania Avenue, Washington
    17, 105, 122, 126, 130, 142
Pennsylvania militia 27, 190
Persia: Evans's fighting in 53
Phaeton, HMS 11
Philadelphia 6, 14, 17, 18, 146, 180,
    190
Pickersgill, Caroline 188, 229
Pickersgill, Mary 188, 229
Pig Point, Virginia 47
Pinkney, Charles 19
Pinkney, Major William 19, 60, 78,
    83, 90
Piper, Captain James 208
Pitch, Anthony 50
Plattsburg, Battle of 231
Pleasonton, Stephen 49–50
plundering: Cockburn's reputation
    for 12; British rules concerning
    33, 122, 145; of Ewell's house 119;
    of Washington 131, 133, 149;
    Codrington's report concerning
    169–70; as object of Cochrane's
    expedition 183; see also discipline:

British; private property: British
    respect for
Plymouth, Devon 22, 237
Poe, Edgar Alan 191
Point Lookout, Maryland 5, 6, 28,
    33, 38
Portsmouth, Hampshire 175
Portsmouth Oracle 159
Potomac River: British fleet
    anchored at entrance of 5, 29;
    advance up 16, 37, 143, 150–3,
    178; Pleasonton's loading of
    White House documents
    alongside 49; Eastern Branch
    Bridge across 64, 70–1, 72, 75–6,
    84, 110; Madison's crossing of
    during flight from Washington
    108, 135; Madison's night at
    Brookville on east bank 148;
    British shelling of Fort
    Washington from 149–50, 153–4;
    British squadron's return down
    161, 168, 170–1, 195; revolt against
    Armstrong among defenders of
    162; see also Alexandria, Virginia;
    bombardment of Fort McHenry
    and Baltimore forts; Navy Yard,
    Washington
Prevost, General George 13
Prince Regent (later King George
    IV) 175–7, 238
Pringle, Major Norman 122
private property: British respect for:
    remarked on 12, 33, 111–12, 119,
    121–3, 129, 138–9, 141, 145, 155
privateering 4, 22, 146, 213

Ragan: battalion of 91
Rain: downpour during
    bombardment of Fort McHenry
    and Baltimore forts 216, 218–23,
    227
regular army, US 26, 84, 94, 98, 234

Renown, HMS 151
Republican party and press 23–4,
  25, 26, 81, 132, 159
Revolutionary War *see* American
  War of Independence
Rhode Island 183
riflemen, US 60, 83, 85, 86, 87, 90,
  102, 198–9, 206, 209
rifles: in relation to muskets 83–4
rocket ships 151, 152, 215
Rodgers, John 190–1
Roosevelt, Theodore 48, 131, 171
Rosenbach, Dr 117
Ross, Elizabeth ('Ly') 2, 9–10,
  171–2, 174, 180, 200, 201, 238
Ross, Major General Robert:
  reservations concerning campaign
  2, 15, 16, 35, 45, 53–4, 55, 56–7,
  58, 128, 171, 174, 182, 183, 193,
  225, 226; concern for his wife,
  Elizabeth 10, 172, 174, 238; early
  career 9–10; first meeting with
  Cockburn at Chesapeake Bay 11;
  under command of Cochrane 13;
  organisation of three brigades
  31–2; landing and encampment at
  Benedict 33–5, 43, 188; advance
  alongside the Patuxent 44–5;
  advance to Upper Marlborough
  48–9; advance towards
  Washington 62, 64–5, 70; shots
  fired at 76, 112–13, 131; ignoring
  of order to abort mission 67–9,
  182, 225; at Bladensburg 77, 78–9,
  82, 84, 85–6, 87, 88, 93, 94, 95,
  97–8, 102, 103; capture of Barney
  98–100, 123; taking of advance
  party into Washington 111–13,
  114, 115; and torching of
  Washington's public buildings
  117–18, 122, 125–6, 127, 128,
  131–2, 137–8, 142, 154, 170, 171–2;
  meeting with and hospitality

offered by James Ewell 119–20,
  136–7; supper with Barbara Suter
  123–4; sparing of Elias Caldwell's
  house 139; concern for victims of
  Greenleaf Point accident 144;
  withdrawal from Washington
  145, 147, 153, 165–8; urged to
  march for Baltimore 146, 147,
  173–4, 178–9, 182, 184; request for
  double promotion of Evans 173,
  238; commendation of Harry
  Smith to Prince Regent 176;
  Elizabeth's delight at news of his
  success 180; advance towards
  Baltimore 193, 197–8; shooting
  and death of 199–202, 238;
  leadership of compared to
  Brooke's 227
Ross of Bladensburg, Kathleen 238
Rossie (Barney's privateer schooner)
  22, 213
Rostrevor (hometown of
  Wellington) 9
Rush, Richard (Attorney General)
  52, 73, 74, 75, 80, 135, 148, 149,
  159

St Helena: Napoleon's exile on 237
St Paul's churchyard, Halifax (Nova
  Scotia) 238
St Sebastian: burning of 118
Salamanca, Battle of 69, 180
Salona, village 135
San Sebastián: siege of 31
Saratoga: surrender at 32
Scorpion (US sloop) 47
Scott, Lieutenant Colonel William
  84, 94, 98
Scott, Lieutenant James: and British
  occupation of Washington 1, 3,
  116, 122, 126–7, 128, 132, 133; on
  Cockburn 11, 13; on Negro
  volunteers 36–7; on Barney's

Scott, Lieutenant James (*cont.*)
flotilla 47; at Cockburn's meeting
with Ross 56; report to
Cochrane 57, 65; despatched
with Cochrane's letter to Ross
and Cockburn 66, 67–8; on
advance to Bladensburg 76–7; at
Bladensburg 82, 88–9, 91; and
advance towards Washington
111, 112, 113; and torching of
Navy Yard 139; and prisoner's
attempt to escape 140; on
Greenleaf Point accident 143; on
delay in advancing on Baltimore
147, 184; on return from
Washington 166; frustration at
not being despatched to London
184–5; on Battle of North Point
205–6, 208–9; and defeat at
Baltimore 222, 223–4, 225, 226;
at New Orleans 232; subsequent
career 237
Seahorse, HMS 151, 152, 195
Senate building 17, 50, 116, 117,
148–9; *see also* Capitol
Severn, HMS 145
sharpshooters 76, 87, 98, 165, 208
Shaw family 198
shrapnel shells 205
Schutz 91
Simmons, William 79–80
Simms, Charles (mayor of
Alexandria) 154–5, 157
Simms, Nancy 157
Sioussat, Jean Pierre ('French John')
107, 108, 234
Skinner, John 35–6, 168, 226
slaves: staffing the White House
20–1, 96; fear of slave rising 27,
36–7, 149; issue of 36; spying for
the British 53, 57; fear that
British would carry them off 153;
Key's opposition to 167; set to

work on defensive ramparts at
Baltimore 190; *see also* Ball,
Charles; Jennings, Paul
Smith, Captain Harry: service
during Peninsular campaign 2,
8–9, 10; on journey up the
Patuxent 30; advocating of assault
on Washington 45, 53–4, 67, 68;
on reckless assault of Bladensburg
bridge 85, 87–8, 102;
participation in assault on
Washington 111, 118; in White
House 127; on torching of White
House 129–30; pursuit of escaped
US prisoner 140; on storm
following sacking of Washington
145; and order to move out of
Washington 147, 166; sent to
London with news of the
expedition's success 172–4, 184,
185; meeting with Bathurst and
the Prince Regent in London
175–7; promotion of 179, 185; on
wife Juana 179–80; arguing
against attack on Baltimore 182,
226; and defeat at New Orleans
232, 233; subsequent career 238
Smith, John (Harry's father) 180
Smith, Juana 9, 173, 175, 179–80,
233, 238
Smith, General Sam: contribution
to restoring American self-belief
3, 230; appointed to superintend
defence of Baltimore 187, 197;
reinforcing of Baltimore's
defences 189–91, 211, 216, 221;
plans for defence of 196, 227, 228;
praise of Stricker 208, 211;
appointment of Captain Webster
to command of Fort Babcock
213; subsequent career 236
Smith, General Walter (and DC
militia): at Long Old Fields 60–1,

64; relocated to Washington 71; ordered to hurry to Bladensburg 74–5; at Bladensburg 79, 84, 94, 100; ordered to retreat to Washington 101; mutiny of men against Armstrong 162

Somerset, Lord Fitzroy 176

Speaker's Chair, House of Representatives 116–17

Stansbury, General Tobias: assembly of force of 1,500 militiamen under 41; deployment of enlarged force to Bladensburg 59; waiting for Major Pinkney's rifle battalion to join him 60; defensive position taken up at Bladensburg 61–2; withdrawal from Bladensburg contrary to orders 71–2, 78; ordered back to Bladensburg 75; repositioned at Bladensburg 79, 84–5; giving command to destroy bridge at Bladensburg 82, 84, 85; during Battle of Bladensburg 91

star-spangled banner 166–7, 229, 230, 233

stars and stripes 188, 229

State Department: Stephen Pleasonton's rescue of documents from 49–50

State Dining Room, White House 19, 108, 126–7

Sterett, Colonel 78, 91–2, 206, 207

Stevens, James 216

Stoddert's Bridge 34, 64, 70, 105

storm: over Washington in wake of British occupation 144–5, 153

Stricker, Major General John 188, 196–8, 202, 203–8, 211

Stuart, Gilbert 19, 108

Sukey (Dolley Madison's personal maid) 107, 108, 136

Surprise, HMS 214

Suter, Barbara 123–4, 132

Suter, Maria 171

Swann, Thomas 5

Tacitus: on Emperor Galba 23

Taylor, President Zachary 236

10th Military District 189

Terror, HMS 215

terrorist attack (11 September 2001) 2, 135

Thackeray, William 235

Thomas, Reverend Joshua 185

Thornton, Anna Maria: friendship with Dolley Madison 3; criticism of Winder 72; flight from Washington 108–9; watching torching of Washington 115, 118; on torching of the White House 130; on William's saving of the Washington Patent Office 141; on fear in Washington of a second attack 158; on futility of resisting the British further 159; on Dolley Madison following the sacking of Washington 161

Thornton, Colonel William 31, 43, 85–9, 96, 97, 102

Thornton, Dr William: early career 72; flight from Washington 108–9; designer of the Capitol 115–16, 140, 234; watching torching of Washington 115, 118; overseeing construction of White House 126; as superintendent of Washington Patent Office 140–1; accused of collaboration 144, 161; curbing of American looters 149; meeting with Madison 159, 160, 161; builder of the Octagon House 234

Times, The 8, 177

Tingey, Commodore Thomas 50, 51, 71, 73, 109–11, 114–15, 139 tobacco: trade 11, 45, 146; taken as booty by British 12, 30, 55, 156; plantations 20, 36

Todd, John Payne 18, 236

Tonnant, HMS 5, 8, 13, 15, 16, 29, 30, 65, 89, 96, 139, 168

Torrens, Colonel 7

Trafalgar, Battle of 5, 15, 65, 183, 195, 222

Treasury Building, Washington 17, 131, 132

Treaty of Ghent 232, 234; *see also* Ghent peace talks and treaty

Trenton, Battle of 39

Upper Marlborough, Maryland: British occupation 48–9, 52–3, 56–9, 67; Stansbury's force ordered towards but failure to reach 59, 60, 61; arrest of William Beanes 166–7

Urquhart, Beauchamp Colclough 128

Van Ness, Major General John 28, 39–40

Vauban, Sébastien Le Prestre, Seigneur de 186

Vermont: joining of the US 188

Victory, HMS 222

Virginia Gazette 159

Virginia militia 27, 60, 72–3, 101, 190

Vitoria, Battle of 9, 10, 79

Volcano, HMS 214, 215, 217

Wainwright, Captain 99, 139, 175

War of Independence 8, 13, 22, 32, 140, 187, 233

War Office: torching of 140–1

'warping': British fleet's laborious process of 152–3

Washington: place accorded to sacking in history 1–2, 4, 233; British reservations concerning attacking 2, 15, 16, 35, 45, 53–4, 55, 56–7, 58, 182, 183, 198, 225; US uncertainty as to whether a potential target 5, 14, 16, 26, 27, 37–9, 48, 59, 70–1; early years as capital 17–21; fear of invasion 21, 25, 26, 28, 37, 42; notorious heat of 29; news of British landing 37; rescuing of papers and military stores from 49–51; decision to advance towards 58; early US retreat to 61–2, 71–2, 78; evacuation of 63–4, 104–11; order to abort attack on 66–9, 147, 182, 183, 225; panic at prospect of invasion 69–70; becomes clear as British target 74–5; US forces retreat to after Battle of Bladensburg 100–1; subsequent retreat from 101, 104; entry of British advance party into 111–13; sacking of 126–42, 153, 158–9, 185, 239; British withdrawal from 145–7; fear of second attack on 157–8; reaction to sacking of 158–64, 171, 172, 176–8, 181, 188–9, 191, 196, 237; defensive measures following sacking of 161; Harry Smith chosen to carry news of sacking back to England 172–3, 174, 185; Prince Regent's questions concerning 176; British hopes that sacking would end war 178–9, 180, 181; impact of sacking on people of Baltimore 185, 188–9, 191; Madison's proclamation concerning sacking 196; sacking negated by British reverse at Baltimore and

Plattsburg 231; *see also* White House

Washington, DC: militia 28, 84, 94, 100, 162

Washington, George: choosing of Washington as capital city 17; portrait of 19, 108, 109; tobacco plantation of 36; leading of troops 51; Thornton's design of the Capitol for 72, 115; Pierre L'Enfant's design of Pennsylvania Avenue for 122; White House as brainchild of 126; death of John Lewis (nephew) 140; purchase of luxury goods from Alexandrian traders 154

Washington Bank: sparing of 121, 138

Waterloo, Battle of 165, 176, 233, 237, 238

Webster, Captain John 99, 213, 216, 219

Weightman, Roger 127, 128

Wellington, Arthur Wellesley 1st Duke of: Peninsula campaign 2, 7, 31, 79, 86, 88, 151, 156, 168, 180; reservations concerning American War 9, 178, 232; contempt for Congreve rockets 89; respect for rules of engagement 130, 156; Harry Smith's meeting with brother 176; appraisal of object of Cochrane's expedition 183; fellow Anglo-Irish officers 201; Gleig's biography of 238

Wells, Private Daniel 199

Whetstone Point, Baltimore 186

Whitbread, Samuel 178, 181

White House: British officers' dining in 1, 2, 3, 126–7, 134; early years as the President's House 17–18; Dolley Madison's redecoration of 19–20; staffed by slaves 20–1; parties at 20, 136; Cockburn's purported threat to burn 22; Madison's meeting with top advisers in 26; Dolley Madison's remaining in 51; planned ball to celebrate defeat of British 62; Dolley Madison urged to leave 63; planned supper 64; Jennings' preparations for dinner 81; rescue of paintings and valuables from 107–8; checked out by Booth 111; American looting 122; occupation and torching of 125–31, 135; flames doused by storm 145; whitewashing 126; burnt-out shell 149; British reaction to burning 177–8; restoration 234–5

Whitney, Eli 140

Wiley's Tavern 135, 136

William III, King 31, 32

Williams, John 101

Williams, Major John 162

Williams, Lieutenant 43, 86

Winchester, David 185

Winder, Governor Levin 25, 27, 187, 189

Winder, Brigadier General William: failure of 3, 125; appointed as commander of military district comprising Washington and Baltimore 25–6; manpower challenge confronted by 26–8, 38, 41; dispute with Van Ness over command of troops 39–40; despatching of cavalry to harry the British 43, 44, 48; meeting at Woodyard with Monroe 46; failed attempt to intercept Ross's main force 48–9; failure to destroy bridges 49, 70, 71, 72, 75–6, 84, 110; arrival with troops

Winder, Brigadier General William
(*cont.*)
at Long Old Fields 52; flurry of
contradictory orders given by
58–62; ignoring orders of 62,
71–2, 78; uncertainty of
concerning British target 70–1,
73; Armstrong's failure to advise
73–4, 75, 80, 84; move to and
deployment of troops at
Bladensburg 74–6, 84, 85; at
Battle of Bladensburg 90, 91–2,
98, 102–3; retreat to Washington
100–1; retreat from Washington
101, 104; appeal to by town
council of Alexandria 142–3;
order to spike guns of Fort
Washington 154; Sam Smith
preferred to as commander of
Baltimore's defence force 189;
role in defence of Baltimore 227;
name cleared in court inquiry 235
Woodyard 34, 43, 46, 48, 49

'Yankee Doodle': striking up of at
Fort McHenry 217
York (modern-day Toronto) 8, 58,
112, 129, 137
York (US coastal town) 5
Yorktown, Virginia 13, 183

From Byron, Austen and Darwin

to some of the most acclaimed and original contemporary writing, John Murray takes pride in bringing you powerful, prizewinning, absorbing and provocative books that will entertain you today and become the classics of tomorrow.

We put a lot of time and passion into what we publish and how we publish it, and we'd like to hear what you think.

Be part of John Murray – share your views with us at:

www.johnmurray.co.uk

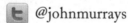 johnmurraybooks

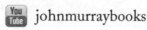 @johnmurrays

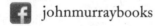 johnmurraybooks